James Baldwin

BLACK LIVES

———

Yale University Press's Black Lives series seeks to tell the fullest range of stories about notable and overlooked Black figures who profoundly shaped world history. Each book is intended to add a chapter to our larger understanding of the breadth of Black people's experiences as these have unfolded through time. Using a variety of approaches, the books in this series trace the indelible contributions that individuals of African descent have made to their worlds, exploring how their lives embodied and shaped the changing conditions of modernity and challenged definitions of race and practices of racism in their societies.

James Baldwin

———

THE LIFE ALBUM

———

Magdalena J. Zaborowska

———

Black Lives

Yale University Press | New Haven and London

The Black Lives series is supported with a gift from
the Germanacos Foundation.

Published with assistance from the foundation established in
memory of James Wesley Cooper of the Class of 1865, Yale College.

Yale University Press books may be purchased in quantity for
educational, business, or promotional use. For information,
please e-mail sales.press@yale.edu (U.S. office) or
sales@yaleup.co.uk (U.K. office).

Set in Freight Text Pro type by Integrated Publishing Solutions.
Printed in the United States of America.

Library of Congress Control Number: 2024943264
ISBN 978-0-300-26220-9 (hardcover : alk. paper)

A catalogue record for this book is available from the British Library.

This paper meets the requirements of ANSI/NISO Z39.48-1992
(Permanence of Paper).

10 9 8 7 6 5 4 3 2 1

For Yeidy—
and in memory of Ali, Leszek, Terri, and all those who have left us, those who passed away peacefully and those who were murdered in cold blood. To those "many thousands gone," from the Middle Passage and the migrants dying in the stormy waters of the Mediterranean to those felled by the pandemic and those suffering from war, hunger, and violence in Congo, Ethiopia, Gaza, Israel, Lebanon, Sudan, Syria, Ukraine, Yemen, and all those other places I may not recall.

CONTENTS

_____

PREFACE ix

INTRODUCTION. I Thought I'd Hit the Jackpot! 1

SIDE A

TRACK 1. Overture 35

TRACK 2. In My Mother's Kitchen 40

TRACK 3. Sissy Boys Don't Belong 57

TRACK 4. At the Blackboard 76

SIDE B

TRACK 1. Through the Door of My Lips 91

TRACK 2. The Prince and His Spiritual Father 97

TRACK 3. Letters to Jewish Editors 115

TRACK 4. A Lover's Kiss Is a Very Strange Event 135

SIDE C

TRACK 1. Because My House Fell Down and I Can't Live There No More . . . 149

TRACK 2. I Am All Those Strangers and a Woman, Too 154

TRACK 3. Traveling through the Country of the Self 177

TRACK 4. The Houses of Baldwin 203

CONTENTS

SIDE D

TRACK 1. Coda Chez Baldwin. 241

CHRONOLOGY 255

NOTES 261

SELECT ONLINE RESOURCES. 277

ACKNOWLEDGMENTS. 281

INDEX 285

PREFACE

———

August 2, 2024

Dear Mr. Baldwin,

We never met in person, yet I've known you for a lifetime. I've read and reread your books, traveled in your footsteps, and taught your works to students on three continents. I've written about your work and spent decades seeking your traces, searching through the papers you left behind. I'd like to thank you for the solace and salvation I have found in your vision of humanity. Please accept this book as my gift to you on your one hundredth birthday.

Today, in these "not-so-united states"—that "burning house," as you once called our home—we turn to you to help us save our country and one another. *Save* was a frequent word on your lips, used for places and people that mattered in your life. Like others, you strove to reconcile irreconcilables—grace, joy, and passion, loss, pain, and despair. You came from Harlem, a true native son, a Black man born into poverty, yet you redefined the norms of racial and sexual identity long before most of us accepted the possibility of doing so. Your differences became your power: a "jackpot," as you once called it.

Driven away from home by racism and homophobia, you labeled yourself a transatlantic commuter. You chose to live abroad to write freely, building new homes and families in faraway places. Though some attacked you for it, you refused to abandon your birthright—to criticize the homeland you loved. From your childhood, you envisioned, described, and fought for a free and equal America. Your humanism is your legacy. Centering each person's uniqueness, sensuality, erotic desire, and creativity, it feeds our imagination, compassion, and pleasure. You worked hard to live up to that humanism in private, while in public you epitomized stylish self-fashioning, cool charisma, and a playful intellect. You never yielded to labeling, groupthink, or the easy way out, though you struggled against these and lost often, as we all do. Your legacy remains, inspiring artists, philosophers, theorists, and politicians.

Thank you for helping us understand that we are all accidents of geography and genetics, and that history is as integral to our being as our DNA. You taught us that though our race, gender, nationality, sexuality, or self-identification might appear dramatically different from that of another, our shared bond of humanity runs deeper. In your own life, you witnessed the way this bond could work for good, but also how it could be used to control, abuse, divide, and corrupt.

I came to your writing for reasons that are personal and political. A bisexual immigrant woman from Cold War Poland, I was the same age when I came to the United States that you were when you first left it. Taken decades apart, our journeys across the Atlantic ran in opposite directions, leading us away from home not because we wanted to go elsewhere but because we had to leave to save ourselves.

I arrived in your American city of New York in 1987, mere weeks before you died in your home in France. But when I read your books, your words reassured me, offering shelter when finding a place for myself seemed impossible, confirming that immigration could somehow lead me home. For more than two decades, you have tasked me with writing about your legacy, a journey that began for me in June 2000 inside your house in Saint-Paul-de-Vence, in the room where you died. It has taken me from France to Turkey and all over the United States—most recently to your rich archive in Harlem, where this book began taking shape.

In *James Baldwin: The Life Album* I excavate the parts of your life that have been obscured by some readers, scholars, even your family. I center your erotic and sexual love for men (and some women), your domestic life, and your authorship as forms of imaginative activism. I extoll your explorations of gender, androgyny, and nonbinary identity that were inspired by your friendships with women and your admiration, not always untroubled, for their ways of being. The humanistic philosophy you forged in your later works sprang out of political lessons you took from Black feminists, family members, and female friends wherever you found them. Mining your private life as potent literary material, in this book I trace your personal struggles to comply with gender and genre expectations as a Black queer man and artist who yearned to live and love without labels.

I call the approach I see in your work Black queer humanism, although I realize that you weren't exactly down with either "Black" or "queer" as labels. But I use "Black" and "queer" in a nod to contemporary audiences, or as you would have called them, the "children." Today we the children embrace your ambivalence about identity stereotypes and heed your call to find our true selves in the face of the world's definitions, labels, and ways of looking. We welcome the dynamism and conundrums inherent in your biography and works, for they help us see the complex and shifting relationships in our own journeys.

The America we live in today may be more divided than ever, yet it is also facing a unique chance at renewal. New generations are weary and angry in the wake of terrorism, police brutality, and attacks on our bodies, reproductive rights, freedom of expression, voting access, the environment, and the raising and education of our children. *James Baldwin: The Life Album* arises out of this historic moment, marred by wars and trauma, and wrapped in sorrow. It comes from my blood and guts, my whole being, for that is how you taught us we must tell stories. You may not like everything I write about you, but I'm sure you would support my right to do so. Your words speak to us all about anger, frustration, and pain, yet they also speak of joy, pleasure, and community. They speak of hope and ability, even power, when we open ourselves to one another, when we do the hard work of building bridges.

In your last essay, "To Crush the Serpent," you caution, "Complexity is our only safety and love is the only key to our maturity. And love is where you find it." I close this letter with the words from your third novel, *Another Country*. Spoken by a Harlem preacher delivering a eulogy for a Black musician, Rufus Scott, they convey a revelatory, indeed a revolutionary point of view in mid-twentieth-century American fiction. They are tender and healing. They carry your spirit and your love; they sustain us as we reshape the world:

> Ain't none of us really strangers. We all here for the same reason. Someone we loved is dead. . . . But don't lose heart, dear ones—don't lose heart. Don't let it make you bitter. Try to understand. . . . The world's already bitter enough, we got to try to be better than the world. . . . You got to remember . . . he was *trying*. Ain't many trying and all that tries must suffer. Be proud of him. You got a right to be proud. And that's all he ever wanted in this world.

Yours truly,
Magda

James Baldwin

Introduction

I Thought I'd Hit the Jackpot!

"WHEN YOU WERE STARTING OUT as a writer, you were black, impoverished, homosexual. You must have said to yourself, 'Gee, how disadvantaged can I get?'" a television interviewer once asked an older, elegantly suited James Baldwin. His forehead pleated, his gap-toothed grin spreading, his left arm gesticulating, the famous man responded, "Oh, no. I thought I'd hit the jackpot! . . . It was so outrageous; you could not go any further. . . . So, you had to find a way to use it." This was the quintessential public Baldwin, the master of the limelight. Framed by a triptych of stereotypes, "black, impoverished, homosexual," he swiftly transformed the interviewer's provocation into a campy summary of his life as one of the twentieth century's greatest writers.

Baldwin's jackpot—his ability to turn his origins into brilliant literary material—brought him fame and financial security. Telling and retelling the story of his life served him well throughout his prolific international career, which spanned the 1940s through the 1980s. His rhetorical dexterity, charismatic delivery, scintillating wit, and sharp dress made him effortlessly seductive to overawed audiences. He wore the celebrity he had achieved as a "race man" and spokesman with panache, facing cameras and fans with studious charm, seamlessly weaving his personal experiences and vulnerabilities into national and global contexts. At rallies, in the pulpit, in lecture halls, or facing an American patrician in a debate at a posh British campus, he held audiences in the palm of his hand. Mixing a preacher's rageful thunder with sharp irony and elegant literary, historical, and political references, he garnered adjectives—*inimitable, passionate, unforgettable*—from fans and critics alike.

Sometimes, though, this world-famous African American author, intellectual, speaker, and civil rights activist seemed to be composed of carefully crafted personae, worn like armor. Sometimes the unguarded Baldwin made an appearance with a trickle of sweat across his temple, a fleeting grimace, an exasperated side eye, a tense shoulder, or the long, stiffly splayed fingers of a beringed hand. In interviews, biographies, and stories told by friends, family, and collaborators, he occasionally emerged as a volatile artist subsisting on cigarettes and whiskey, maniacally pounding at his typewriter through the night; a restless socialite and public speaker who could not refuse an engagement; an absentminded friend who forgot appointments and loans; a demanding guest prone to dogmatic pontificating or sudden, angry outbursts.

Away from public arenas, the private, vulnerable Baldwin doubted whether his origins were indeed the jackpot he claimed for them. As the Caribbean-British writer Caryl Phillips recalled about their private conversations in *The European Tribe*, his friend was often "finding words hard to pin down"; it was as if Phillips were "witnessing a Jimmy 'confession' rather than a Jimmy 'performance.'" Aside from intimate chats, Baldwin rarely disclosed his troubles. Between moments of self-revelation and performance, he was often depressed and beset by traumatic memories, seeking refuge in work, smoking, drinking, and socializing. His long, beautiful letters to family and friends, revealing a sensitive, ruminating, and self-critical writer who relentlessly tested ideas, characters' names, even lines of dialogue in epistolary form, remain unpublished, most resting in various archives, chiefly Yale University's Beinecke Library and the Schomburg Center for Research in Black Culture at the New York Public Library.

As his archives bear out, Baldwin wrote and rewrote tirelessly, usually in longhand. Remixing events, names, and people from his life, he would often split a single draft into several works, as he did for his first three novels, Go Tell It on the Mountain, Giovanni's Room, and Another Country. His creativity seemed boundless. In addition to novels, essays, and plays, he wrote poetry, screenplays, even musicals. His restless mind churned new projects out of thin air; most were never realized. He directed a play in Turkey in 1969, got involved in staging one of his own plays, Blues for Mister Charlie (1964), on Broadway, and dreamt of making movies, for which he wrote several screenplays. His home library indicated that he read voraciously and seemed interested in everything. His interlocutors recalled his thought process as fast and nonlinear, and his rhetoric as merciless. Few could keep up with him. Those who met him never forgot the encounter, no matter how brief.

Today Baldwin's representations spin in digital and analog forms that endlessly amplify his public, performative personae. Online posts, videos, and published works are easily accessible to anyone with a computer or library card. Repackaged as a veritable Baldwin Brand for the information age, the writer has become a popular Black icon for a new generation of readers, students, teachers, fans, community organizers, even those into "woke" self-fashioning. We can watch him in YouTube clips of his television appearances, interviews, lectures, and debates. Podcasts and playlists suffuse the internet, while quotations from his books traverse social media platforms in posts by the American Civil Liberties Union, Vice President Kamala Harris, the poet Saeed Jones, Black Lives Matter (the scholar William Maxwell calls Baldwin "the most tweeted literary authority of BLM"), the Movement for Black Lives, *Crisis* magazine, and Oprah Daily. Hashtags—#thesonofbaldwin, #BaldwinCafe, #EthniciteesLLC, and #jamesbaldwinquotes— compete with countless individual posts extolling his advice on life, love, and politics as "still on brand for being Black in America."

The Brand retails profitably: Baldwin's words and face adorn T-shirts, buttons, and posters, a postage stamp and a Mexican "saint" candle. Mugs, merch, and stickers confer cred on people who never read any of his books. Countless admirers claim to have known, met, or heard "Jimmy" speak, wearing him like an accessory. Online, PBS's *American Masters* joins in the WWJBS (what-would-James-Baldwin-say) game with a page featuring "6 James Baldwin quotes about race." A thirty-three-hour Spotify playlist showcases his musical favorites; an article on his sartorial style advertises an upscale online fashion retailer; an IMDb entry misidentifies him as an actor. A Black-owned, independent Baldwin & Co. coffee and bookstore in New Orleans modeled on the legendary Parisian Shakespeare and Company has become a "community hub." The conservative journalist David Brooks evoked Baldwin's admirable "global humanism" in a 2023 *New York Times* podcast, repeating it in a University of Michigan commencement speech. It is useful to know his name these days.

Dedicated to "Father Baldwin" by the self-designated "Son of Baldwin," Robert Jones, Jr.'s *The Prophets* (2021) is a novel of male queer love under slavery that claims him as an "ancestor" alongside Toni Morrison. Baldwin is an important inspiration for Tomasz Jedrowski's Cold War gay romance *Swimming in the Dark* (2020) and the celebrity trans author Janet Mock's memoir *Reinventing Realness* (2014). Ta-Nehisi Coates's National Book Award–

winning *Between the World and Me* (2015) builds on two of Baldwin's nonfiction volumes, *The Fire Next Time* and *The Evidence of Things Not Seen*. *On James Baldwin* (2024) by the Irish novelist, poet, and essayist Colm Tóibín praises his stylistic mastery and fascination with the "drama of masculinity." Raoul Peck's documentary *I Am Not Your Negro* (2016), ignited by Baldwin's unfinished novel treatment "Remember This House," has been advertised on IMDb as "the book James Baldwin never finished"; the front jacket flap of the book that accompanied the film, which contains excerpts from Baldwin's published works and interviews advertises it as the book that he "never wrote." Barry Jenkins's gorgeous 2018 feature adaptation of Baldwin's novel *If Beale Street Could Talk* (1974) confirms the cinematic appeal of his fiction, what Jenkins calls his "Black ecstatic." In 2023, the Black queer actor and fashion icon Billy Porter was tapped to co-write a screenplay and play Baldwin in a forthcoming biopic.

Since 2014, the James Baldwin Project, founded by the creators of the 1989 documentary—still the best of all—*The Price of the Ticket*, has been bringing screenings and talkbacks to diverse communities. The U.S.-U.K. open-access peer-reviewed academic journal *The James Baldwin Review* promotes scholarship, recovery of archival sources, and Baldwin-related events and people; a special issue commemorating his centenary is in the works. The University of Chicago's 2017 exhibit *James Baldwin among the Philosophers* included Cornel West's definition of him as the "Black American Socrates" who embraced "the perplexity of trying to be a decent human being and thinking person in the face of the pervasive mendacity and hypocrisy of the American empire." The writer Jamie McGhee and scholar Adam Hollowell, authors of *You Mean It or You Don't: James Baldwin's Radical Challenge* (2022), hope to "spur today's progressives from conviction to action" and promote "spiritual activism for racial justice" in both religious and secular communities. In 2023, Lincoln Center held its *Jubilee for Jimmy: A Celebration of James Baldwin* as part of its Summer for the City programming. The Ford Foundation–sponsored *God Made My Face: A Collective Portrait of James Baldwin* centennial symposium and exhibit at the Brooklyn Museum in New York issued a "memorial mosaic" album edited by the critic Hilton Als in 2024. Riffing on Amiri Baraka's eulogy for Baldwin as a "man, spirit, voice," the Schomburg/NYPL opened its *JIMMY! God's Black Revolutionary Mouth* exhibition on the day of his hundredth birthday; a few days earlier, National Public Radio featured a celebratory interview with Robert Jones, Jr., and the scholar Eddie Glaude.

On July 30, 2024, BBC Radio 4 aired *The Lost Archives of James Baldwin* produced by Tony Phillips. It features Jill Hutchinson, who has preserved the writer's vinyl records, books, furniture, typewriters, and artwork for decades, entrusted with this task by his younger brother, David, who inherited Baldwin's house in France. Artists such as Glenn Ligon and Zoe Leonard have used his books and words as material objects, transforming them into canvases and sculptures, and this gives me hope that this important archive, however untraditional, will not remain lost for long. Ligon's 2019 mixed-media exhibition in the Mizzi Palace on the Princes' Islands in Istanbul, Turkey, which framed Baldwin's life there in the 1960s as refracting twenty-first-century "sociopolitical analogies between Turkey and the US," attests to the transnational impact of the material objects of his life.

At the opposite end of pop-culture Baldwiniana, quotefancy .com features five hundred downloadable slides with his words cast against customizable landscapes or abstractions. Updated for convenient mining ("forgiveness," "self-improvement," "education," "civilization"), these slides never reference Baldwin's works (goodreads.com takes care of that), but simply offer a glib "literary" reference for every occasion. In Philip Lopate's critique of

I Am Not Your Negro, he notes that Baldwin's representations solidified circa 1963: "Jimmy the public figure begins to subsume Baldwin the writer," who remains frozen "in the role of prophet . . . posthumous 'witness' and spokesman for our current racial malaise." No one seems interested in the private man who birthed the prophet.

Alongside international academic conferences and publications, social media swag, and marketplace clicks, familiar disagreements about Baldwin's legacy have revived among all audiences. The superiority of his essays over his fiction; the importance of his being gay, bisexual, or queer vis-à-vis his being Black; the authenticity of his works given his love of such dead white males as Henry James and Charles Dickens; his views on HIV/AIDS and the women's movement; the alleged waning of his talent after 1963. And, of course, who owns his story and who should and who should not be telling it and why? In the wake of his centenary and on the cusp of the new Cold War, we are still disagreeing about Baldwin's legacy, our debates recognizable spinoffs of instabilities from his not-so-distant (older?) Cold War time.

Everyone can readily recognize his importance, but who was James Baldwin? Born in Harlem Hospital on August 2, 1924, Baldwin never knew his biological father. His unwed mother, Emma Berdis Jones, hailed from Maryland. She soon married David Baldwin, an older preacher from Louisiana, who gave his last name to her young son, making her a "respectable" married woman. The Reverend Baldwin worked in a factory while Berdis cleaned houses. James helped raise his eight half-siblings and served as a teenage preacher at Pentecostal churches while in high school. He never went to college. After leaving the church at seventeen, he moved to Greenwich Village, worked menial jobs through World War II, and began his career by writing book reviews.

In November 1948, he left the United States and spent most

of his life abroad, especially in France (1949–57, 1971–87) and Turkey (1961–71), but returned often for visits. In the late 1950s through the 1960s, he was a speaker on the fundraising circuits for SNCC (the Student Nonviolent Coordinating Committee), the SCLC (Southern Christian Leadership Conference), and CORE (the Congress of Racial Equality); he traveled through the American South for the first time in 1957. In 1963 he organized a meeting of African American leaders, activists, and artists with Attorney General Robert Kennedy to discuss Black civil rights.

Baldwin's literary stature grew with his well-received first novel, *Go Tell It on the Mountain* (1953), and two essay collections, *Notes of a Native Son* (1955) and *Nobody Knows My Name* (1961). His best-selling second and third novels, *Giovanni's Room* (1956) and *Another Country* (1962), shocked readers with frank depictions of interracial love and homosexuality, while his third book of essays, *The Fire Next Time* (1963), seemingly prophesied national racial unrest, catapulting him to international fame. His first play, *The Amen Corner* (1954–68), was staged by the Howard Players at Howard University in 1955, while the second, *Blues for Mister Charlie* (1964), became a short-lived success on Broadway.

By the late 1960s, Baldwin's hard-won celebrity had begun to wane. His later works—the novels *Tell Me How Long the Train's Been Gone* (1968), *If Beale Street Could Talk* (1974), and *Just above My Head* (1979); the short story collection *Going to Meet the Man* (1965); the essay volumes *No Name in the Street* (1972), *The Devil Finds Work* (1976), and *The Evidence of Things Not Seen* (1985)— were praised abroad and won awards, but were unfavorably reviewed at home. Translated into numerous languages, his books reached readers from Senegal to Japan, Turkey, India, and Poland. In 1986 he received the Légion d'Honneur from the French president and spoke on global racism at the international summit of intellectuals, scientists, and artists in the Soviet Union.

Baldwin died of cancer in late 1987, at sixty-three, in his house in Saint-Paul-de-Vence in southern France. He left a vast archive of unpublished and planned projects, and a household filled with books, furniture, and artwork. Caryl Phillips, who rushed to France to keep vigil by his remains, deems him his "most important single literary influence." Other writers in the United States and beyond, including Hilton Als, Amiri Baraka, Ta-Nehisi Coates, Teju Cole, Nikky Finney, Rachel Kaadzi Ghansah, Tomasz Jedrowski, Randall Kenan, Alain Mabanckou, Toni Morrison, Suzan-Lori Parks, Darryl Pinckney, Jean-Paul Rocchi, Richard Rodriguez, and Shay Youngblood, attested to his inspiration. Baldwin's body returned to rest in Ferncliff Cemetery, north of New York City, where his mother later joined him. A brief eruption of attention following his death waned quickly, and Baldwin disappeared for decades from U.S. media and school syllabi. His house in Saint-Paul-de-Vence, abandoned by his family, was demolished in 2014, an expensive condominium complex rising in its place.

This eclipse of Baldwin's light should not surprise us. The scholar Michele Elam has noted that forgetting Baldwin was a willful act of making him "unknown: less read, cited, anthologized, argued over, taught." The Americanist Maria Diedrich's "James A. Baldwin—Obituaries for a Black Ishmael" (1991) describes "a strange magic" that arose at his funeral on December 8, 1987, at which "his parting praise deprive[d] his knotty, strong trunk of its edges." Thus "domesticated and reincarnated as everybody's Jimmy," the posthumous Baldwin became curated public property—a national Black icon—in "a massive invasion of his integrity." In 1988, the Black poet and the scholar June Jordan and Houston A. Baker, Jr., complained that Baldwin, whom they called "the conscience of his generation," had never received a national literary award. Their condemnation was coupled with a "statement" signed by many African American writers appealing for due recognition of another underacknowledged Black author, Toni Morrison, and appeared in the Books section of the *New York Times*. They blamed the U.S. publishing industry for the systemic devaluation of Black literature. Along with Morrison, Baldwin provided a resonant example of the economics of such devaluation: "How shall we explain the exile of this man who wanted to be loved so much at home? How shall we forget the declaration of this native son who once said, 'I'm worth more dead than alive.'"

While justly targeting the U.S. white literary establishment, though, the Jordan and Baker appeal omitted the rejection of Baldwin by many Black Americans and made no mention of how deeply their attitude had hurt him. The "Black Ishmael" could never satisfy his countryfolk, it seemed. His realization of this fact too often drove him to overextend himself. In "Obituaries," Diedrich explains that his prosperity, even fame, never quenched his hunger for acceptance: "A domicile in southern France might have caused strains and schizophrenic splits in a man who was nonetheless continually called upon to function as a voice of outrage month after month."

In a more positive development, in 1988, having attended Baldwin's funeral, the undergraduate Harvard University poets Sharan Strange and Thomas Sayers Ellis cofounded the Dark Room Reading Series with the poet-composer Janice Lowe of Berklee College to commemorate his legacy. For about a decade, they held workshops and facilitated mentoring and cross-generational community building for Black artists. This was a seed, which has sprouted and flourished since 1998, when new research on Baldwin's life and works began appearing, and the so-called Baldwin Renaissance took root in academe.

Though largely out of public view at first, that scholarly renaissance slowly made its way into public events and commemorations that have been multiplying in anticipation of Baldwin's one hundredth birthday on August 2, 2024. In addition to academic and biographical works by Hilton Als, Lawrie Balfour, Rich Blint, Nicholas Boggs, Herb Boyd, Matt Brim, Cora Caplan, James Campbell, Rachel Cohen, Fern Marja Eckman, Michele Elam, Amy Elias, Douglas Field, Greg Garrett, Ernest Gibson, Eddie Glaude, Jacqueline Goldsby, Mae G. Henderson, E. Patrick Johnson, Randall Kenan, David Leeming, William Maxwell, Dwight McBride, D. Quentin Miller, Bill Mullen, Brian Norman, Robert Reid-Pharr, Marlon Ross, Bill Schwarz, Lynn Orilla Scott, Colm Tóibín, Joseph Vogel, W. J. Weatherby, and myself, digests of fragments and quotations—*Memorable Quotations: James Baldwin* (2012), *Baldwin for Our Times: Writings from James Baldwin for an Age of Sorrow and Struggle* (2016), *James Baldwin's Little Book of Selected Quotes* (2021)—expand, explode, and sometimes entomb the race man's "timeless wisdom."

For Baldwin's ninetieth birthday in 2014, the choreographer Bill T. Jones spearheaded a festival, *James Baldwin, This Time!*, at New York City's Live Arts Theater, which also inaugurated the "Year of Baldwin." Multiple events featured actors, dancers, musicians, critics, and writers at Harlem Stage, Columbia University, and other venues, drawing large audiences. That August the writer was given a landmark in his Harlem neighborhood when a stretch of 128th Street between 5th Avenue and Madison was named James Baldwin Place. The brick house at 81 Horatio Street where he lived intermittently from 1958 to 1961 bears a plaque affixed during a public ceremony on October 7, 2015, by the Greenwich Village Society for Historic Preservation; in 2020, New York City LGBT Historic Sites Project commemorated the James Baldwin Lawn in St. Nicholas Park in Harlem. In 2021, the Baldwin residence at 137 West 71st Street in New York, which the writer had bought for his mother, received a Cultural Medallion from the Historic Landmarks Preservation Center. In France, the site of his house in Saint-

Paul-de-Vence attracted brief media attention in 2015 after developers bulldozed it to build expensive condominiums. There is no writer's house museum for James Arthur Baldwin anywhere.

At the cusp between Baldwin's century and ours, Percival Everett's novel *Erasure* (2001) satirized racialized expectations that Baldwin had found crushing as the "Negro writer" half a century earlier. *Erasure*'s first-person Black male novelist-narrator recalls a literary agent advising him to portray "true, gritty real stories of black life" instead of "retellings of Euripides and parodies of French poststructuralists." Everett's protagonist is aware that racial "realism" sells and confesses that he doesn't think much of or even "believe in race," though those who do believe in it "may shoot me or hang me or cheat me." By 2023, *Erasure* had inspired a brilliant cinematic adaptation, *American Fiction,* whose title echoed Baldwin's views on the U.S. racial binary as a requisite for good writing. Today, though freely satirized, racial literary realism continues as a profitable commodity, while James Baldwin the Black Icon has become a brand.

Baldwin's late essay "Here Be Dragons" (1985) is the inspiration for my biography, which centers not Baldwin the public man—the Baldwin I described above—but Baldwin the obscured private man. Originally published in *Playboy* magazine as "Freaks and the American Ideal of Manhood," "Here Be Dragons" placed U.S. identity formation within a distorted view of the national past that privileged men and whiteness. Because "all countries . . . make of their trials a legend . . . a dubious romance called 'history,'" Baldwin explained, Americans received a fantasy rather than an account of true events. Resembling a seductive feature film, à la D. W. Griffith's racist blockbuster *The Birth of a Nation* (1915), this version of history blinded Americans to the racism and violence they uncritically accepted as the "key to [their] . . . imagination." Adapting W. E. B. Du Bois's concept of double consciousness, Baldwin showed how profoundly twentieth-century visual culture served that version and how it shaped individual minds. At the beginning of the twentieth century, Du Bois explained that Black Americans saw themselves through visions of caste manufactured by their white brethren in power. At the essay's end, Baldwin summed up the devastating consequences of this reality: "We all exist . . . in the eye of the beholder. We all react to and, to whatever extent, *become* what that eye sees."

Baldwin's statement on racial becoming in the public eye has not lost its power. While the ubiquitous public writer flickers on screens, the private man dwells out of sight. He can be found in hefty boxes of manuscripts, unpublished letters, correspondence with agents, editors, and lawyers, bills, journals, notes, and photographs at the Schomburg Center and other archives. Other glimpses of the private Baldwin in film footage and photographs rest in institutional and individual collections from New York, New Haven, Cambridge, Massachusetts, and Atlanta, Georgia, to Vence, Guillaumes, and Saint-Paul-de-Vence in France. Though most of them are theoretically open to all, these venues are not easily accessible given their remoteness from one another.

Readers all over the world can conjure up their own Baldwin from his works on paper, screen, or in audible formats. Fans may feed their imaginations in the domestic and international locations he inhabited; for example, La Maison Baldwin—a U.S.-French organization that advertises itself as a "sanctuary for writers"— held an upscale centennial festival, *Baldwin and Black Legacy: Truth, Liberation, Activism,* in Saint-Paul-de-Vence and Paris in September 2024. There is no writer's museum, though, no simulacrum of his study—what he called his "dungeon" and "torture chamber"—where we can imagine Baldwin's work routine by looking at his everyday objects. Salvaged from his house in Saint-

Paul-de-Vence before it was demolished, books, typewriters, art-work, posters, clothing, jewelry, knickknacks, vinyl records, post-cards, and photographs remain inaccessible. Collected by private individuals, the surviving matter of his life is disparate, an incomplete portrait, some digitized in a collection at the University of Michigan Library, others on display at the National Museum of African American History and Culture (NMAAHC)/Smithsonian.

James Baldwin: The Life Album encompasses all Baldwin's incarnations, and especially the more private, vulnerable, and messy man. A brief biography, it highlights the aspects of his life and works that have been understated, obscured, even erased: his troubled childhood, struggles with sexuality and gender, and the influence of women, Jews, and queers on his authorship. Spotlighting lesser-known archival sources, relationships, and contexts, in this book I seek out the complex human behind the memorialized and monumentalized public personae—Son of Harlem, Black Icon, Great Twentieth-Century Writer, Race Man, Civil Rights Activist, Prophet, Witness. I peek behind their armor, convinced that his vulnerabilities show us more of the man. Reassembling, rotating, and rearranging well-known pieces of his portrait, I make space for previously muted stories, sites, actors, and approaches to his works.

Famous lives are usually told in a linear fashion. Bracketed by births and deaths, punctuated with recognized achievements and relationships, such biographies embrace orderly temporal progressions. Baldwin's preoccupation with remixing the various elements of his origins—"black, impoverished, homosexual"—has inspired me to forgo such an approach. While aware that no account can offer a full version of a person's life, here I purposefully embrace Baldwin's broken-record reliance on autobiographical, even auto-ethnographical (a term often used to reference critical, even academic life writing) repetition and his stubbornly cyclical, often achronological narrative style—what Caryl Phillips calls his "gracefully lilting sentences . . . mutable words, and elliptical phrases, endlessly circl[ing] back on themselves."

As the scholar Jacqueline Goldsby explains, Baldwin deliberately challenged temporalities and genres, reshaping the experience of writing and reading for all involved; in his underappreciated *Tell Me How Long the Train's Been Gone*, "novel-writing and novel-reading . . . provoke the openness and reciprocity that theatre aims to foster through the medium of radical, embodied presence." Noting that he has been regarded too narrowly in terms of genre by literary critics, the scholar D. Quentin Miller argues that Baldwin's writing should be considered in the context of the "confessional school of poetry" explored by the likes of Robert Lowell, and as "politically efficacious as any speech. . . . Poets can be warriors, too." Baldwin's insistence on the importance, immediacy, and messiness of memory and private life resonates with today's idea of "auto-theory." Referring to writing that combines theoretical reflections with accounts of autobiographical, embodied experience, "auto-theory" focuses on the cyclical and achronological way we experience memory. We might see it as an organic approach to telling stories. In one form or another, auto-theory has existed since humans invented storytelling. It pervaded Baldwin's oeuvre as he reinvented it for his century and ours. In this book, auto-theory helps shed light on more elusive aspects of Baldwin's private life, especially the influence of women.

Since the 1970s, Black feminist writers, poets, activists, and theorists have centered private life in similar ways. Maya Angelou, Nikki Giovanni, Audre Lorde, Alice Walker, and scholars like Barbara Christian and bell hooks, among others, promoted auto-theoretical interpretations of culture by elevating women's experience, creativity, and ways of knowing. These contemporaries of Baldwin's embraced gender and sexuality, working-class pursuits, and unglamorous locations as artistic subjects. Younger Black writers Baldwin influenced, such as Toni Morrison, Sonia Sanchez, and Suzan-Lori Parks, similarly politicized the private in ways that resonated with and enriched Baldwin's ideas. We have not heard much about such affinities because gender segregation has dominated teaching and research on African American literature. In *James Baldwin* I challenge such divisions by showing how important women were to Baldwin's authorship and how he often struggled with this need.

Often symbolized by black-and-white photographs of marchers carrying, or wearing, signs that read "I AM A MAN," the Civil Rights Movement projected a Black, male, straight image. Nonconforming individuals were not good for the movement's publicity; they also disturbed the carefully curated politics of mid-twentieth-century African American respectability. Baldwin, who never hid his sexuality, could not pass for straight. Yet he often took his place alongside other leaders under the guise of the so-called "race man." He was excluded from speaking at the famous March on Washington in 1963 for being too inflammatory, though Bayard Rustin, who was also queer, was not, as he was one of the March's key organizers. Rustin spoke briefly, soon coming under attack by politicians. Keeping the gays out of sight, the movement relied on the unacknowledged labor of Black women while men served in the public-facing roles. Baldwin took a long minute to understand this in conjunction with African American feminist ideas on these matters. As *The Life Album* shows, this delay is surprising, given the childhood roots of his writing life as his mother's right-hand man.

Baldwin's sexuality and mannerisms made him an obvious and frequent object of criticism, ridicule, even surveillance (he had a copious FBI file) during the Cold War. Read today, reviews of his works ring with homophobia and racism that were then standard.

Langston Hughes's 1956 assessment of Baldwin's first essay collection, *Notes of a Native Son*, for example, characterized his style with backhanded compliments—"thought-provoking, tantalizing, irritating, abusing and amusing." To Hughes, Baldwin used "words as the sea uses waves, to flow and beat, advance and retreat, rise and take a bow in disappearing." Praising his essays over his sealike fiction, Hughes diagnosed Baldwin's abilities as fragmented, his viewpoints as "half American, half Afro-American, incompletely fused." Baldwin came across as a confused sissy, too fluid and indeterminate; Hughes wished that he would become "a straight-from-the-shoulder writer" one day. (This review came in the wake of a personal letter Hughes wrote to Baldwin on March 7, 1953, in which Hughes expressed admiration for Baldwin's "critical writing," concluding, "the more fences young writers jump over, the better. More power to you!")

As if hyperbolizing Hughes's critique of *Notes*, the literary critic F. W. Dupee painted Baldwin as an aggrieved, gender-bending incarnation of Nathaniel Hawthorne's ostracized heroine Hester Prynne in *The Scarlet Letter* (1850). Reviewing Baldwin's best-selling *The Fire Next Time*, Dupee saw its author as Hester in blackface—an angry "Negro in extremis." When a photograph of Baldwin's serious face graced the cover of *Time* magazine that same year, the text inside described him as a "nervous, slight, almost fragile figure, filled with frets and fears . . . effeminate in manner." In 1967, a weary Baldwin told the Turkish literary journal *Cep Dergisi,* "I have been criticized for so many things, and for so long, that I am quite unable to look at the possibility of being criticized as a danger." This "homosexual funkiness," as the scholar Robert Reid-Pharr described the Baldwin effect in his home country, characterized his later works, which, Reid-Pharr noted elsewhere, "threw into confusion . . . the boundaries of (Black) normality."

His critics' desire that Baldwin straighten out is among the reasons why in *James Baldwin* I tell his life story in a deliberately unstraightforward, even queer, manner. To honor who he was, and how he viewed and wrote about himself, I revisit his life both chronologically and achronologically, and at times by mixing the two approaches. A brilliant stylist of the English language, Baldwin leaned on repetition and revolution, even re-evolution, of themes, phrases, and points of view, some of which were inspired by Black English and music. Exploding traditional syntax, style, and genre expectations, his long sentences remixed ideas, characters, events, and locations, embracing what he called "the beat." Fascinated with how experience and emotion drove embodied imagination, will, and speech, he channeled their restless dance into his works, syncopating dates, locations, and personae, repeating riffs and refrains like a virtuoso improviser.

Since his earliest writing attempts, Baldwin sought to describe what being a Black queer person in America and the world felt like. As Lynn Orilla Scott's pioneering *James Baldwin's Later Fiction* (2002) concludes, "He described not only the social landscape but also the human heart, giving testimony to our desires and dreams for a new identity and a new nation." He also understood that audiences (including the closeted Langston Hughes) expected straightforward, muscular prose from him. Like gender and sexuality, race was supposed to shape his style, indeed serve as his primary motivator. In terms of cultural capital and market value, Black writing in Baldwin's time was expected to explore gritty social conditions through stories rooted in history and politics. Baldwin's broken-record penchant for auto-theory, psychological introspection, and bold homosexual sex scenes in his fiction made many critics and readers uncomfortable. Their demands and rejections were a frequent source of anguish to the writer, as reported by Baldwin's friend and frequent host the novelist William Styron. In Karen Thorsen's *The Price of the Ticket* documentary, Styron referred to Baldwin's late-night riffs and rants as physically draining "schizoid wrenching." In 1963, Baldwin told *Mademoiselle* magazine that the ability to write and maintain his public persona came at the cost of being "penalized for trying to remain in touch with yourself."

David Leeming's 1992 biography describes how U.S. critics panned Baldwin's last and longest novel, *Just above My Head* (1979), for its lack of "realism." Misunderstanding its sophisticated, hybrid form of a "parable in the form of confession . . . [a] philosophy . . . [and] the sorrow song," the reviewers dismissed the book without placing it inside its author's complex literary career. Baldwin considered *Just above My Head* an elaborate "lyric" and his best novel. France agreed. With the French title rendered as *Harlem Quartet: La Cosmopolite, Just above My Head* was an award-winning hit. Noting the resurgence of European interest in Baldwin, the novelist Alain Mabanckou in his introduction to the 2017 French edition calls it a timely "literary testament," each page singing about "brotherhood, love, hope, and redemption."

Since childhood, Baldwin "had wanted to be a musician . . . a painter . . . an actor," as he told the writer and translator Jordan Elgrably, and in this biography I explore these aspirations in his literary work and in his life. His famous contemporaries, such as Harry Belafonte, Miles Davis, Beauford Delaney, and Sidney Poitier, appeared in essays and inflected fictional characters: Richard, Sonny, Rufus, and Arthur from his first play, *The Amen Corner*, through the short story "Sonny's Blues," to his novels *Another Country*, and *Just above My Head*. Artists of all kinds abound in his works: in unpublished drafts, a painter named Sylvester mirrored Beauford Delaney, Baldwin's Greenwich Village mentor and lifelong artistic father figure; another Delaney-like figure, white this time, is about to leave his Black lover, Ruth, in the short story "Come Out the Wilderness" published in *Mademoiselle* in 1958; a famous bisexual Black actor named Leo Proudhammer narrates Baldwin's fourth novel, *Tell Me How Long the Train's Been Gone*. Leo comes after Eric, a white queer southern thespian in *Another Country*. Both these characters are their author's porte-paroles and precursors to the Creole diva Edith Hemings of Baldwin's last, unpublished play, "The Welcome Table" (1987).

Despite his love of many kinds of art, it was the special role of writing in society that anchored Baldwin's life and is a theme in this book. His two straight-shooting essays on U.S. literature at mid-twentieth century, "Everybody's Protest Novel," published in the Paris literary magazine *Zero* in 1949, and "As Much Truth as One Can Bear," published in the *New York Times* in 1962, laid down his terms. In the first essay, he attacked stereotypical and sentimental portrayals of Black characters as dehumanizing. "Everybody's Protest Novel" placed Richard Wright's groundbreaking novel *Native Son* (1942) in the "protest" and "sentimental" tradition of Harriet Beecher Stowe's abolitionist fiction *Uncle Tom's Cabin* (1852) that it condemned. Wright was Baldwin's benefactor and literary mentor, and a transatlantic literary scandal ensued. "Everybody's Protest Novel" was considered a father-figure assassination by the twenty-five-year-old rising author. The literary scene could not envision more than one leading Black author. Nor could the white intelligentsia conceive that Baldwin and Wright, given that they were both Black American writers, might disagree.

Baldwin's radical views on fiction are evident in the later essay, "As Much Truth as One Can Bear," in which he critiqued the U.S. national literary canon. He included Ernest Hemingway and his "sexless and manufactured" heroines alongside other white men such as William Faulkner, John Dos Passos, F. Scott Fitzgerald, even the "mighty" Henry James, his personal favorite. These white modernists were anachronistically echoing the "songs of the plains, the memory of the virgin continent, mysteriously despoiled," he opined. Bemoaning lost innocence and the American Dream that never materialized for most folks in the Promised Land, those authors failed their readers and offered no inspiration to their descendants. "As Much Truth as One Can Bear" argued that artists had to disturb the peace by shaking off their fellow citizens' complacency and indifference. Societies were "never able to examine [and] to overhaul themselves," so "ferment [and] disturbance [were] the responsibility, and the necessity, of writers." Calling on the "handful" of new authors to speak for their inarticulate audiences, Baldwin wanted them to "turn [their] backs" on the mythologized past. Based in truth, a new literary tradition could redeem America: "Not everything that is faced can be changed; but nothing can be changed until it is faced."

Passionate about his ideas, Baldwin was sometimes unable to face his own limitations. His changing views and contradictions are among the themes driving my biography. His discussion of the national literary scene in "Everybody's Protest Novel" and "As Much Truth as One Can Bear," for example, rather ironically bolstered the American white male canon that he so passionately criticized. By excluding Black and women writers from his discussion in the latter, he may have been displaying ignorance of their works. At the same time, a denial of their existence accompanied a denial of his own experience—the influence of women on his literary development, which he had begun acknowledging in the former piece.

Baldwin included Stowe, that "impassioned pamphleteer," in "Everybody's Protest Novel" because he read Uncle Tom's Cabin obsessively as a child, and because it could be found in many working-class Black households of the day. In his mind, the comparison between Stowe and Wright made sense intellectually, for it targeted writing Black people as stereotypes. But in the context of late 1940s and Wright and Baldwin's private connection, his comparison was doubly offensive to Wright: Stowe was white; worse, female authors were generally considered inferior to male writers in literary circles; it was a compounded insult. The truth Baldwin failed to recognize in both these essays—any more than the literary critic Henry Louis Gates, Jr., did in his *New York Times* review essay of 2006, "Cabin Fever," in which he branded Baldwin Stowe's "true 20th-century literary heir"—was how deeply misogyny was naturalized in the racist literary culture Baldwin yearned to reshape.

Baldwin's own long-term struggle with gender—and his tendency to duck the issue—is in evidence in an earlier piece that probably inspired "As Much Truth"—"A Word from Writer Directly to Reader" (1959). In it, Baldwin insisted that Americans' lives unfolded under the "fearful pressures . . . to lie about one's own experience." Novels were necessary to preserve the truth and its transformative potential, he argued, for their authors provided a voice for "a speechless people," their books expressing "what the citizens of this time and place actually feel and think." This radical reversal of the truth-vs.-fiction binary drove Baldwin's lifelong ethics and literary aesthetics, culminating in the humanistic philosophy of his later works.

But if novels preserve the truth, what are we to make of Baldwin's sexist and heterosexist fictional characters, such as David and Giovanni in *Giovanni's Room,* or Rufus, Richard, Yves, and Vivaldo in *Another Country?* Whose truth do they represent? Were the misogynists in his own novels embodiments of the widely accepted male privilege he was criticizing? Or did they perhaps reflect his own struggles with gender and women's place in society? With his own masculinity and sexism? In this book I offer answers and hypotheses, interpretations and close readings of papers and published works that shed light on such complex issues.

Literary labor and technique interested Baldwin as a practitioner and especially as a person who came into his own without the support of a college degree or writing seminars. He demanded that authors embrace a professional paradox arising from their social responsibility. Like his adoption of fiction-as-truth as his artistic creed, his insistence on accepting the conundrums and ambivalences of authorship was a signature move. In "A Word from Writer Directly to Reader," he explained that a writer had to be a rebel, "outrageous, independent, anarchical," and a consummate professional—"thoroughly disciplined"—at the same time. Good fiction arose from life experience, hard-won self-knowledge, voracious reading, and passionate work.

In an undated letter to John A. Williams, author of the 1961 novel *The Night Song,* based on the life of the jazz great Charlie Parker, Baldwin directly linked this concept of anarchical discipline to "the achievement of what is called technique." He insisted that "either you master your material, or your material masters you." For "beneath this cliche," he added, "sleeps an awful truth, which is, simply, that your material is nothing more and nothing less than your private relation to your private life." Pointing to Williams's *Night Song*—"you know more, vastly more, than you are willing to tell"—Baldwin concluded, "You can only tell about others what you are willing to face about yourself."

In 1980, at fifty-six, he told the editor and writer Wolfgang Binder that he had been staging "a kind of return to my own beginnings," a self-search if you will, throughout his fiction. Spanning 1953 to 1979, his six novels "come full circle from *Go Tell It on the Mountain* to *Just Above My Head,*" he insisted. That is why a similar cyclicality guides the storytelling in *James Baldwin,* for we must mine his auto-theoretical novels for fragments of his life story. Read today, the novels sample and echo one another, loop in and out of events signposting Baldwin's private life.

In November 1987, in his last interview with Quincy Troupe,

he explained that in his final novel, *Just above My Head*, "I tried to deal with what I was most afraid of" and that "the vehicle of the book is music. Because music was and is my salvation." In the essay "Of the Sorrow Songs" (1979), on the Black musicians he admired, artists like Ma Rainey, Jerry Roll Morton, Billie Holiday, the Duke (Ellington), and the Count (Basie), Baldwin explained that great art was about listening for revelation and revolution, about seeking elucidation and enlightenment, and telling stories about it: "Music is our witness, and our ally. The 'beat' is the confession which recognizes, changes, and conquers time. Then, history becomes a garment we can wear, and share, and not a cloak in which to hide; and time becomes a friend." Echoing and radically revising Walt Whitman's nineteenth-century poetic self-affirmations in these words, the twentieth-century Black queer writer sang of his own selves and multitudes, of his communities at home and abroad. In an interview, "Disturber of the Peace," he claimed "all those strangers called Jimmy Baldwin," alongside "the brightest boy in the house"—the wounded, precocious child he never ceased to be.

Being around him "was like a movie or a fairy tale," recalls David Linx, a talented Belgian jazz musician, vocalist, and composer whom Baldwin helped seek refuge from a difficult father in 1980s. Linx lived for a while in the writer's French house and with his family in New York while finishing his education. Having heard Baldwin sing in 1986, the nineteen-year-old Linx invited the writer to make a record with him and the Belgian jazz guitarist Pierre Van Dormael. Finished only weeks before Baldwin's death, that album, *A Lover's Question* (Label Bleu 1991, 1999) features Linx's music and Baldwin's "spoken word performances." As the scholar Douglas Field remarks, that album embodies Baldwin's inextinguishable thirst for experimentation and collaboration. Interestingly, *A Lover's Question* also recycled and sampled sources in

Baldwin's signature record-like style. The title and second track referenced a poem included in Baldwin's only poetry book, *Jimmy's Blues* (1983), and that poem was probably a remix of Clyde McPhatter's 1958 hit R&B single under the same title. It might also echo the 1978 country remix of McPhatter's song by Jacky Ward or riff on Shakespeare's narrative poem told in a female voice, "A Lover's Complaint," in which lovers, questions, and complaints revolve freely. Linx saw Baldwin as a sage and a father figure, a lonely, strong, and passionate man, who taught him about "love, rhythm, then dealing with yourself . . . how to live my life . . . how not to go under, and above all, how to stay in the light."

Baldwin's faith in our imaginative potential opens the possibility of a humanistic revolution. His words from *Another Country* are this revolution's antiviolent, antiracist motto. "We can be better than we are, and do better than we do." As the Harlem preacher in that scene explains, we have a choice about how to be: "The world's already bitter enough, we got to try to be better than the world." An affirmation of what I call Baldwin's Black queer humanism, these words convey a generous orientation to the world, to oneself, and to other people. Multiply marked by sexuality, gender, and race, Baldwin's linkage of his life experience to wisdom, aesthetics, and ethics drove his writing. Arising from a deep consideration of what art, beauty, and morality entailed, his philosophy of Black queer humanism sings of the complex confusions and conflicts of his private, vulnerable selves.

In "Family Secrets," Baldwin's longtime admirer and descendant, the Black queer writer Hilton Als, admits that Baldwin's "various contradictions" are "one of the most valuable features of his work." In full agreement, in this book I let Baldwin's conundrums, vulnerabilities, and conflicts guide the pace and shape of the story it tells. Key parts of his biography—childhood, education, travel, exile, search for home—constantly replay throughout his works. Similarly, themes related to these parts revolve, reappear, and resound like tracks on a phonograph record. An aficionado of vinyl, Baldwin loved playing and replaying his favorite records. His collection is now in private hands in France; documented by Gerald O'Grady, it is "a balm of sorts when one is writing," as Ikechúkwú Onyewuenyi, the curator of the Hammer Museum in Los Angeles, described it in an interview.

Baldwin loved singing and always wrote with favorite soundscapes playing on his turntable in the background. Thus, I have designed this book as a two-disc vinyl LP album, of the kind he kept in his private collection. *The Life Album* spins out Baldwin's philosophy of Black queer humanism as the unifying motif of this record.

In 1984, Baldwin told Jordan Elgrably and George Plimpton of the *Paris Review*, "I've changed precisely because America has not." An idealist and a romantic, Baldwin saw himself as always in progress, "badly placed in time," and "victimized by my own legend," as he told the writer Quincy Troupe in his last interview. Recorded in November 1987, their conversation echoes with final statements, as Baldwin insisted, "I was right . . . I was trying to tell the truth," and regretted "an estrangement between myself and my generation." All he wanted was the impossible, for everyone to trust him. He yearned to change his country and the world by endowing people with what he valued most—the power of language and humanizing stories. This was a personal, humanist quest that failed as often as it succeeded, as his hastily scribbled notes emphasize: "I am not at all ashamed of having loved anyone I've loved, or of having been loved. I am ashamed of the times I've failed love." Literature was a tool for "learning to love one another." He understood love as a deep connection with others, including erotic attraction, sexual desire, and spirituality. Its complex workings propel his humanistic philosophy and pervade Baldwin's more private published works as well as obscure items in his archive: unpublished letters, notes, and drafts that drive this biography.

I first defined Black queer humanism in my earlier book, *Me and My House: James Baldwin's Last Decade in France* (2018). The philosophy reflects the paradoxical revolutions and unexpected symmetries between Baldwin's time and ours. His later twentieth century saw a sharp repolarization of racialized identities and their representations, just as we are seeing in our century. He anticipated the explosion of fluid, trans, and nonbinary identities that we have been experiencing for over a decade now. Attending to Baldwin's Black queer humanism helps us discern the powerful potential of his more private works, the buried parts of his archive, and the many physical features that contemporaries criticized in him—his illegitimacy, life abroad, small frame and swishy walk, prominent eyes, dark skin, and nervous mannerisms. A tribute to his auto-theoretical remix of the "jackpot" of his disadvantaged origins—"black, impoverished, homosexual"—this book revolves around the Black queer humanism philosophy.

The interactions of the three terms—"Black," "queer," and "humanism"—connect Baldwin's time to ours, when the importance and scarcity of private life grow as quickly as the National Security Agency's data storage tries to take it away. To start with the last, most capacious, term, Baldwin's vision reworks the old-fashioned Western philosophical concept of humanism that finds the meaning of human life in art and science, rather than in religious dogma. His years in Harlem churches and his gift for language helped him depict each individual life as rooted in personal experience and knowable through critical thinking and auto-theoretical multisensory imagination.

Key to Baldwin's humanism was his rejection of all labels and fixed notions of identity as "myths" or "lies." Baldwin believed that fictions about human difference exploited superficial variations of body shape, skin color, facial features, and hair texture, and were falsely broadcast as "facts" by politicians, teachers, pseudo-scholars, and priests. These fictions have functioned as mutually exclusive, divisive binaries of race (Black/white), gender (masculine/feminine), class and social status (low/high), and sexuality (hetero-/homo-), to name a few. They served institutions of power such as organized religion and the state. Handy for divide-and-conquer, fear-based politics, they have been used to justify slavery, war, mass incarceration, police brutality, economic and environmental exploitation, and sexual and gender violence.

Instead of harping on the untruth of identity labels and binaries, Baldwin explored the way they worked and why they held power over people and their imagination. Religiosity, misogyny, homophobia, colorism, nationalism, and classism corroded all human lives, including—Baldwin insisted—within African American communities. His airing of Black America's dirty laundry and his rejection of exclusionary conceptions of Americanness did not endear him to cultural and political elites on either side of the color line. No Black publisher in Harlem would hire him or publish his work in the 1940s. In the 1960s, he came across as angry, unwieldy, or extremist to some white reviewers, while Black publications either muted or reviled his sexuality for the sake of respectability, racial nationalism, or both. Echoing John and Robert Kennedy's joke about him, Baldwin was christened "Martin Luther Queen." The nickname caught, conflating racism, misogyny, and homophobia, as noted by the journalist W. J. Weatherby and scholars Lee Edelman, Douglas Field, and Marlon Ross (Baldwin as "an acclaimed homo sissy artist and activist" redefined the tele-visual in Ross's recent book). Yet Baldwin held on to moral and aesthetic rigor. In 1978, at City College in New York, the "Queen" was awarded the Martin Luther King Memorial Medal for his "lifelong dedication to humanitarian ideals." Black, homosexual, and increasingly foreign to his divisive compatriots, he made his odd-man-out status an engine of his writing.

My first term, "Black," took the place of "Negro" during Baldwin's lifetime; it later evolved into "Afro-American," "Afroamerican," and "African-American" (with or without a hyphen), and has recently returned to the capitalized "Black." All these terms refer to Americans of African diasporic descent and have been associated with generational and cultural shifts. In the 1960s, for example, the Black Panthers provided an edgier alternative to the National Association for the Advancement of Colored People (NAACP) and its politics of respectability. Baldwin grew up with "Negro," which he uses, alongside the N-word, in his writings and speeches. Later replaced by the above-mentioned terms, "Negro" now carries derogatory connotations, as do "mulatto" and "colored." Always wary of labels, Baldwin wrote about the term "Afro-American" as containing "two confusions" and two "undefinable proper nouns" in *No Name in the Street* (1972). Amid "cultural pretensions of history," he saw terms like these as merely "a mask for power," while intellect and imagination were individual responsibility, for "what is called civilization lives first of all in the mind."

In the 1970s and 1980s, deploying a somewhat similar unmasking tactic, Black feminists, lesbians, and queers articulated new understandings of race, gender, and sexuality as interlinked and interdependent. The novelist Alice Walker coined the term "womanism" to center female experience, love, and ways of being. Womanism also affirmed Black, southern, working-class, and immigrant cultural contributions. Artists and authors like Gloria Anzaldúa, bell hooks, Audre Lorde, and Cherríe Moraga coined another umbrella term—"feminist of color"—to distinguish their approach from both white middle-class feminism and Black, Latino, and other heteropatriarchal nationalisms.

The middle term in Baldwin's philosophy, "queer," was used during his youth to denote men who were sexually attracted to other men. Later replaced by "homosexual" and "gay," in the 1980s and early 1990s, "queer" reemerged when "gay," "lesbian," and "bisexual" were deemed inadequate to express the complexities of modern identity and identification. "Queer" now signifies multiple nonconforming, anti-heteronormative, and other nonbinary and norm-defying identities (e.g., genderqueer, member of Queer Nation). Semantically, "queer" communicates the transgression of social norms, the bending and crossing of boundaries. It rejects bourgeois traditions, gender roles, and family models. Widely established by the early 2000s, the term has been used in acronyms such as LGBTQ+ (lesbian, gay, bi-, trans, queer, and more) or LGBTQIA (lesbian, gay, bi-, trans, queer, intersex, and asexual). "Queer" also welcomes pronouns denoting non-cisgender and nonbinary identities and identifications of all hues: "they"/"them"/ "theirs," "hir"/"hirs"/"hirself," "Ze"/"Zir"/"Zirs"/"Zirself," and so on. In the early 2000s in academia, Black Queer Studies legitimated a new kind of inquiry into figures such as Baldwin. Its emergence as a new scholarly field in works by Roderick Ferguson, Mae G. Henderson, Sharon P. Holland, E. Patrick Johnson, Dwight McBride, Robert Reid-Pharr, Marlon B. Ross, Lynn O. Scott, myself, and others critiqued the traditional heteropatriarchal and essentialist underpinnings of African American Studies that dated to the 1970s.

A sharp-witted theorist and fierce cultural critic, Baldwin reconceptualized how Black authors were expected to write and how Black men could behave and live. His works help us comprehend the ways in which race-, gender-, and sex-based systems of oppression come together and how they also break apart, together. He understood the power of racialized sexuality in the United States decades before academics began incorporating his ideas into terms like "intersectionality" or "disidentification"; he wrote about androgyny in his late essay "Here Be Dragons." His ideas now trickle into debates between theorists of trans- versus nonbinary identities. Two recent celebrity memoirs, RuPaul's *The House of Hidden Meanings* (2024) and Billy Porter's *Unprotected* (2022), confirm his influence on today's gender-nonconforming artists.

Baldwin abhorred violence and machismo yet came to a sustained critique of masculinity only in later life, inspired by feminists of color. His alternative family model at his home in Saint-Paul-de-Vence reimagined traditional domesticity around Black and queer values. In "The Welcome Table," his last, unpublished play, for example, his stand-in is a Black woman singer, while his own house provides the setting. Sisters in art and thought including Maya Angelou, Nikki Giovanni, Florence Ladd, Audre Lorde, Vertamae Smart-Grosvenor, and Eleanor Traylor helped him feel valued when men, including members of Black Power organizations, asserted their masculinity by denigrating his. Alice Walker's *The Color Purple* and *In Search of Our Mothers' Gardens* held center place in his home library. (The author of *Just above My Head* and "The Welcome Table" would not have minded being called a womanist.)

Today, Baldwin's Black queer humanism helps us reconceive what it means to be human as the new Cold War and populism are reshaping our century. Affirming kaleidoscopic identities in the United States and beyond, it can serve as a lens through which to reexamine our history, culture, and relationships with our own selves and others. While virtual reality and artificial intelligence are being touted as substitutes for writers, artists, and teachers, we all yearn for real, rooted, body-affirming, multisensory language and vibrant imagination. The multiple cycles, rhythms, thoughts, and sensations driving us inspired Baldwin's creative descendant, the Nigerian American writer and photographer Teju Cole, who in *Blind Spot* (2017) imitates Baldwin's embodied, multisensory, organic approach to stories: "I begin to hear what I see."

In a somewhat similar vein, the sides and tracks of *James Baldwin: The Life Album* offer an untraditional, nonlinear biography. Like a phonograph record from Baldwin's own collection, this book can be experienced in sequence or sampled in sections. As it revolves around the central theme of Baldwin's Black queer humanism, each side and its tracks explore an influence in his life that becomes an important remixed and reinterpreted theme in his later writings. The achronological sampling of Baldwin's works in this LP-album-book allows us, for example, to hear from an older Baldwin reflecting on his experiences as a young child on Side A, Track 2. Similarly, his persistent memories of the Reverend Baldwin's abuse on Side C, Track 2 invite us to listen to the much younger Baldwin who flees into writing to process his pain and fear on Side A, Track 3.

Though despairing of its happening in his lifetime, Baldwin believed that we could create a world where each person was indeed judged on the content of their character. His faith was a stubborn act of hope that some called naïveté. Can we find the fortitude to read him deeply, embrace his humanism, and do the imaginative work he asks of us? As this book spins through the tracks of Baldwin's life, resonating with his complexities and uncontainable intellect, I invite my readers to compose their own variations using the sides and tracks that follow.

Side A

TRACK 1

———

Overture

I N A LONG, undated letter from the mid-1950s, James Baldwin wrote to his mother, Berdis, about his dramatic transformation as a published author: "When I was young . . . I thought that I would never be loved because I was so weak and ugly." In his thirties, hardly a titan of physical prowess, but with a well-received first novel, essay collection, and play to his credit, he explained, "No one, now, thinks of me as weak. They think, on the contrary, judging from the great demands they make on it, that my strength is inexhaustible." Baldwin continued, "Nor does anyone think of me as ugly anymore," for "I am considered so strong and so striking that I am quite beyond needing what other people need; and people tell me their troubles but they never seem to suspect that I have any of my own." Lapped in public adoration, he could entrust his woes only to his mother, "occasionally, at three o'clock in the morning." He did not mention feeling loved by anyone but her.

Baldwin had a deep and tender relationship with his mother, a compassionate, open-minded parent who loved him unconditionally. While Leeming mentions "minor disagreements" between them in his biography, they always maintained a "constructive dialogue" despite her deep religiosity. In 1980 Baldwin told Wolfgang Binder that it took him decades to understand her: "I would not describe my mother as a saint . . . how she managed that block, those streets, that subway, nine children. No saint would have gotten through it! . . . She saved all our lives. She is somebody." The mother also inadvertently gave his first lessons in literary metaphor when he was about five: Baldwin recalls in *No Name in the Street* a moment when he saw her studying a piece of black velvet. Murmuring to herself, "'That *is* a good idea' . . . she carefully placed this bit of cloth in the closet." In the imaginative child's mind, the swath of fabric magically transformed into a symbol—the material manifestation of meaning—an "idea." A literary metaphor was born, and along with it a special kind of narrator—tender, vulnerable, and filled with wonder.

Berdis, who might not have always understood her son's life choices and, indeed, some of his ideas, was always a patient listener. In a clip included in Karen Thorsen's documentary *James Baldwin: The Price of the Ticket,* she appears to be middle-aged, and she addresses the fraught issue of her son's vocation, explaining, "I knew he *had* to write." She nurtured his talent, enduring confrontations with her religiously authoritarian and homophobic husband, the Reverend David Baldwin. A minister and deacon, the reverend disapproved of books, movies, and theater, and he saw his stepson as irrevocably tainted by his illegitimacy. Although Baldwin details his mother's courage and perseverance at great length in several unpublished drafts, his printed words in *No Name in the Street* state the truth of her situation succinctly: "It did not take me long, nor did the children, as they came tumbling into this world, take long to discover that our mother paid an immense price for standing between us and our father."

Echoing these childhood sorrows, an early draft related to his first novel, *Go Tell It on the Mountain,* a 1947 sketch titled "I, John," fictionalizes Baldwin's relationship with his mother, framing her influence on its young narrator's personality. Young John associates his mama's voice with sunlight, song, and "mystery," "since the sun moved so freely over the room." Their mornings bloom after his father leaves for work. The boy often tumbles playfully in his sheets, then leaves the bed "barefoot, and open[s] the closet" door to "play . . . with his mother's shoes or stockings or hat or belts." When she later finds him "fallen asleep amidst the ruins," she picks him up and scolds him "soundly, telling him that he was the worst child in creation." Her love is tough but unfailing. "Though she slapped his fingers and, washing his face, scrubbed it with an unusual harshness, he was not really frightened, for he knew she was not angry." When he asked her, "*Mama?* Then she held him from her, looking at him; she hugged him tight, she kissed him and told him he was wound around her heart-strings."

John's father, though, "was always angry and . . . told him that he was the ugliest child in the world," claiming that John and his mother looked alike. "Then I'm the ugliest woman," the mother would retort. The boy confirmed their affinity: "dark (but not as dark as his father) with the same enormous, protruding eyes, the same flat, broad forehead, even the same widows' peak, the same wide mouth." A crossed-out sentence that follows in the manuscript foreshadows the boy's growth into manhood as her physical extension: "His mouth was to achieve in time the same bitter and defensive humor as her mouth; it was never to achieve the patience." His "slightly cleft" chin, which John dislikes, "was where an angel had kissed him just before he left heaven and became her little boy," his mother tells him, proclaiming his birth to be a miracle. With the same religion in mind, his father sees the cleft chin as "the mark left by the devil's little finger." The boy's world is forever split between his two parents.

Probably penned during time spent in both Harlem and France, "I, John" spotlights a young child and his imaginative awakening, a Black boy who is hypersensitive and vulnerable. John feels safe only with his mother, and his closeness to her confuses others. When John's Aunt Florence explains to a frowning family friend, the stern Sister McCandless, that he is a timid boy, for example, the sister concludes, "Don't look to me like he's real bright. Makes me nervous . . . hiding in a corner at the least little thing. That ain't no way for a boy to be." Little John finds himself outside socially accepted gender roles even before he knows what they mean, or where he would like to belong. By the time *Go Tell It on the Mountain* was published by Knopf—Baldwin dedicated it "For my Mother and Father"—its fourteen-year-old protagonist had lost much of his earlier innocence. And Baldwin had to give up his ambition to openly portray his protagonist's sexuality. Later in the story, John wrestles with the first pangs of sexual desire for a male deacon, which hit him, curiously enough, while he is also experiencing a religious awakening. As noted by his biographer W. J. Weatherby, one of the manuscripts ended with John's un-equivocal coming-out statement, "I want a man," which was removed by the editors. The published version was a compromise.

Baldwin never hid the strong autobiographical slant of his first novel, suggesting that his childhood and adolescence were similar to John's, at the same time as he claimed it as a fiction. As he soon realized, he had little choice over how others would see him and how they would classify his writing. He was lucky, for his public school teachers, such as Gertrude Ayer, Orilla "Bill" Miller, Horace Porter, and Abel Meeropol recognized his talent and encouraged him to mold his origins (and deconstruct the stereotypes they evoked) into literary material. In time, his self-reflective approach became his "ticket," "gimmick," or "jackpot," as he variously named his talent in many essays and interviews. With a little help from these teachers, both white and Black, he realized that he was intelligent and had a gift for language. Despite his painful awareness of his difference from his classmates, a desire to belong and succeed drove how he represented his life—the only story he knew firsthand when he embarked on his writing career. This helps explain why he constantly returned to representations of his life, and especially his childhood, throughout his works—an important theme that spins through the tracks on this side of his life album.

Recalling his childhood in unpublished undated autobiographical notes written much later than "I, John," Baldwin acknowledges its "darkness." In his usual dramatic fashion, he worries that he "received a wound so deep that it was all but mortal." Aware of the unreliability of memory, he suggests dark possibilities, "a feeling that something happened to me which should not have happened to any child [and that] my consciousness somehow smuggled it away." His past "walks up and down my sleeping & my waking hours," he muses, translating the feeling into writing. The questions prompted by this mysterious childhood wound multiply in the reader's mind: What was that injury and what caused it? Being born to an unwed mother? His bitter conflict with his stepfather? His ambivalence about his sexuality? A bodily or psychological trauma too unspeakable to name, or recall? All the above? The answers could have produced melodrama. In Baldwin's hands, they become vehicles for writing that disturbs, delights, and nurtures.

TRACK 2

———

In My Mother's Kitchen

BALDWIN'S FIRST CONSCIOUS experience of linking objects, thoughts, people, and literary expression came with the piece of black velvet he described in a scene from the story "I, John." A boy is pretending to be asleep while keenly observing his mother. She is leaning out of the window—something she has severely forbidden him to do—talking to a neighbor across their tenement building's air shaft. The neighbor is a strict "church lady" who sometimes babysits John. His mother, "with that admirable recklessness which characterized grown-ups . . . sat in the window talking to sister McCandless, who sat in the opposite window." The women often visited this way, each remaining in her own space. Once Sister McCandless gave his mother something, "and both women had leaned far out of their windows, and their hands met in the air." They passed something between them, which the boy could not see, "The something *was an idea*: a piece of black velvet cloth with stars. 'Thank you,' said his mother, looking at it, 'that's a wonderful idea.'—'You mighty welcome, said sister McCandless, I sure ain't got no use for it.'"

Returning to the scene a quarter of a century later, in *No Name in the Street*, Baldwin may have spun the memory with Duke Ellington's 1940 "Harlem Air Shaft" playing in the background, as his biographer the poet and scholar Ed Pavlić suggests. The mother's sentence—"That *is* a good idea"—opens Baldwin's book, thus making her words pivotal. The use of the black velvet prop between "I, John" and *No Name in the Street* illustrates how Baldwin's return and rewrite, record and remix method fuses experience and memory into literature. In "I, John," Sister McCandless has "no use for it" and passes the black cloth to the narrator's imaginative mother, who finds it a "wonderful idea." Useless to the former, interesting to the latter, the same object means different things to the two women. As the fascinated boy observes them, he is seeing not only two Black women but how meaning is made between the mother he loves and the neighbor he dislikes. But in 1972, Baldwin recalled this childhood epiphany with mock exasperation: "We can guess how old I must have been from the fact that for years afterward I thought that an 'idea' was a piece of black velvet." A silly piece of cloth, a mundane event, and a precocious boy's imagination add up to something written and beautiful.

Baldwin's mother, the heroine of the black velvet passage and a strong presence throughout his oeuvre, hailed from coastal Maryland's fishing community of Deal Island and came to New York City seeking work. She bore James Arthur out of wedlock at age twenty-two, in Harlem Hospital, on August 2, 1924. Baldwin probably never learned his biological father's name. David Leeming recalls, however, that Berdis, who was afraid of flying and thus had never visited her son in France, called him before his death in 1987 to disclose his father's identity. Apparently Baldwin never shared that information with anyone.

In his first novel, *Go Tell It on the Mountain*, John Grimes's missing father, Richard, is his mother Elizabeth's first great love; he works as a bellhop, jokes about her faith in God, and calls her "Little-bit." Sensitive and vulnerable, the bookish Richard dies before his son is born. Falsely accused of robbery, Richard is sent to prison, where he is severely beaten. After he is released, ignorant of Elizabeth's pregnancy, he kills himself. John is then raised by Richard's opposite—a preacher his mother marries after her son's birth—and remains unaware that the man he recognizes as his father is not biologically related to him.

In unpublished biographical notes later adopted as the preface to *Notes of a Native Son,* Baldwin wrote of his childhood as "the usual bleak fantasy . . . we can dismiss . . . with the restrained observation that I certainly would not consider living it again." When he was a toddler, Berdis married David Baldwin, a Pentecostal preacher from Louisiana who made his living as a factory worker. The preacher man gave her son a new last name, and James in time made it his own. Until his teenage years, when he accidentally overheard a conversation between his parents concerning his illegitimacy, Baldwin assumed that the reverend was his biological father. The novel and the life played on parallel tracks, while the important themes of illegitimacy and difficult fathers reverberate throughout his many woks.

Berdis and David Baldwin had eight children together—five girls and three boys born between 1928 and 1943—making Baldwin the eldest of nine. The precocious big brother proudly catalogues their births and his own, writing them into American literary history in *No Name in the Street:* "I, James, in August. George, in January. Barbara, in August. Wilmer, in October, David in December. Gloria, Ruth, Elizabeth, and (when we thought it was over!) Paula Maria, named by me, born on the day our father died, all in the summertime." As he wrote in the autobiographical notes that were later published by the Library of America, he "began plotting novels at about the time I learned to read" and wrote his first story, about the Spanish Civil War, as a tween; it won a prize and was published in "an extremely short-lived church newspaper." He was outraged that it had been "censored" by "the lady editor." From the beginning, his desire to write created conflict between his parents: "My mother was delighted by all these goings-on, but my father wasn't; he wanted me to be a preacher." In *No Name in the Street,* Baldwin recalls "being terrified of the man we called my father . . . whom I did not understand till he was past understanding." (This theme plays in Track 3.)

David Baldwin's mother, Barbara, who was born into slavery in Louisiana and bore twelve children by different white and Black men, came to spend her last years with the family in their tenement apartment. "She was so old that she never moved from her bed," her grandson remembers in *No Name in the Street.* "Pale and gaunt . . . she must have worn a kerchief because I don't remember her hair. . . . She loved me; she used to scold her son about the way he treated me; and he was a little afraid of her." Her death broke his heart. Not only because the legacy she left him was a disappointment—an old metal box that he thought was full of candy contained needles and thread instead—but because even more than his mother, whose "strength was only to be called on in an emergency," Grandma Barbara was a powerful woman who could control her son, and young Baldwin depended on her: "I knew—children *must* know—that she would always protect me with all her strength."

Protection was scarce in the Baldwin household, where the autocratic father made their mother, who "was always in the hospital, having another baby," "suffer quite beyond our ken." The children, who welcomed every newborn with open arms, "soon learned to depend on each other and became a kind of wordless conspiracy to protect *her.* (We were all, absolutely and mercilessly, united against our father.)" Racism and the harsh economy of the country helped keep Baldwin and his siblings in dire poverty. He was five at the time of the Great Crash on Wall Street in

1929. In an unpublished interview with the journalist Arthur Crossman, he recalled their living conditions as "hard to describe": "The first things I do remember were my father shoveling snow and the winter-time. I remember the houses and the tenements in which we lived, the broken windows and roaches and the rats and the falling plaster. I remember fights—our fights with the landlord to get these things corrected, we never won." Discipline at home came in two forms—his mother's expressive eyes and his father's strap—and brought unsurprising consequences: "She controlled us far better than our father ever could, for all he could do was beat us and beating a child simply hardens and sharpens the child," he told Crossman.

Baldwin's childhood lessons in social and economic status belonged to every "poor kid," he wrote in his unpublished notes. Always intertwined with race and class, as he realized later, gender and sexuality were much harder for him to understand while growing up in the poorest parts of Harlem. Men and manhood stood at the center of families, churches, and struggles for racial equality. The omnipresent Founding Father mythology pervaded the history taught in schools and memorialized in public places. It left little room for Black queer boys like him: "All you have to figure out is how you are going to outwit those forces which are determined to destroy you," he wrote, looking back at his impoverished, solitary youth. "You watch it trying to destroy your father and your mother and other people," yet your "father's the first person who makes it real to you." Raised in a conservative, heteropatriarchal culture, Baldwin valued his father's efforts and suffering. His mother's and other women's labors would too often go unnoticed or, at best, remain undervalued.

Yet it was the world of mothers, and spaces traditionally gendered feminine, that provided shelter for young Baldwin. In his mother's kitchen, "I read, without the remotest discrimination, everything that I could get my hands on," Baldwin recalled of his nanny duties, "with the book in one hand, the newest baby on my hipbone." He especially remembered reading *Uncle Tom's Cabin* around the age of seven. "I knew I did not really understand it," he explains in the *The Devil Finds Work*. That lack of understanding prompted the intensely curious child to reread Stowe's book obsessively, which worried his mother, who hid it. But soon she saw the futility of her efforts—he always found it and read it again. Soon, "in fear and trembling, [she] began to let me go," releasing her firstborn to the power of fiction.

A page-turner and runaway best seller in the United States and England, Stowe's novel contributed to the cultural work of the mid-nineteenth-century white abolitionist movement. Although Baldwin sharply criticized it in his essay "Everybody's Protest Novel," *Uncle Tom's Cabin* is a groundbreaking specimen of the vexed sentimental genre. Often in epistolary form, penned by predominantly female authors, sentimental novels had served didactic and entertainment purposes since the eighteenth century. (Nathaniel Hawthorne derided its creators as "the damned mob of scribbling women.") Stowe's strident antislavery message, sensational plot and characters, and melodramatic turns spawned an explosion of pirated copies alongside imitations and adaptations: stage performances, sheet music, children's books, toys, and illustrations, as well as, later, cinematic versions. *Uncle Tom's Cabin* sparked contention in the pre–Civil War United States, where many chose to disbelieve the cruelty and violence it portrayed.

Allegedly teased by Abraham Lincoln as the "little lady" who started the Civil War in 1861, Stowe was forced by its polarized reception to compile *A Key to Uncle Tom's Cabin* in 1854. Its subtitle explained her purpose: "Presenting the Original Facts and Documents upon Which the Story Is Founded, Together with Corroborative Statements Verifying the Truth of the Work." Filled with newspaper clippings, bills of sale, advertisements for "runaway slaves," and letters she solicited from enslaved and formerly enslaved people and their descendants, the hefty companion volume bolstered the novel's historical claims. It is unlikely that Baldwin read it, for he would presumably have mentioned it vis-à-vis his concerns with literary verisimilitude; it was also not as widely available as the novel or its children's version. In the later twentieth century, *Uncle Tom's Cabin* was rarely read but nearly uniformly reviled for its white pieties about slavery. It was blamed for employing racist stereotypes—Sambo, Mammy, Topsy (who embodied a Black child, a "pickanniny"), Eliza, and the tragic "mulatta" Cassy—and its titular Uncle Tom became an epithet for self-hating Black sellouts such as Uncle Ruckus in Aaron McGruder's cartoon and television series *The Boondocks* (2005).

To young Baldwin, Stowe's novel became an obsession; a 1967 edition surviving from his home library in France is in tatters. (He also owned a xeroxed copy of Richard Wright's first book, *Uncle Tom's Children*.) As Baldwin explained in an unpublished piece, as a child he associated *Uncle Tom's Cabin,* "somewhat desperately, with my bed-ridden grand-mother, who had, as I was told, been born a slave." He was astounded that at such an early age he managed to "associate my *grand-mother* with a *book,* and the book with slavery and slavery with *me.*" The complex connections he made between the women in his family, American history, books, race, and himself proved that he was no ordinary child. By the time he had penned "Everybody's Protest Novel," however, he was keen to break both into manhood and onto the publishing scene, where sentiment and domesticity played badly.

A sensitive, imaginative boy, Baldwin found 1930s–40s Harlem fertile ground for literary inspiration. Filled with transplanted Black southerners and immigrants, the neighborhood resounded with Spanish, Yiddish, Black English, and Slavic languages. Its people often kept to their tightly woven ethnic groups and were suspicious of others, especially those who did not share a religion or language. The area was overflowing with multitudinous sensations that floated up and down the avenues—cooking smells and noises, colorful clothing, singing, shouts, songs, and radio and phonograph music. In 1944, Duke Ellington explained his "Harlem Air Shaft" orchestral piece as employing a tenement architectural feature to express that richness: "You get the full essence of Harlem . . . your neighbor's laundry . . . janitor's dogs . . . people praying, fighting, snoring. . . . An air shaft is one great big loudspeaker." Baldwin, familiar with Ellington's composition and fond of synecdoche (the literary device of using the part for the whole), wrote about Harlem in his sole children's book, *Little Man, Little Man: A Story of Childhood* (1976), in similar ways. To its young narrator, TJ, home was beauty, excitement, joy, and violence, addiction, abuse, and danger in equal measure.

The Harlem streets blazed with a spectrum of human types: working people and church matrons, "bums," prostitutes, racketeers and other criminals; dandies, artists, students; doctors, professors, authors, and lawyers up on fashionable Sugar Hill. Everywhere children played on stoops, in the gutters, and in the streets. Neighbors and friends looked out for one another. A tacit understanding among parents was that other adults could discipline unruly children as long as the parents of the offender were later informed about it. Yet they did little to warn the kids about the dangers predatory strangers posed to them. As we will see, a sense of being left unguided and unprotected often tempers the multisensory richness of Baldwin's Harlem childhood memories, flashing painfully throughout his writings.

In 1948 when he was only twenty-four, Baldwin published the first piece inspired by his birthplace, "The Harlem Ghetto: Winter 1948." Subtitled unambiguously "The Vicious Circle of Frustration and Prejudice," this early essay explored Jewish-Black relations. It appeared in *Commentary* magazine, which was founded by the American Jewish Committee in 1945. Under Elliot E. Cohen's liberal editorship, *Commentary* offered a heady mix of political, cultural, and social views, with contributors ranging from the anti-Stalinist left to conservatives; Baldwin's being published there as an aspiring writer meant that he was noticed in New York's intellectual circles. In 1970, recalling his thinking then, Baldwin told the feminist anthropologist Margaret Mead that it was "the greatest crisis in my whole life. This whole Jewish/black thing." His Harlem, he writes in 1948, is slow to change, and often feels claustrophobic and alienating to an aspiring Black writer. Baldwin sounds angry, for example, because Black publishers in Harlem refused to hire him without a college degree. He criticizes the fact that Black churchgoers both identified with the persecuted Jews of the Old Testament and were taught to despise their descendants as white landlords and store owners. He analyzes Jewish-Black relationships astutely: "Caught in the American crossfire," where "a society must have a scapegoat . . . [and] hatred must have a symbol," he explains, "the Negro, facing a Jew, hates . . . not his Jewishness but the color of his skin." In the divisive U.S. national politics, "Georgia has the Negro and Harlem has the Jew."

In later essays, published in *The Fire Next Time* and *No Name in the Street,* Baldwin focused on material aspects of his Harlem childhood and how they formed his imagination and sense of self: "the rats, the murders on Lenox Avenue, the whores who lived downstairs," "wine-stained and urine-splashed hallway," "every knife and pistol fight . . . every disastrous bulletin: a cousin, mother of six, suddenly gone mad," "a slow, agonizing death in a terrible small room; someone's bright son blown into eternity by his own hand; another turned robber and carried off to jail." To its young, the neighborhood offered only two choices: the street

or the church. Neither was what Baldwin wanted, dreaming as he
was of writing his way out in novels, poems, and plays.

In his fiction, Harlem is a formative space for his characters,
even as they long to escape it. Its religious rituals, churches, and
families are central in *Go Tell It on the Mountain*. In contrast, it is
a distant, somewhat exotic counterpart to the bohemian Greenwich Village of *Another Country*. Filled with corrupt police, colorism, and religious fanaticism, Harlem is the place that many
young people, including Tish and Fonny in *If Beale Street Could
Talk* and the protagonists of *Just above My Head*, yearn to leave.
Baldwin's children's book *Little Man, Little Man* portrays the neighborhood through the eyes of several young characters inspired by
his family.

Among them, Blinky, a bookish tomboy of eight stands out.
Her glasses are described as "blinking just like the sun.... She ...
the color of sun-light when your eyes closed ... when ... open, she
the color of real black coffee, early in the morning." Blinky's difference, maturity, and "funny color" suggest she may be her cre-
ator's androgynous avatar; she has "unfulfilled queer potential,"
as I tell my students. TJ, the narrator, describes her as gender-
nonconforming, "She don't like nothing that wears dresses ...
always in blue jeans. Look like she do everything she can to be a
boy. But she ain't no boy." Written as a gift to his nephews and
nieces, gorgeously illustrated by Baldwin's close friend and unrequited love, the French painter Yoran Cazac, *Little Man* is primarily a book for adults. It voices Baldwin's conviction, based on
his own formative experience, that the place where children grow
up, and how and with whom, imprints them for life.

Baldwin's childhood also included childrearing as his mother's
helper. In *No Name in the Street*, we find some of the most striking
passages about babies ever written by a man. The narrator catalogues the many subtle sounds infants make, the fleeting mo-

ments of wonder as their bodies develop, the way sturdy love blooms amid the drudgery of chores: "It gives you a toothless smile when you come near it, gurgles or giggles when you pick it up, holds you tight by the thumb or the eyeball or the hair. . . . You begin the extraordinary journey of beginning to know and to control this creature." Baldwin's deep love for his brothers and sisters is evident in this passage, as is his embrace of mothering as something a boy or man could do.

The epilogue to *No Name in the Street* centers childbirth and midwifery as metaphors for a new world symbolized by a homoerotic embrace of the "alabaster Mary" and the "despised black mother," both impregnated by the Holy Ghost. This unholy family reflects Baldwin's love for his mother and sisters, his homage to their generative power, and perhaps even some envy of that power, as his letters and conversations with feminists that I examine on Side C will show. Interpretations of *No Name in the Street* have usually highlighted its explorations of the carceral state and criticized its cyclical, impressionistic structure. But the nonfiction volume's feminine themes and cyclical format signal Baldwin's growing awareness of the workings of gender and memory alongside alternative family models. The scholar Trudier Harris takes him to task for excluding lesbians and for continuing to "draw in [women's] potential for growth on the short rein of possibility" in the world dominated by men "whose egos are too fragile to grant their equality." As in *Little Man,* he leaves women's queer potential unexplored.

Though not always foregrounded as a strong, liberated presence, Baldwin's mother inflected his whole oeuvre. Several characters in his novels echo Berdis's quiet demeanor, physical appearance, and gentle personality: Elizabeth in *Go Tell It on the Mountain,* Rufus and Ida Scott's mother in *Another Country,* Sharon in *If Beale Street Could Talk,* and Florence and perhaps Amy in *Just above My Head.* In an unrealized story treatment that bears no date, "Victoria Lorraine St. John," hastily handwritten in black marker on a yellow pad, the title character is young, pregnant, and unmarried. A likely prototype for Tish, the nineteen-year-old first-person narrator of *If Beale Street Could Talk,* Victoria describes herself as "small & skinny and ugly and very black . . . sexy." Unashamed of her body and her condition, she physically resembles Berdis, whose petite stature Baldwin inherited; he was about 5′6″ and 135 pounds.

Victoria is among several women storytellers he planned in his later years to turn into protagonists of novels, plays, musicals, and screenplays. In another archived draft, titled "The Deathbed Conversion," the mother character resembles Berdis as much as the author: "Mama. Big eyes, a smile which she reached for everyday that she faced her children (this smile she gave to no one else)." Her size and unassuming presence disguise resilience: "She was smaller than our father, indeed she did not long remain much bigger than me. The smile counselled patience, from moment to moment, hour to hour, day to day; and year to year, if we should be so lucky as to be comforted." The overworked, often pregnant mother lacked time and energy for many tender moments with her children.

Like John Grimes, the protagonist of *Go Tell It on the Mountain,* Baldwin often associated his physical appearance with women, especially his mother, writing in an early draft of that first novel: "My father appeared to hate my mother, because of her eyes—he said she was ugly; but I thought she was beautiful, my mother, exactly because of those enormous eyes, which conveyed, when we were starving, so much, to all of us, even to the infant, without a word." In the draft of "The Deathbed Conversion," a novel he intended to write for his brother David, he throws his views on appearance against the white beauty standards made ubiquitous by mid-century American cinema. He recalls in a letter to Maya Angelou dated November 20, 1970, "Bette Davis, pop-eyed, over champagne, in close-up, in the Renaissance Theater.... And I fell in love with her because she was so ugly—our father said, because I look so much like my mother, and have those same big eyes, that I was the ugliest child he had ever seen."

The boy, his mother, and the white movie star blend into a hybrid creature in this instance of disidentification—the term popularized by the scholar José Muñoz's *Disidentifications* (1999). Inspired by Baldwin's writings on cinema, Muñoz's disidentification referred to how marginalized Americans negotiated the dominant culture's oppressive elements—racial or class stereotypes, posters of movie stars, beauty product ads, and so on. In the absence of bodies that looked like their own in prominent social spaces, gay men and women, people of color, immigrants, and artists could creatively recycle and "diss" omnipresent representations of whiteness, wealth, and body type to imagine their own identities.

Another, early deployment of Baldwin's disidentification appears in a late 1940s–early 1950s draft, "The Prisoner." In it, Baldwin described Johnnie, a young man who resembles John Grimes of *Go Tell It on the Mountain*, and Peter in his early short story "Previous Condition" (1948). At twenty-one, Johnnie wants to appear manly. Remembering himself vividly as a child, though, he intensely dislikes and wants to squelch that image: "He was small, scrawny, plain, and worn. No face, no body. ('Johnnie's gonna be a smart boy when he grows up' his mother used to say ... defensively? 'Ugliest chile I ever did see! I bet that's the ugliest ol' boy in the world,' his father had laughed)." The persistent memory of the parents' diverging visions of the boy carries into the final version of *Go Tell It on the Mountain*, where John Grimes not only believes his father's judgment but also links his ugliness to masturbation and his budding homosexuality.

Unable to disidentify from the image of himself given by his father, Gabriel, John staggers under the power of that parental condemnation. Unlike several of its drafts, in the published novel, Baldwin relegated the mother Elizabeth's love for John to the background. And yet, like her quiet gift of coins on her son's birthday given behind her husband's back, like her kind words and embrace after his father rejects John following his "threshing floor" religious conversion, that love proves stronger. For as Baldwin wrote his mother in the letter with which I began Side A, his writing made him everything he failed to be in his father's eyes.

Born with a curved lower spine that gave him a swaying, "swishy" walk, Baldwin was branded a sissy, his hypervisibility immediately attracting bullies. The Reverend Baldwin wanted his sons to be strong and "manly," and he increasingly despised his stepson as the boy matured into his mannerisms. In time, the precocious child who believed his father's judgments and, as he wrote in his autobiographical notes, "put pennies on [his] eyes every night to make them go back," began to question these paternal verdicts. He would seek affinities with groups that were rejected or marginalized by the reverend and his church—unreligious women, artists, queers. His yearning to belong among people who accepted and embraced him, who were like him and liked him, spurred his later search for a model of human identity that would fit everyone. But the young Baldwin was unable to verbalize what he was experiencing. Although he understood racism and economic exploitation, other forms of discrimination—sexism, misogyny, homophobia—were unfamiliar or harder to articulate. Even though he experienced similar oppression himself, or saw his mother and sisters suffer from it, misogyny and homophobia were often swept under the rug in Harlem, dismissed and disidentified from as white folks' problems. That's how it was then; sometimes it was easier and safer to close one's eyes and ears to what was reviled even though it could be an integral part of oneself.

Shaped by such circumstances and his desire to belong, Baldwin adapted his Black queer origins according to his audience, changing them to fit different needs. At times, he disidentified from them, using rhetoric associated with traditional family dynamics—in an interview clip in Thorsen's documentary, for example, he refers to "my woman, my children"—at others he claimed them as his jackpot; at still others he seemed to succumb to their depressive weight in private correspondence. In his unpublished autobiographical confession, his childhood appears as a period of profound confusion, split between spaces ruled by men and those ruled by women, with the attendant gender stereotypes. He writes, "[My] private life seems always to have been menaced by my circumstances, and my pride, and also a feminine, & total ignorance."

But whereas this remark seems to associate ignorance with the feminine, elsewhere he dates his birth to the historic moment marked by the emergence of several "skinny black girls" he clearly admired: "Josephine Baker—from St. Louis [who] went to France, just about the time that another skinny black girl—Ethel Waters—was singing *Supper-Time*." He mentions Zora Neale Hurston, "Jessie Huff-Fauset" (that is, Jessie Redmon Fauset, the literary editor of *The Crisis* magazine), and Ella Fitzgerald, whom he first heard when he was "selling shopping bags on 125th St." He recalls, "Bessie Smith was still alive, though I didn't know it, had never heard of her." Other famous Black artists he mentions in this manuscript include the Black male poets and writers Countee Cullen, Langston Hughes, and Jean Toomer.

As a child, Baldwin could not have known these artists associated with the Harlem Renaissance. His father's religiosity forbade participation in the Black creativity that made that part of the city central to an explosion in music, literature, and visual arts that Baldwin would come to admire. The glittering Apollo Theater and Hotel Theresa hosted many cultural events and were within an easy walking distance of the Baldwins' apartment located in the neighborhood of Fifth Avenue and 130th Street. In recounting the details of his life in these confessional notes, Baldwin thus inserts himself into national literary history in hindsight. He deliberately places his hardscrabble origins as a descendant of southern migrants in proximity to the "skinny black girls" like Hurston and Baker, perhaps preferring their company to that of men like Cullen, Hughes, and Toomer. Though his first, intuitive affinity was with the skinny black girls who looked like his mother, these talented Black men, whose sexual orientation he learned of only later (and some of whom he eventually met), became his idols once he entered school.

Looking back at his childhood and adolescence in his unpublished notes, Baldwin realized that he, and all Harlem and the United States, were locked in "the trap of history and sex and color," confinements that "no child can be expected to know." This confusion later led him, a voracious reader, to grapple with gender, as the demands and exclusions of identity and identification, so achingly troubling to a teen, spurred him to seek a means of springing this trap in his books. An autodidact who "read everything," as his biographer and friend David Leeming mentioned in our interview, he taught himself critical thinking and would soon expound on how gender and sexuality, as much as class and religion, were inextricably interwoven with race. His autobiographical notes confirm what his published essays rearticulate, "One writes out of one thing only—one's experience." Then comes grueling work that no talent alone can fuel: "everything depends on how relentlessly one forces from this experience the last drop, sweet or bitter, it can possibly give."

Baldwin's sometimes obsessive cycling back to the well-worn grooves of his troubled early life confirms not only its importance to his artistic evolution, but also how dramatically it shaped his thinking about humanism. It also helps us see how his return-and-rewrite handling of specific memories emerged as a lifelong literary method. Reading, writing, schoolwork, and many domestic labors operated for young Baldwin like themes in an Ellington composition. In addition to minding babies, he cleaned the family's four-room apartment, cooked, ran errands, and attended church, where he preached as a high schooler. With his father gone for most of the day, he was the man of the house, forced to mature too fast, seeking solace and enjoyment in reading and later writing, missing a carefree childhood like all the impoverished children whose stories never become books.

TRACK 3

_____

Sissy Boys Don't Belong

B ALDWIN CONSIDERED his tall, dark-skinned stepfather, the Reverend David Baldwin, handsome and even beautiful, and yearned for his love and acceptance, which never came. His own gender identity, so offensive to the minister, often puzzled him, for until he started school he had no alternative models of masculinity. Painfully self-conscious that his small frame and bookishness made him a target of other boys, he remained sensitive about his appearance and sensibilities, adopting the more relaxed, effeminate look he loved only in his later years in France. Like the one with his mother, Baldwin's relationship with his father, whom he assumed to be his biological parent until he was in high school, profoundly affected his work, sense of himself, sexuality, and relationships with other family members, lovers, and friends.

His father's physical and emotional abuse scarred Baldwin deeply, and memories of it play throughout his drafts and published works in a painful counterpoint to his mother's loving support. In a 1976 interview he described his father's "silence, rigidity ... beating us ... madness." Reverend Baldwin was the inspiration for John's father, Gabriel, in _Go Tell It on the Mountain_, who vows to beat his son's effeminate nature out of him; he may have echoed in Julia Miller's cruel father, Joel, in *Just above My Head*. Marked by his father's punishing hand, Baldwin abhorred and feared violence his whole life but was also attracted to strong, powerfully built, "straight-looking" men.

David Baldwin's violent treatment of his family, and especially of his stepson, demonstrated the fragility of that imposing man in a society and church that Baldwin would soon recognize as morally bankrupt. While the racism and poverty he endured did not excuse the reverend's abusive behavior—much less ameliorate the harm it caused his family—they partially explained the stress he was under. Unbeknownst to him, David Baldwin's actions may have been related to a genetically determined mental illness that later killed him. In time, the adult James Baldwin recognized his stepfather's tragic condition, even pitied him, though this recognition could not erase his childhood trauma and its physical and psychological effects.

A memory of a particularly brutal beating disrupts the flow of a late essay, "Here Be Dragons": "Once, my father gave me a dime . . . to go to the store for kerosene for the stove, and I fell on the icy streets and dropped the dime and lost it. My father beat me with an iron cord from the kitchen to the back room and back again, until I lay, half-conscious, on my belly on the floor." In a 1969 interview he described David Baldwin as an autocrat, "righteous in the pulpit and a monster in the house. . . . And it wasn't so much a matter of punishment with him: *he was trying to kill us. I've hated a few people, but actually I've hated only one person, and that was my father*. . . . I was not his son. I was a bastard." The beatings imprinted Baldwin's frail body with trauma years before he knew about his illegitimacy, contributing to his lifelong fear of violence, episodes of depression, and alcoholic self-medicating. In the 1989 documentary by Karen Thorsen, he recounts in a voiceover that his father "frightened" him "so badly" that nothing much seemed as terrifying in later life.

In unpublished handwritten notes probably dating to the 1970s–80s, Baldwin recalls that his stepfather had him circumcised at the age of five as a way of somehow erasing the sin of his illegitimacy: "I was little, and yet somewhat too old to be circumcised." The scar "I carry still looks as if my fore-skin had been hacked off with a broken bottle." He identifies the event as "an outrageous act of hostility against a helpless child." Worse still, the long-term effects of that wounding resulted in self-harm common among children whose physical bodies were violated: "Perhaps I thus then discovered that I was helpless and turned in on myself." He calls the taking of his foreskin "a species of rape" that had impressed itself on him "as a devastating punishment." In *Go Tell It on the Mountain,* a Baldwinian twist on a well-known Old Testament scene featuring the exposure of Noah's nakedness to his children has John utterly terrified: he glimpses his father's mighty penis in a bath while scrubbing Gabriel's back. John's own genitals lead him to masturbation, and thus are immediately associated with sin, but also offer pleasurable escape. John's autoerotic teenage pursuits are a contradiction—"that wickedness for which his father beat him and to which he clung in order to withstand his father."

Looking farther into Baldwin's past, the draft of "I, John" dwells on a young child's terror in the face of his father's anger at what he has missed during Sunday school. The father asks him about the text from the Bible, and the boy "did not dare to answer the question, for his father would surely know if he told a lie, his father would slap him if he said he could not remember." The terrified child stares at the card with the Bible verse, "which he could no longer see, for it was joined to his father's thumb, his father's wrist-bone." As the terrifying parent continues to interrogate John: "His entire body was hot, hot tears were just beneath his lashes. He made a last effort, not yet daring to look up, for to look up would be surrender, to let his father see that he was crying already." The father persists, berating the boy, who "began to be afraid that he would wet his pants"—his penis now implicated in his weakness and defeat. The scene ends with the man dismissing the boy, who is holding his hands to his face and squeezing his knees together: "'I'll *give* you something to cry about.' . . . If you ain't a sorry sight,' he said." In "Crying Holy," a later draft related to the same novel, Baldwin describes a nightmare in which the boy's father is chasing him as their Harlem church and street close in on him, crushing him.

Busy with his factory job and religious pursuits, the Reverend Baldwin had little time for his perplexing stepson, except to express displeasure and contempt. Baldwin's mother did what she could to protect and nurture her firstborn while they worked side by side. Often left alone and sent on errands unsupervised and unwarned about the possible dangers to a young boy, he was assaulted by a child molester as a tween. The incident was his first, brutal lesson about sex, money, and power.

As he describes in his unpublished notes, on one occasion, a man who appeared to be about thirty or forty years old called to Baldwin to run to the store for him. Baldwin went with him willingly to fetch money from the man's nearby apartment, hoping to make a dime, which was common for children his age. Once they were alone on the stairway landing, the man told him he was a cute boy and touched his face. Baldwin recalls, "His eyes got darker and darker, and he did not seem to be looking at me. I became more and more frightened; and silence, like waves, gathered and gathered on the landing, breaking over my head." The terror became amplified, for he had no idea what was happening, yet instinctively knew he was in danger. No one had told him that strangers could be predators; even less did he realize that some of them could have been victims of abuse like himself.

In a risky passage, he explains that when he felt the man's greedy hands on his body, handling his private parts, he was flooded with both fear and arousal, as his body responded to the man's touch: "I was entirely at his mercy, and if he had known anything about seduction, if he had looked at me, if he had taken me in his arms and kissed me, he might have been able to take me, I might have been able to give myself." What that terrifying encounter revealed to the young Baldwin—and what he could finally now tell, with bruising honesty in this unpublished manuscript—was that his own sexual nature and need for love made him easy prey for those who could manipulate them. After he got away and ran back home, he felt shamed and dirtied: "I locked myself in the bathroom, and threw the money—a quarter & two dimes—out of the bath-room window. I thought that I would never be clean again." Because he had had no knowledge that such experiences even existed, he wrote, "I did not know what was happening in me, and there was no one I could ask."

This painful encounter reappears in several published essays and interviews, and most significantly, in Baldwin's last novel, *Just above My Head*, in which a younger brother, the singer Arthur, describes an identical assault he experienced to the narrator, his older brother, Hall. They are both adults when Arthur finally unburdens himself, and Hall is shocked, not only to learn about the assault but because Arthur had no one to turn to in its aftermath. Hall feels guilty that he had not been able to protect little Arthur, who, doubly traumatized by the attack and by his family's inability to help him, plunges into religion and music as escapes. The brothers realize that their parents' silence about sex and their failure to warn their sons of such dangers make them partially

responsible for Arthur's trauma. The difficulty of Arthur's situation, like young Baldwin's, is exacerbated by his subsequent realization that he is sexually attracted to men. This sets him up to
fear and hate his body and its desires, to shun his longing for
homoerotic pleasure.

In his last published nonfiction volume, *The Evidence of Things
Not Seen*, Baldwin returns to the subject of children's vulnerability
and the responsibility of adults to teach them about their bodies
and protect them from sexual predators. In 1979–80, research on
the subject took him to Atlanta, where he investigated the murders and rapes of Black children, "mostly boys," according to the
FBI website about the crimes. *The Evidence of Things Not Seen*,
though still somewhat underappreciated, is a poignant statement
on the nature of law enforcement and on the American state's
shortcomings in its care for children and youth. Baldwin specu-
lates that whoever the serial killer and rapist was benefited from
his victims' ignorance and trust in public figures like teachers and
ministers. Like himself decades earlier, some of those children may
not have been taught anything about sexuality by their religiously
repressed parents.

Though filled with hardships, Baldwin's boyhood also contained much play, pleasure, and joy. Despite his parents' religious
devotion, for instance, the tenderhearted, dreamy, precocious
youngster was no stranger to boy-on-boy infatuations. In fact, he
met some of his heartthrobs in church. As he writes with gentle
humor in his confessional notes, "I remember, for example, that
when I was around nine or ten, I was very much in love with a boy
my age, named Romeo Clarke." The object of his affections was
very handsome and gentle, and, he writes, "we were so clearly &
openly in love that we were known as Romeo & Juliet." An echo
of that attachment returns in *Just above My Head* with the characters of Crunch and Arthur.

Young Baldwin's first romance with Romeo Clarke initiated a period of pubescent erotic experimentation. Baldwin as Juliet discovers sensory delights in the body of another, along with opportunities for everyday intimacy: "We lived, practically, in each other's nostrils. I remember him poking my belly-button. I remember him sitting in the toilet." They were children, "energetic and curious." Though Baldwin recalls doing nothing overtly sexual, he is certain they must have "looked at or touched or kissed the other's sex." His romance with Romeo did not last, however, as the other boy's family moved away abruptly. Baldwin did not realize until much later that their elders may have decided to separate them. Heartbroken, Baldwin went so deeply "Juliet" after losing his Romeo that he cried in despair on his beloved's former doorstep.

This love story became something of a warning concerning his budding erotic nature, especially after he entered school. There he was offered little education about his own and others' bodies, not to mention rules of respect, consent, and the existence of sexual and gender differences. Baldwin immediately stood out, which made him vulnerable without his fully understanding why. An older boy, he continued in the notes, "cornered me in the bathroom & pulled out his cock and ordered me to suck it." He sensed that as an effeminate male child, he had to protect himself: "No hero, I am yet no fool. I wouldn't do it—not only because I didn't like him enough, but because if he could make me do it once, he could make me do it all the time." Baldwin feared the bully would tell others, "and a life already miserable would have been made unbearable." Though his genitalia were obviously essential parts of his body to those who abused and harassed him—his stepfather, the pedophile, and the bathroom bully—as a victim, young Baldwin was disassociated from his body, its beauty, and its potential for pleasure. As he put it, "I didn't know, for a very long time, that I had a cock." He did love and desire as a child, though, without understanding his feelings, and suppressed his bodily urges out of self-preservation.

Soon after the bathroom incident, another object of his boyish affections taught him how to protect himself by, paradoxically, getting religion. In confessional notes, Baldwin muses that one of the reasons he entered the church to preach at fourteen was that he fell in love with a boy he calls "Ned," who was about a year older. The actual object of that infatuation was a childhood friend, Arthur Moore. Young Baldwin confused his love for Ned with a yearning for God: "All of my passion . . . translated itself into a tyrannical concern for his [Ned's] soul's salvation." Moore was also responsible for Baldwin's meeting Bishop Rosa Artemis Horn of Mount Calvary of the Pentecostal Faith church, where Moore's family worshipped.

Mother Horn, as she was known, was a transplanted southerner via Illinois, who came to Harlem in the 1930s. Her adopted white Scandinavian daughter later followed in her footsteps, becoming Bishop Gladys Brandhagen, known as the "white angel." Horn asked young Baldwin a question upon meeting him that he later repeated in several works: "Whose little boy are you?" To which "his heart replied at once, 'Why, yours.'" The charismatic, maternal preacher seemed to offer protection and hope, and he felt drawn to her, yearning to belong with her. Horn would later inspire the character of Sister Margaret, a powerful, conflicted preacher in Baldwin's first play, *The Amen Corner*. Rejected by the Reverend Baldwin, he was embraced by a maternal figure of no less authority.

The church offered a refuge where Baldwin could hide from his new, confusing sexual feelings. Later he mourned that his infatuation with Moore was stifled by religious propriety: "Poor him, poor me, when we should have been making love, discovering something real about each other, we were crying holy before the Lord," he wrote in an unpublished piece. Not discovering something real about each other meant a missed opportunity, a gap in his development that he would have to fill. He realized that children their age were experimenting with their bodies, "the laying on of hands—with the girls," but, unaware of same-sex love, he could not imagine boys doing something similar with each other. He chuckles at the person he was then, "so holy that no one would have dared to mention [sex and homosexuality] to me." On a camping trip, he and Arthur Moore once "lay on their backs in a tent and talked about sex and we both had wet dreams. We both repented to heaven, and we went on a purifying fast." Later, the boys corresponded, though they never explicitly discussed their mutual attraction. Baldwin used Moore as a model for the character of the handsome deacon Elisha in *Go Tell It on the Mountain* with whom John Grimes falls in love, confusing erotic passion with religious calling.

As he wrote in *The Fire Next Time*, the sinful street was not an option for the timid boy he was then; the only choice for the teenage Baldwin was a life in the church. He began preaching at his family's neighborhood Fireside Pentecostal Assembly at fourteen. His family also worshipped in other Harlem churches, including the Abyssinian Baptist Church on 138th Street and Mount Calvary of the Pentecostal Faith. Becoming a "saint" and a preacher required being "saved." Like John in *Go Tell It on the Mountain*, Baldwin found himself writhing in spiritual ecstasy on the "threshing floor" during a church service. Though his first novel paints that scene in unmistakably erotic terms, its author used his three years of preaching to hide his sexual longings. A refuge, the pulpit functioned similarly to a closet, where he locked himself away, shunning the temptations of the world. Afraid of where his confusing erotic desires could lead, he was "incredibly dedicated, &

remained a virgin, much to the surprise, if not the definite and horrified amusement of most of my fellow ministers," as he admits in the unpublished confessional notes. Always precocious, he had to admit to himself that he was hiding from the unavoidable hormonal upheavals plaguing his body. In his late essay "To Crush the Serpent" (1987), in which he retells the story of his psychosexual origins against the background of late twentieth-century American televangelist culture, he pondered his failure to escape desire as both its subject and object: "The young male preacher is a sexual prize in quite another way than the female; and congregations are made up of men and women."

Baldwin's juvenilia, published in the middle and high school literary magazines *The Pilot* and *The Magpie*, came out of some of these upheavals, and they offer insights into his teen struggles with his circumstances, internal as well as external. They echo his conflict with his father, his sexual confusion, the poverty and crime but also many enchantments and inspirations of his neighborhood, and a growing ambivalence about the church. He was also exploring homosexuality and homoerotic attraction in writings marred by much sentimental phrasing and exclamations of longing for love both in Jesus's and in another boy's arms. His 1941 play *These Two* is a prime example of this phase in his writing, as David Leeming notes. The play is quite melodramatic, with Stowe's influence unrepressed; its boy protagonists in love die tragically at the end following a run-in with the police. Victims of class and racial contempt, they are in the wrong place at the wrong time. In addition, their ignorance of their mutual attraction creates another tragedy.

These Two reflects Baldwin's growing social awareness as well, his never-ending fear for his life as a young Black queer man. Naturally anxious, he was learning about Black people who had been killed by police, drugs, and gang violence, or who had died by suicide. In an interview with David Frost in 1970, he summarizes the brutality of those statistics: "For every Sammy Davis, for every Jimmy Baldwin, for every black cat you have heard of in the history of this country, there are a hundred of us dead."

High school was also the place where Baldwin became aware of adult Black queer people. The poet Countee Cullen, who taught him French at Frederick Douglass Junior High, was gay, though closeted; Baldwin may have guessed Cullen's sexuality. Like all children at that age, he had crushes on friends in school and church. In Baldwin's hormonal adolescent imagination, his teachers, classmates, even fellow worshippers may have inspired erotic fantasies that the budding writer used as material. A steamy, incomplete, unpublished, undated, untitled handwritten piece of erotica stashed away among unrelated archival material at the Schomburg Center confirms that possibility. While the style suggests that it was written sometime after he finished high school, possibly years later, its setting—inside a teacher's office—points to Baldwin's school years as an inspiration. It begins on page 9 (the rest may have been lost), with an explicit sex scene between a teacher and a mature student athlete. Soon after, a sexual encounter ensues between two male teachers, an English instructor named Charlie, "heavy and black, and also from Alabama," and a white man named Kent. The men meet in Kent's office, which Charlie enters as the student exits; at first Charlie seems to be threatening to expose Kent's sexuality before coming on to him himself.

Baldwin explores the men's simultaneous, paradoxical yearning for passionate, macho sex bordering on violence and for soft, nearly (stereotypically) feminine affection. The draft combines vulnerability and sensuality with forceful desire fulfilled in graphically described sexual intercourse. Charlie, who instigated the sex, especially "treated Kent with a surprising and very moving tenderness," and when "Kent lay his head in Charlie's lap . . .

Charlie held him there." As if enacting an interracial sexual healing that anticipates Baldwin's harangue against the toxicity of the "American ideal of manhood" in "Here Be Dragons," this piece extolls "a very powerful affection between" American men who only appear to be straight. Baldwin would run variations on this trope in *Giovanni's Room, Another Country, Tell Me How Long the Train's Been Gone,* and *Just above My Head,* in which, as in his own life, religion, desire, and sexual passion revolved to the beat of achronological recall.

Baldwin's popularity as a charismatic preacher challenged his father's status as a deacon and absolute ruler in their home and in the house of the Lord alike. As a teen, Baldwin looked younger than his age because of his slight frame, and also because his father forbade him to wear long pants. He graduated to adult trousers after he entered the pulpit, but he had to buy his first pair with his own money. He enjoyed the sense of manly power the pulpit offered, and, oblivious to the oedipal context of his standoff with the Reverend Baldwin, he used the experience, not altogether consciously as he confessed later, to restore and cultivate his masculine pride.

In his unpublished confessional notes Baldwin writes bluntly about lording his newly found power over his violent stepfather: "My entry into the church was the definitive beginning of my father's decline." He admits that he both recognized this and "was pitiless about it . . . paying him back." His success in the pulpit was his revenge, one he took with grim determination: "In all but the most bluntly literal sense, I killed him." He felt that he had no choice in his actions, for "he had already tried to kill me." The young James Baldwin was unable to articulate these disturbing feelings when he "first climbed the stairs to the pulpit & entered my father's arena." Something in him knew, however, that "only one of us was going to be carried alive" out of there, and he was certain that the reverend knew it, too. His accidental discovery around the same time that he was not David Baldwin's biological son amplified these feelings.

Baldwin's church-fueled fear of sex, its dangers and its temptations, may have delayed his erotic awakening, but it did not stifle his natural curiosity. There was no lack of "opportunity" to overcome what he admitted in the notes was his deep "ignorance," or "excuse" concerning sexuality. He internalized the church's casting of the body as innately sinful and of the sexual act as dirty. Soaking up Christianity's misogyny and homophobia, he used them against himself and others. When he saw "girls who showed their pussy on the fire-escape," and "whores, in hall-ways, with their skirts above their head," they seemed barely human. They appeared to him as interchangeable body parts, receptacles for men's lust, which was no less disgusting and defiling. He remembered vividly "men & boys pissing everywhere, creaking beds, the groaning of our parents in their room, the dirty comic-books, & the births in our house." Carnal knowledge included, for him, reproduction, whose consequences he and his siblings witnessed at home with every new baby's arrival. Less lurid, these memories echo in the *The Fire Next Time,* whose "Down at the Cross" opens with horrors of puberty and a teenager's angst at the "whores and pimps and racketeers on the Avenue [who] had become a personal menace."

With no sex education at school, Baldwin knew nothing about women's sexuality, desire, and pleasure either. He was astounded, for example, when one of the "sisters" at the Fireside church wanted to strip the incorruptible young minister of his innocence. As he told David Leeming later, she used the "presence of her flesh" in the house of the Lord, pretending to be writhing in religious ecstasy to draw his attention. She then sent him a faked "sick call" that required him to visit her apartment late at night, presumably to deliver personal ministrations in the form of the laying on of hands. A late bloomer, he feared his arousal and women's sexuality even more.

At seventeen, though, Baldwin could not endure his holy insulation any longer. The church was the arena in which to fight his key struggles—his sexual awakening and "slugging it out with Daddy," as he defined his relationship with the reverend in an interview. Bored with preaching, in high school he began preparing himself to become a writer. A short story grew out of these efforts. "The Death of the Prophet," later published in *Commentary* (March 1950), blends a teen protagonist's memories of corporal punishment with his homoerotic longings. Its narrator, Johnnie, curses God in despair over his family's poverty. As punishment, his father "stripped him naked and beat him until he lay on the splintery floor, in feverish sobbing and in terror of death." Later, when a Jewish friend, David—probably inspired by Baldwin's high school crush—comes by, the anti-Semitic father insults him. Johnnie realizes that his father hates him for his friendship with a Jew, and for having made "his home in the populous Sodom," thus domesticating the two forms of discrimination expressed in this scene.

Soon afterward, having read "too much" in high school, Johnnie leaves home. At eighteen, neither a child nor religious any longer, at his mother's request he visits his dying father in the hospital. Finally free of the man's power, he feels palpable relief: "No more would this violent man possess him; this arm would never be raised again." Yet his father's death cannot erase his traumatic memories or his isolation. "Now he was the man, the conqueror, alone on the tilting earth," he reassures himself. Yet he still feels like a terrorized "two-year-old . . . sprawled on his face and belly and burning knees . . . screaming with that unutterably astounded, apocalyptic terror of a child." Overwhelmed by grief and a brutal flashback, Johnnie faints. The story ends when he comes to, alone with his pain, fury, and terror, with no father or god to accept and protect him.

For all the church gave Baldwin, it proved ultimately hollow. The cadences and imagery of the King James Bible verses he shouted in the pulpit made him a man. His influence over his congregation helped him embrace his rhetorical talents, yet this very power led him to realize that he was beginning to cheat at, or merely perform, his faith and ministry. Decades later, in *The Devil Finds Work* he explained, "When I entered the church, I ceased going to the theater. It took me awhile to realize that I was working in one." He also understood that his stepfather had been possessed by "his pain, his hatred, and frustration," and capable of only a "narrow and ugly perversion of faith." Baldwin was smarter than that and did not want to follow in those footsteps. He needed another option.

In *The Fire Next Time,* he juxtaposed most vividly his favorite metaphor of the street versus the church, one that represented his conviction that Harlem offered him two life choices only. The street encompassed the Black sinners of his neighborhood he feared and the predominantly white, Western realm of arts and culture that he loved and excelled at in school. The church meant the omnipresent eye of other believers in the fires of hell who desired his pound of flesh as a preacher—Young Brother Baldwin— in his father's terrifying house; it meant performing a role he no longer wanted. By the 1970s, he had begun to articulate, sometimes indirectly, an alternative to both—his art rooted in his complex self. In *The Devil Finds Work,* he returns to the theme of leaving the pulpit, casting his decision in the context of movies he watched as a teen and that of the secular street, "I could not stay in the pulpit . . . I could not make my peace with that particular lie— a lie, in any case, for me. I did not want to become Baby-Face

Martin—I could see that coming . . . since I found myself sur-rounded by what I was certain to become." Baby-Face Martin was a rough character played by Humphrey Bogart in a 1937 crime drama, *Dead End,* that Baldwin examines in the essay, remixing his thoughts about his childhood in Harlem yet again.

The black-and-white movie concerns a rich mobster who re-turns to his impoverished, but now quickly gentrifying, immi-grant neighborhood to visit his pious mother. When she rejects him as a sinner, Martin, filled with wounded pride, becomes vio-lent, endangering the local children. Baldwin recognizes that story: "I had seen the gangster . . . in *my* streets, with his one-hundred-dollar suits, and his silk shirts, and his hat: sometimes he was a pimp and sometimes he was a preacher and often he was both." His allusion to Bogart's hard-boiled character is more than a ref-erence to the movie's unrealistic plot and its ending (Martin's death in a shootout with the police); it is also another take on his rough childhood in the world where men like Martin ruled over children and women. Martin's demise and the children's rescue at the movie's conclusion, owing to his denunciation by a noble hero, seem utterly unrealistic to Baldwin: "In my streets, we never called the cops" and "I had never seen any children saved . . . be-cause . . . those who really wished to save the children became themselves, immediately, the target of the police." He seems to have forgotten his own happy ending. Or rather, as he did increas-ingly in his later works, he lets the reader discover a third option—his self-made salvation from the street-church dichotomy—in the lines of his gorgeous prose: a complex, and not entirely happy ending as the tracks to come will show.

Movies require surrender to fantasies and precisely for that reason offer a pleasurable escape from reality. In a paradoxical twist, Baldwin left the church by means of one when he was seventeen. One day in 1941 his best friend, Emile Capouya, "an American Jew, of Spanish descent . . . one of the most honest and honorable people I have ever known," dared him to attend a matinee right in the middle of a usual time of worship. Though a year younger, Capouya was a confidant and knew "to what extent my ministry tormented me," Baldwin recalled. (He was also the first person to whom Baldwin revealed his illegitimacy.) The film he and Capouya saw at the St. James Theater was *Native Son,* based on Richard Wright's novel. Directed by Orson Welles, whose staging of an all-Black cast in *Macbeth* had enchanted Baldwin as a child, the movie was a revelation. As Baldwin writes in *The Devil Finds Work,* at the movie's end he stood up abruptly in the balcony where he and Emile had been seated, and nearly fell "headlong . . . to the pit." He wanted to write not only novels but also plays and screenplays. Walking out of the church was a true leap of faith, and "demanded that I commit myself to the clear impossibility of becoming a writer." Making that impossibility a reality became his new vocation.

Baldwin preached his last sermon on his stepfather's favorite Bible verse, "Set thy house in order," addressing the reverend, who was probably sitting in front. The verse resonated fifteen years later in his extraordinary 1955 essay "Me and My House," later retitled "Notes of a Native Son." In it, Baldwin comes to terms with his father's death, sets his course as a moral writer, and ponders for the first time his ethical choices and Black queer humanist approach to identity. Though he returned to the church on visits and always loved Black religious music and sociability, by 1963, he was writing in *The Fire Next Time* that it was time Americans got rid of god. This was never forgiven, as Teju Cole remarks ironically in *Blind Spot* because Baldwin was a queer "writing for *The New Yorker* . . . talking black liberation while fucking white boys."

Baldwin's reasons for leaving the pulpit were deeply personal and had moral and material underpinnings. His triumph as a preacher did not prevent him from noticing the smug arrogance of some of the "saints" who applauded his preaching and their indifference to those excluded from the congregation. Such attitudes grated on him as much as the discovery that some church elders valued their homes and Cadillacs more than the well-being of a closeted queer youth like himself. He enjoyed his "manly" stature in the pulpit yet knew that he could never be cynical enough to embrace the church as a lucrative profession. Worst of all, he felt the sanctified fear and hatred of the body and the senses required by the church beginning to poison his own mind.

To his increasing horror, he was noticing how the fear of carnality, erotic desire, and pleasure were being translated into a universal, condemnatory suspicion of creativity, originality, and joy anywhere outside of worship. Members could get the spirit and writhe in physical ecstasy, as John Grimes does in his orgasmic religious conversion on the threshing floor in *Go Tell It on the Mountain*, but they were publicly shamed and punished for "walking disorderly"—real or imagined transgressions of acceptable conduct outside the church. Baldwin would later sum up that attitude as anti-sexual and antihuman, naming it "mortification of the flesh" in *The Devil Finds Work*, and return to it time and again in his works. Sexual repression destroys lives in nearly all his works, and especially his play *The Amen Corner* and novels *Giovanni's Room*, *If Beale Street Could Talk*, and *Just above My Head*.

His leap away from church happened a few years after Baldwin had ended his close relationship with Orilla "Bill" Miller, a beloved elementary school teacher. She had taken him to see the all-Black-cast performance of *Macbeth* and was the first adult who believed in his literary talent, encouraging, critiquing, and directing the first play he wrote. He never forgot her disappointment at his decision to forgo writing for preaching. In another revolution of his life story, years later they reconciled, and they remained close until his death.

At seventeen, however, he could not understand human limitations; he simply wanted to escape the prison that was the house of the Lord, the reverend's home, and the neighborhood where he did not feel he belonged. The street beckoned, with all the excitement and confusion it represented—books, bodies, movies, and theater—and through and beyond it loomed his own path.

TRACK 4

———

At the Blackboard

I N A 1963 INTERVIEW for *Life* magazine, Baldwin described his childhood fascination with literature: "You think your pain and your heartbreak are unprecedented in the history of the world, but then you read. It was Dostoyevsky and Dickens who taught me that the things that tormented me most were the very things that connected me with all the people who were alive, or who ever had been alive." The discovery that literature could forge an intimate connection between oneself and the rest of humanity pointed Baldwin toward his third life option, which became his own path. His creative journey beyond the church and the street centered his writing and became the heart of his philosophy.

Young Baldwin's voracious reading took him on that path to New York City's great public library, especially the 135th Street branch. As he wrote in his unpublished autobiographical notes, "There were two public libraries in Harlem and I read everything in both of them by the time I was thirteen. . . . The Schomburg collection had books about Africa which I had never really heard of and so I was fascinated by that." Though most of the books he read first were part of the "white world" in which he initially saw himself as an interloper, he quickly made that world his own, responding to its influences, imagining new possibilities. In an early book review of Maxim Gorky's *Mother*, he wrote that art "has its roots in the lives of human beings: the weakness, the strength, the absurdity. . . . It belongs to all of us, and this includes our foes, who are as desperate and as vacuous and as blind as we are and who can only be as evil as we are ourselves." His formal education ended in high school, but he remained an avid reader and autodidact for the rest of his life.

Educated in the New York City public school system at P.S. 24 and Frederick Douglass Junior High, Baldwin proved to be precocious in the classroom, thanks in part to that love of reading. Later, he traveled across town, virtually migrating into another world, to attend the prestigious DeWitt Clinton High School in the Bronx, where he was one of the few Black students. At P.S. 24, he encountered "Gertrude E. Ayer . . . *the first black Principal in the history of New York schools*. I did not know, then, what this meant: but, in 1963, doctor Kenneth Clark informed me that she was, until 1963, the only one," he recalled in the autobiographical notes. In response to a Christmas card he sent Ayer from Turkey in 1966, she wrote him an aerogram, recalling his P.S. 24 self as "Jimmy." The two kept in touch; Ayer wrote to him about her granddaughters, asking, "If you have time, write me. . . . Tell me a little more about Turkey and how you are being received. . . . I still have a snap of you taken in P.S. 24th. You are standing beside the student judge of the School City Court. You were Clerk of the Court. Remember?" She signed it, "Love." Possibly the first teacher who noticed his abilities in front of others—she once singled out his writing on the blackboard as exemplary—she helped Baldwin embrace his talent and trust it.

Another teacher Baldwin loved was Orilla "Bill" Miller (later Orilla Winfield). She was a white communist from Galva, Illinois, the lucky daughter of a progressive man who wanted her to be educated. The 1929 crash ended Bill's time in college and upended her family. One of her sisters was sent to live with relatives, as her parents could not afford to feed her. Forced to work, Miller came to New York as a teacher when she was about nineteen or twenty. A social idealist and ardent believer in democratic education, she chose to work in Harlem's elementary schools, where she created theater projects for the New Deal Works Progress Administration (WPA). She found young James Baldwin to be immensely bright, and immediately took him under her wing. She treated him as her "assistant" and talked to him with seriousness and respect, always calling him "James," while he and other students called her "Bill." Years later, in *The Devil Finds Work*, Baldwin wrote that she "directed my first play and endured my first theatrical tantrums and had then decided to escort me into the world." They read and heatedly discussed Dickens's novels *Bleak House* and *Oliver Twist*, and, after she married and he grew older, politics, history, and current events, "about Spain . . . and Ethiopia, and Italy, and the German Third Reich."

Bill took him to plays and movies "to which no one else would have dreamed of taking a ten-year-old boy," despite his father's disapproval. Berdis was happy for her son to have such opportunities, though, and David Baldwin did not dare refuse a white woman in a position of authority. That is how young Baldwin saw, at the Lafayette Theater on 132nd Street, Orson Welles's acclaimed stage production of *Macbeth* with its all-Black cast, set on a fictional Caribbean island during the Haitian Revolution. He had read the play in preparation for the performance and was thrilled at his discovery of the stage. Bill also took him to the movies, where *A Tale of Two Cities* and *20,000 Years in Sing Sing* impressed him deeply. Baldwin came to love Bill as a surrogate mother who could give him what his biological mother could not, crushed as she was by domestic duties and labor for others. Bill had Berdis's approval, gratitude, and friendship. The women corresponded, continuing even after Baldwin's death. Berdis also exchanged letters with Bill's sister Henrietta, who became part of young Baldwin's extended school family, along with Bill's husband, Evan Winfield. Baldwin, who called Henrietta Miller "Henry," came to love the entire family, not minding that they were white, and he considered their apartment his intellectual refuge, a second home of sorts.

He fell out with Bill at fourteen, however, after he was "saved" and joined the church. He went to her apartment to tell her that he had decided to become a preacher. If this declaration was a part of an age-appropriate rebellion against a mother figure, neither of them realized it. Barely a decade older than Baldwin, Bill was deeply disappointed. She perceived his decision as a cowardly turning away from the intellectual and secular vocations in which his talents lay, and she expressed her loss of respect for him in no uncertain terms. They were out of touch for a long while. By the time he left the church some three years later, she had moved to California; they did not rekindle their connection until the mid-1950s.

In *The Devil Finds Work*, Baldwin explains that Bill Miller was one of the reasons he could never hate whites as a group or a racialized category. Like his mother, Bill taught him never to judge others by the color of their skin: "I was a child . . . and, therefore, unsophisticated. I don't seem ever to have had any innate need to . . . distrust people: and so I took Bill Miller as she was, or as she appeared to be to me. . . . From Miss Miller . . . I began to suspect that white people did not act as they did because they were white, but for some other reason, and I began to try to locate and understand that reason. She, too, anyway, was treated like a n[-]r, especially by the cops, and she had no love of landlords." Their reunion was sparked by Baldwin's masterful essay "Me and My House." Bill saw her name mentioned on the first page when it appeared in *Harper's* magazine in 1955. She wrote to the publisher, who forwarded her letter to Baldwin. (It is now in his archive at Beinecke Library at Yale University.)

It was not until the early 1960s that Bill and her husband Evan finally saw Baldwin in person again. They were mesmerized when they heard him speak on tour with CORE in Southern California, where they then lived. Bill's niece Lynn Orilla Scott interviewed her aunt in the early 1990s for a dissertation on Baldwin, and Bill reported that she had been "utterly surprised" by Baldwin's charisma as an adult. He was "an absolutely stunning and dramatic speaker. He had the whole audience in the palm of his hand." To the regret of both, the reunited friends were unable to visit for more than a few minutes after his speech was over. Baldwin was whisked away to a fundraiser soon after they first hugged. Bill was immediately concerned about his health, as she had been when he was a kid. He seemed to her "the most exhausted looking person I've ever seen," she wrote to him in one of the letters that followed.

Along with Principal Ayer, Bill was the first teacher to ignite Baldwin's passion for writing and take his creative ambitions seriously. She helped him believe in himself. Even though he could not afford to go to college, she taught her beloved student that not only was it possible for him to become a writer with only his tough origins as capital, but also that he had every right to use his writing to shape American culture. In a May 15, 1963, letter, Bill explained tenderly, "I am writing this note while the impact of the L.A. . . . meeting is still fresh. It was hearing you and touching you that completed the picture." His teacher still, she elaborated, "I want to tell you that the . . . promise of the wonderful child has been fulfilled in the man. I am not referring alone to the development of your writing ability. . . . I am referring to the moral you—in that broad sense of one's individual relationship to man around him. That Evan and I had a small part in your life adds to the value of ours. I also say, thank you, that there is this James Baldwin in America in the year 1963." In our 2017 interview, Ken Winfield, Bill and Evan's son, explained that he had heard a lot about Baldwin while growing up. He remembered his mother using the formal "James" when referring to him, rather than the familiar "Jimmy" flaunted by too many of the writer's lesser acquaintances. Bill's two sons accepted that Baldwin was their mother's "first son," and were comfortable with the deep bond between the two.

Ken also witnessed the last meeting between the teacher and her student in 1986. Baldwin was lecturing at the University of California, Santa Barbara, and came to pay a visit. He might have begun to suspect that his cancer was terminal, for the meeting was intensely emotional. Evan had already died, and in our interview, Ken recalls Baldwin being focused on Bill the whole time. "It was like sitting in a gallery . . . he went to Mom's rocker and held her hand for two hours without letting go . . . [as they] talked about their years together in Harlem." According to many who knew them both, Bill and Baldwin shared many qualities; they were people who were open, curious about the world, and interested in others. Charismatic and warm, they attracted followers. As Bill's niece explained to me, Bill was admired for her charisma and activism, and had developed her "own entourage . . . mostly women," who followed her, even moving from their home states to stay close to her. After her husband's death, Bill moved to Michigan. She remained tremendously proud of Baldwin's work, especially his civil rights activism. She may have inspired him to try his own hand at teaching, first in Turkey and then during intermittent visits to the United States in the 1980s.

In unpublished notes, Baldwin wrote about his schooling and how much his eclectic education had influenced his intellectual development and shaped his politics. He considered himself "luckier in school than the children are today," noting that his "situation, however grim, was, also, relatively coherent." Though most of his teachers were white, "many were black (or, in those days, *Negro*, or *colored*). It is worth pointing out that some of the white teachers—not many, but some—were very definitely on the Left: opposed Franco's Spain, for example, and Mussolini's Italy, and Hitler's Third Reich." He soon learned that for their views, which the U.S. government and especially its leaders, such as Senator Joseph McCarthy, considered extreme and dangerous, "they were, not so very much later . . . placed on black-lists and drummed out of the academic community: to the everlasting shame of that community."

Among Baldwin's other educators was a radical southern socialist, Wilmer Stone, who also noticed his literary talent, and Abel Meeropol, a child of Russian-Jewish immigrants, a communist, and a poet, lyricist, librettist, and musician. Meeropol taught English at DeWitt Clinton High School. Publishing poetry under the pen name Lewis Allan, Meeropol set his 1937 poem "Bitter Fruit" to music, creating the famous song "Strange Fruit" that Billie Holiday and Nina Simone performed to great acclaim. Meeropol also adopted Julius and Ethel Rosenberg's children, Michael and Robert, who were orphaned when their parents were executed in the infamous Soviet espionage trial in 1953. In a September 5, 1974, letter, Meeropol reminds Baldwin of one classroom assignment, recalling "a small boy with big eyes." Meeropol would "send groups of boys to the blackboard to write one paragraph on a particular subject and then have a general discussion with the class as to how well each boy expressed his thoughts and feelings in the paragraph." Baldwin was "to describe some aspects of a scene of nature," and Meeropol's letter recalled a lovely metaphor: "You chose a winter scene in the country and the one phrase I never forgot was 'the houses in their little white overcoats.' It was a beautiful imaginative expression from a little boy."

Moved by their epistolary reunion, Baldwin responded on September 29, thanking Meeropol for teaching him "the connection between one human life and another." The only things Baldwin remembered from that day in school, alas, were the "black-board" and the "bottomless terror" in which he lived as a shy and "strange" child. "But if I wrote the line which you remember, then I must have trusted you," he concluded. By then, Baldwin's ideas were circling in on a humanistic philosophy: "Each of us, whether or not we know it, or can face it, is tied to the other," he wrote Meeropol. Yet his conviction was a tough sell to others, for "the attempt to state such a thing is banal: better, simply, to trust it and recognize it as unanswerable." Ostracized by keepers of racialized virtue on both sides of the U.S. color line in the 1970s, Baldwin waited to express this sentiment publicly until 1985, when he published the essay "Freaks and the American Ideal of Manhood" (later retitled "Here Be Dragons") in *Playboy*.

Meeropol's teachings echoed those of Bill Miller, who, as Baldwin recalled in *The Devil Finds Work*, "tried to suggest to me the extent to which the world's social and economic arrangements are responsible for (and to) the world's victims. But a victim may or may not have a color, just as he may or may not have virtue." His realization that victims need not be good, or that suffering does not create virtue was a "difficult . . . unpopular notion, for nearly everyone prefers to be defined by his status, which, unlike his virtue, is ready to wear." Baldwin's responsiveness to his teachers also resonated with his own unrequited desire to become a parent, an impossibility for him at that time. The friends of his whom I interviewed in the United States and Turkey in 2001–7—David Leeming, Sedat Pakay, Engin Cezzar, Zeynep Oral, and Gülriz Sururi—assured me that they were convinced he would have made a marvelous father. But Baldwin had to console himself by spoiling his many nephews and nieces. (His intellectual interest in child psychology blossomed within a friendship with the renowned African American social scientists Kenneth and Mamie Clark, who were instrumental in the 1954 *Brown v. Board of Education* litigation that ended public school segregation in the United States.)

Baldwin was surprised to find that the author of "Strange Fruit"—a song considered quintessentially Black—was Jewish. Nor, as Baldwin wrote in his September 29 letter to Meeropol, "could it possibly have occurred to me that one of my teachers raised the Rosenberg children. It's a perfectly senseless thing to say, but I'll say it anyway: it makes me very proud." In a 1975 letter, one of those children, Michael Meeropol, mentions Baldwin's "break with the NY literary establishment around my parents' case," a break that might have been due to a publication that he and his brother hoped would help clear their family name. As his father Abel Meeropol explained in strong terms to Baldwin in a letter of October 28, 1974, they were all "delighted . . . with your warm, sympathetic understanding of the frame-up of the Rosenbergs and the unconscionable psychological torture two little children were subjected to by the judenrats of these dreadful witchhunting days."

Having experienced hatred and homophobia from his own people and FBI surveillance courtesy of his homeland, Baldwin could understand Meeropol's thinking. He certainly shared his old teacher's views on the treatment of minorities in America. "I happen to be Jewish," Meeropol wrote, "but there have been judenrats even in Nazi Germany and as you very well know our whitewashed history is honeycombed with the most vicious cruelty beginning with the American Indian." Their epistolary call-and-response echoes Baldwin's early views on Black-Jewish relationships in the 1948 "Harlem Ghetto" essay and the trajectory of his thinking in later pieces such as "Negroes Are Anti-Semitic Because They're Anti-White."

Among Baldwin's Black teachers, "never . . . to be forgotten," was his math instructor at Frederick Douglass Junior High, Herman W. Porter, as he reports in his unpublished autobiographical notes. Harvard-educated, Porter was a father figure of sorts, just as Bill Miller had served as a mother figure in Baldwin's younger years. Porter "soon gave up any attempt to teach me Math," Baldwin's account continues, for "[I] had been born, apparently, with some kind of deformity which resulted in a total inability to count: from arithmetic to geometry, I never passed a single test." His learning disorder was never diagnosed, but Porter wisely channeled his student's abilities in a direction where he could shine, helping him run the school magazine. "He assigned me a story for this magazine, concerning Harlem . . . that demanded serious research," Baldwin recalls. Porter took him downtown to the 42nd Street library and waited for him while he studied. The student remembers the event for both the academic and the psychosomatic effects it had on him: Mr. Porter "was very proud of this story I eventually turned in, but, I remember, I was so terrified that after-noon that, as we were descending again into the subway, I vomited all over his shoes."

Baldwin's biographer David Leeming narrates that trip to the library differently. Like Bill Miller before him, Herman Porter met Baldwin's father when picking the boy up at the family's Harlem apartment. Unlike Bill, however, Porter was insulted and accused of corrupting the boy "with books by white devils," for the reverend felt free to unleash his wrath against a Black teacher. David Baldwin's behavior upset his son so much that the child vomited in the street, after he and Porter had left the apartment. Unlike the much younger Bill Miller, Herman Porter was aware of the reverend's hostility and understood the racial, class, and especially religious complexities of the family's situation that were likely incomprehensible to the atheist Bill.

Another important Black teacher at Frederick Douglass, the

celebrated poet Countee Cullen, also provided some semi-parental care and encouragement to pursue writing. Cullen advised Baldwin on poetry and prose, once chiding him that he wrote too much like Langston Hughes, which was not to the more formalist Cullen's taste. Baldwin was convinced, though, that he was imitating his mentor—Cullen. Both Porter and Cullen gave Baldwin his first editorial job. Porter secured the editor-in-chief position for him at the school's literary magazine, *The Douglass Pilot,* which had been founded by Cullen.

A Schomburg Center folder contains Baldwin's first business card with a decorative green border: "*The Douglass Pilot* School Magazine—June 1938—James Baldwin, Editor-in-chief, Class 9B1." His stories include "Be the Best," inspired by Douglas Malloch's motivational poem about a "little scrub," and "One Sunday Afternoon," about a white "bum" who talks about his life's disappointments. Baldwin's nameless narrator introduces himself as a member of a boys' club, the "Super Secret Service Men of the United States." The task of this mysterious society is to collect random strangers' stories. His goes like this: The "bum" became homeless after his parents, "true New Englanders—bleak and cold," prevented him from realizing his dream of becoming an actor. "That's the most important thing in Life, doing what you can do well, the way you ought to do it," he admonishes the young narrator. "Don't you ever forget what I've said. You see before you a man who is a failure in life because he wasn't courageous enough to stare opposition in the face and stare it down."

Baldwin also penned another didactic *Pilot* piece, "Success Story," about the Black actor Alvin Childress from Meridian, Mississippi, a member of Harlem's Lafayette Players. Childress, who later became known for the *The Amos 'n' Andy Show* on CBS, remained forever typecast. He had intended in college to become a physician but then joined the Federal Theatre Project and appeared in a production of *Haiti* by William DuBois in 1938. We do not know whether Baldwin saw that production, but it is possible that the enterprising young editor and writer cleverly recycled Childress's life story as an inspiration for "One Sunday Afternoon"— an early example of his dexterous literary imagination.

When Baldwin left Douglass for DeWitt Clinton High School, which he attended from 1938 to 1942, he continued his editorial work at that school's literary magazine, *The Magpie*. Clinton was at the time a boys' school, and there he met youngsters who became close friends and adolescent crushes; some also became prominent writers and artists: Sol Stein, Emile Capouya, and Richard Avedon. (Other famous alumni include the painter Romare Bearden, Stan Lee of Marvel Comics, the poet Gil Scott-Heron, the photographer Robert Mark Altman, and the journalist Robert Warshow, who later became Baldwin's editor at *Commentary*.) His closest friend, who saw him through adolescent heartbreaks, was Emile Capouya. Later part of the New York City intellectual and leftist circles that Baldwin would also enter as a budding book reviewer, Capouya became a successful writer and publisher. Like another buddy of the *Magpie* circle, Sol Stein, Capouya fought in World War II, while Baldwin was exempted from service as his family's breadwinner.

The Magpie featured Baldwin's and his friends' poems, short stories, and editorials. One issue housed at the Schomburg Center includes a World War II–inspired short story, "Peace on Earth," which opens with a black-and-white drawing by an artist named "Jon Baldwin" of a dying soldier held up by two others, while a third soldier looks up from a dugout. It is unclear whether Baldwin was the artist; occasional sketches and doodles throughout his archived papers make it plausible. The "Peace on Earth" characters are young Black men: Stan, Pete, and the unnamed first-person narrator. They are all "part of that much ridiculed class of people known as 'Holy-Rollers'"; their white comrade, Jonny, is "the youngest and most religious of us," the narrator clarifies. While they talk about girls and how they miss home, Pete dies in a sudden explosion. *The Magpie* issues held in the Beinecke Library collection at Yale contain another World War II story, "An Incident in London," that features Baldwin's Clinton buddies Avedon, Capouya, and Stein. Another story, "Mississippi Legend," has "a woman of magic" as its main character. In yet another, a storyteller speaks to the narrator in what seems to be Baldwin's early attempt at Black English or a southern dialect. A poem about the gaiety of youth appears as an early attempt at verse.

At the all-male Clinton, Baldwin's closest friends were nearly all white and Jewish. He had crushes on several of them, especially Capouya, and possibly Avedon. Perhaps an early inspiration for the tender masculinity Baldwin imagined in his juvenilia, Emile Capouya understood Baldwin's torment after the discovery of his illegitimacy and his inner turmoil when the pulpit lost its allure. The former star student, Baldwin began failing at school and had to take an extra year to graduate. After finishing, he and Capouya looked for their first jobs together. Capouya's extraordinary compassion and care for his friend's needs perhaps signaled that he welcomed and reciprocated Baldwin's love to some degree.

Capouya also helped Baldwin take the leap of faith into writing by introducing him to a new mentor, a Black artist who was possibly as complex as the young Baldwin. A year before he preached his last sermon, Baldwin had traveled to Greenwich Village to meet the painter Beauford Delaney. Capouya had already met Delaney and deemed him the role model his friend needed on his new path. Delaney's affection and patience would save and shape Baldwin's life in extraordinary ways. A protégé and surrogate son, Baldwin would enrich Delaney's no less profoundly, as we'll discover on Side B.

Side B

TRACK 1

Through the Door of My Lips

I N THE TITULAR ESSAY, "The Price of the Ticket" (1985), which opens a collected nonfiction volume published shortly before his death, Baldwin recalls a momentous day in 1940. On that day the budding writer's labors in his mother's kitchen, his teachers' lessons in solidarity and humanism, and the trauma his father caused him encountered a new artistic force. As Baldwin stood on the threshold of the Black painter Beauford Delaney's Greenwich Village studio at 181 Greene Street, "A short, round brown man . . . looked at me. He had the most extraordinary eyes I'd ever seen." The older artist's powerful gaze oversaw Baldwin's further literary evolution and directed his changing self-image. His comment about Delaney—"He opened the door all right"— echoes a church spiritual, "Lord, Open the Unusual Door," as well as Psalm 141:3–4, "Set a guard over my mouth, Lord; / keep watch over the door of my lips. // Do not let my heart be drawn to what is evil / so that I take part in wicked deeds." Sounding the importance of their meeting, this opening signaled a new chapter in Baldwin's journey.

Beyond that door, Delaney's studio became both home and workspace. The painter loved vivid colors, and embraced white—a necessary background, contrast, and lighting—in his art. Baldwin's passage into this light-filled space brought him face-to-face with multisensory creativity. He writes in "The Price of the Ticket" that he "walked . . . into Beauford's colors—on the easel, on the pallet, against the wall—sometimes turned to the wall—and sometimes (in limbo?) covered by white sheets." In the same essay, he vividly recalled the "small studio (but it didn't seem small) with a black pot-bellied stove somewhere near the two windows." The space telescoped him into a world filled with new places, sounds, and people:

> There *was* a fire escape which Beauford, simply by his presence, had transmuted into the most exclusive terrace in Manhattan or Bombay. I walked into music. I had grown up with music, but, now, on Beauford's small black record player, I began to hear what I had never dared or been able to hear. . . . I really began to *hear* Ella Fitzgerald, Ma Rainey, Louis Armstrong, Bessie Smith, Ethel Waters, Paul Robeson, Lena Horne, Fats Waller . . . Duke Ellington and W.C. Handy, and Josh White . . . Frankie Newton. . . . And these people were not meant to be looked on by me as celebrities, but as a part of Beauford's life and as part of my inheritance.

In a letter of May 30, 1963, Baldwin wrote to the actor Harry Belafonte to enlist his support for an exhibit of Delaney's paintings. Comparing his mentor to great European modernists, he expressed his debt to Delaney, "my spiritual father": "It is impossible, probably, to describe his work. There is something in it of Cezanne and Van Gogh, and it owes a great deal to the blues. But this is only to suggest, and very weakly, that he brings great light out of the terrible darkness of his journey, and makes his journey, and his endeavors, and his triumph, ours." The meeting with Delaney marked another jackpot moment. The painter contained "all the stars, all the constellations, all the angels . . . [and] the universal brotherhood of man," as Henry Miller described him in 1945. Baldwin called Delaney his "principal witness."

A self-supporting artist, Delaney was a fortuitous male role model for the impressionable, conflicted teenager. His lessons about Black manhood diverged dramatically from what Baldwin had learned in his father's house and at church. In Delaney's studio, he was accepted as a Black queer artist, encouraged, and nurtured to embrace his writing vocation. Hybrid, often experimental, always evolving, Delaney's art radically engaged and transformed the Western models he had studied in school. Helping to confirm Baldwin's own choice of a creative path and desire to find his unique voice, it provided the teenager with an inheritance—a new patrimony that amply compensated for the university education he was missing. Surrounded by music, dance, paintings, textiles, and sculptures that propelled the painter's creativity, Baldwin soaked it all up like a sponge. In letters to friends, he wrote about learning "Life," as he called the novel universe accessed through Delaney's door: secular culture, visual arts, exciting friends, dating, music, sex, love, and previously forbidden drinking and smoking.

By the time they met, Delaney had already held some one-man shows. The subject of a 1938 *Life* magazine feature, he was part of the modernist Black arts scene known as the Harlem Renaissance. For his part, working at "a Dickensian job, after school, in a sweatshop on Canal Street," Baldwin "was getting on so badly at home" that he dreaded returning. Delaney understood his protégé's hunger for affection and acceptance. He saw that Baldwin was both drawn to and intimidated by the intellectual and artistic circles of the Village, which offered more than Harlem's street vs. church choices. This more liberal, bohemian neighborhood became Baldwin's new home. Delaney named Baldwin "Prince," and sat him down for a portrait.

To the teenager, that sitting probably revealed what he never felt he could own: beauty, desirability, even exceptionalism. A freshly minted royal, Baldwin eagerly took all that his spiritual father offered, embracing multisensory creative pursuits and stimuli that fed his budding writer's desire. Now he could build on, even flaunt, his impoverished, Black, queer origins. Prince Baldwin could write whatever he pleased, turning the experience and memories of his earlier years into literature. Disconnecting from his old home, earning his own money, and writing as much as possible was neither romantic nor easy. To do it, he had to work a variety of often backbreaking blue-collar jobs while he was still in high school and after graduation. Having accepted economic responsibility for his large family as the eldest son, he regularly sent money to his mother.

In "The Price of the Ticket," Baldwin identified the conflict that marked his early Village years under Delaney's tutelage: "I became a kind of a two-headed monstrosity of a problem." With no college degree, how could he find the means to live and write freely without selling his soul? Working during the day, he wrote at night. His letters and juvenilia from this period detail his coming to terms with his roots in Harlem and with the individual and social responsibilities of the artist. Intrigued by what he called "the private life," he examined his identity, Blackness, and literary vocation in two masterful essays, "The Harlem Ghetto" (1948) and "Notes of a Native Son" (1955). Published within seven years of each other, they reflect his evolution as a someone who had to navigate two incompatible yet interdependent realms: art and money.

In 1943, when Baldwin's stepfather died of complications of tuberculosis and mental illness, Baldwin's last tie with the house of the Lord broke. Delaney was there to comfort him. Years later Baldwin wrote to his mother about those days, marveling at the kindness of the man, and describing him as "calming me and dry-ing my tears and putting me to sleep in his own bed and going out, in his best clothes, to Harlem, to raise money for Daddy's funeral." For the rest of his life, Baldwin found himself caught between two irreconcilable Black father figures: David Baldwin, a heteropatriarchal religious fundamentalist who despised him, and Beauford Delaney, a queer bohemian artist who loved and nurtured him. Neither was related to him by blood; both suffered from mental illness and had a deep impact on his literary imagination. After the Reverend Baldwin's death, Delaney remained Baldwin's father figure until his death in 1979. When that happened, the shattered Baldwin, who took care of Delaney in his late years, was so distraught that he was unable to attend the funeral. Painful memories of this paternal dichotomy, of those two deaths, etched deep grooves throughout his works, which remixed childhood memories of violent confrontations and constant fear with the love and beauty he found behind Beauford's door.

Baldwin had other male mentors besides Delaney, though none was as crucial to his artistic evolution. The intellectual and literary world he yearned to join in the 1940s was dominated by men. Most of them were white, and some were Jewish, but others were Black. These men were the writers, editors, managers, and publishers of the journals that gave Baldwin his first writing assignments as a book reviewer. Some of them became role models and teachers: Sol Levitas of the *New Leader,* Randall Jarrell of the *Nation,* and Robert Warshow of *Commentary.* In 1948–50, as Baldwin labored over his first essay, "The Harlem Ghetto: Winter 1948," and short stories, "Previous Condition" and "The Death of the Prophet," for *Commentary,* Warshow encouraged him. Other men he encountered at the time functioned as interlocutors he would argue with, but still find helpful, like the older Richard Wright, whose 1940 novel *Native Son* established him as the premier Black writer. In time, some of the men in Baldwin's sphere would criticize or even dismiss him, among them Eldridge Cleaver of the Black Panthers, whose *Soul on Ice* (1968) branded Baldwin a traitor to Blackness because of his homosexuality.

Baldwin passed from his mother's kitchen into a male-dominated, homosocial literary world when he was too young to realize the importance and usefulness of the early lessons he learned from women. Armed with Berdis's and his teacher Bill Miller's faith in his abilities, he carried a knowledge forged by domestic labor, movies, and theater, driven by voracious reading and a lot of early writing. Burdened with supporting his family, he needed father figures to guide him in the professional and creative worlds. He also longed for guidance as he confronted his repressed sexual desires and fell into his first love affairs and erotic experiments. It was his Black queer painter mentor and the other men whose influence provided a kind of alternative family and haven for Baldwin whom we shall examine on this side of his Life Album—men who helped him begin the journey toward a fuller recognition of himself. Much as Delaney did with his pigments, Baldwin swirled the colors of his origins to create a self-portrait filled with humanistic love, beauty, and the power of the pen.

TRACK 2

The Prince and His Spiritual Father

THE FIRST PORTRAIT Delaney painted of Baldwin, *Dark Rapture* (1941), features the teenager's nude, erect, and—to some beholders—slightly averted body. (Some of us may see young Baldwin's nude body as communicating a barely perceptible aversion at being so portrayed.) Unique among the likenesses of his protégé that Delaney created over the years, it shows Baldwin's facial features as undefined, perhaps undefinable as yet. It is unclear whether Baldwin is looking at us or turning his gaze away in shy vulnerability. His face is a blur of lines shot through with bright sunshine. Floating on top of the erect torso, his head is a vessel filled with light and possibility. Darkly luminous, his figure is splendid and self-contained. Speckled with colors reflecting the background, which is part summer landscape, part his brightly striped seat, this is the body of a young man whom the painter loved and cherished. That body may once have been desired by the man who held the brush. Yet perhaps because Baldwin never reciprocated his mentor's attraction, it remains a mystery; it communicates an expression of longing. The later portraits move away from the youth's body and focus on the face and the eyes of the man who would gradually emerge from that first blurred, sylvan figure.

Delaney's painting captures Baldwin's vulnerability as he was about to finish high school. Traumatized by his stepfather's abuse and by the encounter with the pedophile, the youth was unsure of himself and fearful of other men's attention. He disliked his body, his looks, and his budding sexuality. Delaney's brush paints Baldwin as only partially formed, as if the canvas were reflecting the teenager's inability to look squarely back at the world. The position of the body communicates indecisiveness and slight physical discomfort: he is sitting with his right leg bent, with his foot under his left knee. The left foot is firmly planted on the floor, the calf flexed. His right hand is hidden behind the bent knee with his elbow slightly curved, while his left palm is strongly planted in front, ready to push on the seat to get up.

Delaney masterfully captured the tension between vulnerability and shame, pride and sinewy strength in his model. Baldwin is motionless yet dynamic, sparkling with light and energy, yet afraid and uncertain. In Delaney's eye, the "Prince" is both a wounded child and an erotically charged demi-god at whose feet, if we push this over-the-top reading, he positions the beholder's gaze. Given the date of this portrait, Delaney may have also captured the traces of psychic wounds inflicted by Baldwin's homophobic, violent stepfather.

Under Delaney's tutelage, Baldwin realized that his feelings about the reverend were consuming him. He needed to neutralize them, to create writing that would turn his painful experience into publishable prose. Since no free mental health services were available and seeing a therapist was considered a vice of the white bourgeoisie, Baldwin had only himself and his friends to help him. In *Dark Rapture*, Baldwin perhaps saw himself through Delaney's loving eyes. It was a momentous self-discovery, for the Prince glowing on that canvas was attractive, filled with possibility, even power. In a sense, Delaney had given Baldwin his body back through the portrait. For the first time, the young man who believed himself irredeemably ugly and sinful could see himself as beautiful and lovable. The stepfather's story of a sissy stepson who chose to become an author in the white Sodom was retold by Delaney's colorful, loving masterstrokes.

Baldwin's new life in the Village made it possible for him to write all that he had been unable to express as a child, leading to drafts of stories and a novel. Although he could not erase his Blackness and sexuality and their material consequences in the racist and homophobic world, he could turn his life into literature, into a radical artistic and political statement. The peaks and valleys of his creative process reflected his history, mixing euphoria and distress, which turned into depression, doubt, and emotional breakdowns. Delaney's later paintings of Baldwin—up to *Portrait of James Baldwin, 1971*—provide a visual interpretation of the process of the writer coming to terms with both his origins and his creative labors.

Being gifted, imaginative, and hypersensitive in addition to being Black and queer often spelled solitude. In a 1986 interview, Baldwin told the Black journalist Arthur Crossman that he felt burdened by his peculiar imagination. Like many artists and geniuses, he had an easier time dealing with abstract and metaphorical, rather than material, problems: "I have, unhappily, the sort of intelligence, which, immediately upon being presented with a problem . . . a 'real' problem, that is, a problem neither esthetic nor intellectual nor abstract, but a problem simply of one's life, of life itself . . . promptly snaps tight, like a lock, hides, curled in the dark, like a worm and will not function in the least." Through the influence of his mentor, though, Delaney's troubled young apprentice learned discipline and a work ethic that propelled his literary labors toward a full-time career.

Although Delaney was much older and had been born in Tennessee, his early life helped him understand his young protégé's struggles. One of four surviving children of the ten his mother bore, young Beauford had battled disease and the effects of poor living conditions. Like Baldwin, he was a preacher's son and sexually attracted to men. His mother, Delia, was born a slave and was illiterate, yet she instilled a deep respect for education and social justice in her children, much as Berdis had done for James. Encouraged and helped by an older local white artist, Delaney traveled to Boston, where he completed a solid artistic education that gave him not only professional confidence but also the credentials Baldwin never gained. Delaney's creative trajectory made him a perfect spiritual father figure for the younger artist, whose own career would resound with his mentor's complex influence.

By 1929, Delaney was in New York City, then humming with Harlem Renaissance energies. Working blue-collar jobs to pay for his studio, he embraced the multiracial, bohemian arts world, though it initially meant living in poverty. He painted while learning to negotiate with the white people who helped him exhibit and sell his art and had achieved some economic stability by the time Baldwin entered his life. Delaney was a pragmatist who felt his vocation was to be a hard-working painter rather than a reluctant revolutionary, as Leeming notes in his biography of the artist, *Amazing Grace* (1998), but this balanced approach was nevertheless insufficient to stabilize his mental health and drinking whenever he stopped working. This may explain why Delaney's sober attitude toward his vocation failed to instill a similar balance in Baldwin as an artist. The younger man struggled with fear of rejection by his deeply religious family, who remained uneasy about his lifestyle. Like Delaney, Baldwin felt wounded by Black rejection. Unlike him, Baldwin turned to activism to pay his dues, which took time from his writing and brought him criticism from both Black and white audiences. Combined with his fears and anxieties, these efforts to find balance between work and being a Black spokesperson would later negatively impact Baldwin's health and productivity.

Delaney's textured paintings from their Village period beckoned with a dynamic world of color, sound, and movement. Baldwin fell into that world headfirst, entranced by the older artist's striking streetscapes, characters, landscapes, and abstractions. Beauford's urban scenes offer a mesmerizing, original portrait of New York City neighborhoods, juke joints, bars, squares, and dance halls. He also painted rural Tennessee, in addition to portraits and rich experimental abstractions, all filled with complex sensations, motion, and light that still grip the viewer. In Delaney's eye, humans appeared unbound by hierarchies; they were living out loud and possessed by creative, democratic passions and joys. He captured them all: musicians, dancers, street vendors, actors, and all the unusual characters who made the city a vibrant cultural mecca. That human mix, bolstered by Delaney's methodological admonition "Don't describe it, show it," would enchant Baldwin, reappearing in his best works.

Delaney's introverted, quiet personality belied the explosive sensuality and eroticism of his artworks. This contradictory mentor—understated yet powerful, queer though closeted— eventually helped the younger man embrace his literary talent and sexual ambivalence. Delaney moved in the largely white male gay circles of Greenwich Village and revealed his sexuality only among close friends. He hid it especially carefully whenever he was in Harlem, where racial and sexual coding often linked homosexuals to whiteness, secular excess, and "foreign" licentiousness. Shaped by the Harlem Renaissance he embraced as a youth, Delaney mirrored that movement's secrets and contradictions in his paintings and personality. In the estimation of Henry Louis Gates, Jr., the Renaissance, of "emblematic importance to later movements of black creativity," was "surely as gay as it was Black, not that it was exclusively either of these." Writing about the British filmmaker Isaac Julien's brilliant *Looking for Langston* (1989), Gates also acknowledges the "powerful current of homophobia in black letters" that was Hughes's as much as Baldwin's lot.

Julien's impressionistic cinematography in *Looking for Langston* helps viewers imagine Delaney's life, which, like that film's mise-en-scène, hid a queer underground of private and public spaces where same-sex love, art, passion, and beauty blended. As Leeming explains in *Amazing Grace,* when Delaney met Baldwin, his sphere included his lover "Dante and their bohemian friends," the "Negro art" circles, and "a third life centered around . . . the aesthetics and development of modernism in Europe and the United States." All three cast their influence on his canvases as much as on his young apprentice. Though enchanted by them all, the apprentice disliked one aspect of his mentor's life: being closeted. Baldwin had not fully developed his rejection of identity labels or his humanist vision at this age, and he judged Delaney's life to be a lie. Driven by youthful idealism, Baldwin considered the personal, inner life and honesty about it the most important topic for an artist—one he would remix and refine lifelong.

Although he remained reticent about himself, Delaney's many self-portraits read like eloquent pages from a diary recording different periods in his life: sometimes he appears in a golden Renaissance artist's costume; sometimes his sickly face is dominated by a distorted, wandering eye. Upon meeting him in New York, the painter Georgia O'Keeffe found him to be exceptional. She greatly admired his art and did several portraits of him, including a powerful charcoal in 1943. Its disembodied, floating face is that of a saint; its liquid gaze helps viewers see some of the qualities Leeming describes: "On the surface Beauford . . . was all tranquility and wisdom. People came to him . . . as to a guru who could solve their problems. And Beauford gave them wisdom and solace; he could do so not because he was above pain but because he was suffused by it."

Like Baldwin's, Delaney's suffering stemmed from his experiences as a man doubly victimized by race and sexuality. It also resulted from hypersensitivity and vulnerability, qualities the two shared that were useful to artists but often impractical for dealing with daily life. Delaney was liberally using drink and marijuana to dull his senses when the first stirrings of mental illness began visiting him. As he grew older, he started hearing voices; later it would become clear that he suffered from acute paranoia and schizophrenia. Too long untreated, his illness progressed during the late 1950s and the 1960s.

Baldwin was awed by Delaney's artistic pedigree and bohemian lifestyle and threw himself into imitating him, taking up drinking and smoking. He considered going to college—either at City College of New York or the New School for Social Research—but his finances and low grades (which added a year to his high school studies) marred his chances. Delaney convinced him that a writer did not need a college degree to start a career. Baldwin therefore took his education into his own hands, continuing the autodidactic practices he had begun in his childhood, and making a living among working-class men just as his preacher–factory laborer stepfather had done. His exit from Harlem first led him to Delaney's studio, then to rented rooms and roommates in Greenwich Village and New Jersey.

Delaney found Baldwin his first job as a dishwasher-waiter in a small Village restaurant, the Calypso, where Connie Williams, a warm, maternal woman from Trinidad, took him under her wing. She fed him and his siblings when they dropped by and let him stay overnight on occasion. Like many other cafés and restaurants in the Village—the San Remo, White Horse Tavern, Joe's Diner—

the Calypso attracted a mixed crowd of drifters, artists, and leftist intellectuals who were white, Jewish, Black, Puerto Rican, and sometimes queer or sexually ambivalent. Patrons of the Calypso included writers, activists, and musicians: C. L. R. James, Claude McKay, Alain Locke, Eartha Kitt, Marlon Brando, Stan Weir, Malcolm X, Paul Robeson, and Delaney and his friends, such as the young Black writer Smith Oliver, and a striking teenage waitress, Ruth Robinson, who was of Cherokee, African American, and African-Scottish descent, and who was everyone's favorite, as Leeming notes.

His father's death in 1943 forced Baldwin to return home to help his family. He could not write there, however, and soon left, working blue-collar jobs to help support his mother and eight half-brothers and sisters. A long list of these jobs appears in Baldwin's biographical papers: "a laborer in a New Jersey Quartermaster Depot . . . for the Army . . . in shipyards, factories, icehouses, docks, restaurants, trucking firms, a meat packing house: as assistant welder, as handyman, truck driver's helper, stock clerk, shipping clerk, office boy, messenger, elevator boy, waiter, and dishwasher. Etc." For a while, he and his friend Emile Capouya lived in Rocky Hill with an Irish-American couple, Tom and Florence Martin, who shared their love of literature. In a letter to Tom Martin dated September 2, 1944, Baldwin describes writing "under exceedingly adverse conditions" during his shift as a "galley boy in the Composing Room of the *Morning Telegraph*." The publication he mentions was devoted to movie stars—"Bette Davis is fornicating with Robert Taylor," "Veronica Lake just had an abortion"—and he is clearly embarrassed by its lowbrow nature. Baldwin writes about being surrounded by "model Americans of our time." These men, presumably, are deemed "successful" because they have held the same job "for the last fifty years. They are all very proud of it," he states disdainfully.

Baldwin's long list of employers indicated his poor suitability for menial jobs. Capouya, who found them both decently paid work in Belle Mead, New Jersey, and roomed with Baldwin in 1942, witnessed how much his friend disliked the work. Baldwin's distaste had to do with more than his small size, lack of ability, and desire to be an artist. In "The Harlem Ghetto" Baldwin explains that it was only when he worked as a Black laborer that he began to understand his stepfather's hatred of the "white devils." In the same essay, he calls New Jersey "New Georgia" for its influx of white southerners who targeted his "'uppity' ways, his sardonic wit, and his Northern-Negro lack of 'respect.'" When confronted with racism and segregationist practices, Baldwin felt rage and hatred that seemed out of control. Discrimination that marred the South existed in the North, too, though it may have seemed less apparent there, or simply more insidious. In New Jersey, it was blatant, to a far greater degree than in New York City. When bars and restaurants refused to serve him, Baldwin discovered that such exclusions made him feel murderous, and he feared that his reaction to the bigotry would get him killed.

No matter how hard he worked his body, he soon found that he could not lift his family out of poverty. His punishing work ethic as an author forced him to write "all the time," before, during, and especially after work, as he noted in "The Price of the Ticket." After Cullen, his teacher-poet, Delaney was "the first walking, living proof, for me, that a black man could be an artist." In the letter to his mother I quoted in the Overture, he explains how helpful Delaney was in his pursuit of a full-time writing life, "telling me that there was no point in my trying to work in factories—there were people who *could* and there were people who *couldn't*—and I couldn't and the sooner I accepted this fact and stopped feeling guilty about it and started doing what I *could* do, the better." Though their artistic media were different, he credited Delaney with teaching him how to look and see deeply, how to notice detail and how to read into it in order to make it real in his writing. For books, he increasingly believed, would be his ticket to economic security.

Baldwin learned to see the world through Delaney's eyes by following him on walks through the Village. "In a warmer time, and less blasphemous place," he wrote in "The Price of the Ticket," evoking ancient Greek ideals and their homoerotic overtones, "he would have been recognized as my Master and I as his Pupil." In a 1984 interview with Jordan Elgrably and George Plimpton, he recalls a moment of enlightenment when Delaney taught him a new way of reading their urban landscape: "I remember standing on a street corner with . . . Beauford . . . down in the Village, waiting for the light to change, and he pointed down and said, 'Look.' I looked and all I saw was water. And he said, 'Look again,' which I did, and I saw oil on the water and the city reflected in the puddle. It was a great revelation to me. I can't explain it. He taught me how to see, and how to trust what I saw." In this master-student dynamic, the teenager must repeat the action of looking to understand what he needs to see before he can find his own vision. To the adult Baldwin, Delaney remained "an example of courage and integrity, humility and passion. . . . I saw him shaken many times and I lived to see him broken but I never saw him bow." These ethical qualities would color Baldwin's own authorial ethics and shape his Black queer humanism.

Above all, Delaney introduced Baldwin to his Black cultural inheritance, creative freedom, and self-confidence. He accomplished this by loving Baldwin in ways his stepfather would and could not, and by exposing him to people who came from similar circumstances and embraced their artistic calling. He also introduced him to Village life. They went to clubs to listen to jazz; one of these appears in Delaney's *Jazz Quartet* (1946). Delaney let his protégé indulge in some of the vices his family worried about. He smoked weed and drank with Baldwin and his friends, teaching the young man a valuable lesson about marijuana that Baldwin sums up in "The Price of the Ticket": "I simply could not write if I were 'high.'" Some of the people Baldwin met on these outings inspired fictional characters he drew on for years in his works: Delaney, for example, appears as Sylvester, who is sometimes a painter, sometimes a musician, and once a Brazilian bartender in the unpublished manuscripts "What Little I Had" and "Any Boot-Legger" that Baldwin planned to turn into novels.

Like Delaney, Sylvester has "big, slanted eyes . . . and the big, long, massive nose—how he has always hated his nose! . . . and his wide, bitter, laughing mouth." Sometimes he appears as a hybrid of Baldwin and Delaney, with "all that tight, black, kinky hair, with . . . little gray in it." Sylvester could also be a composite of Delaney and Baldwin's younger brother David. He is a misogynist; occasionally he is unhinged. In one version, he is dying of cancer; in another, his nephew JimJim is having an affair with his younger white wife, Elaine. Delaney and his passionate, sexually frustrated friendships with an Italian-American singer and a Black painter, neither of whom knew about the other, inspired juvenilia that explored homoerotic desire, passion, and sexual initiation. In all these stories, all the characters stay up long into the night, drinking, smoking incessantly, and discussing "life."

Not all of Baldwin's inheritance from this spiritual father was good for him. Baldwin became a virtual alcoholic, possibly encouraged by Delaney's example, often experiencing bouts of drunkenness and depression following unhappy love affairs and breakups. He would sometimes feel insecure about his family's acceptance of him and let guilt drive him to riskier behavior. The nocturnal writing habit that he followed lifelong was established while he lived in the Village, as the only time he had to write came between day jobs and evening outings with Delaney and friends. Some of his extended family tried to convert him to a healthier lifestyle: Leeming, an assistant and protégé of Baldwin's in the 1960s in Turkey and later his authorized biographer, repeatedly tried to persuade Baldwin to strike a better balance but never succeeded. Baldwin addresses these efforts as "your lectures" in a 1965 letter from Istanbul, writing to Leeming somewhat melodramatically, "Understand that, if you tame me, you will also have killed me. The nature of my impossibilities come with the territory. And I will kill to redeem my territory." Protective of his ways, Baldwin saw his writing as a journey to a self-knowledge whose conquest yielded art: "I know much more about myself as a writer than even you can know. Only I know the territory, since it's only I who can conquer it. But when it's conquered, one's got a map. . . . I intend to draw that map, and not even death will stop me now."

Though by the 1970s Baldwin was openly labeling himself a "freak," as he did in *No Name in the Street,* as a teenager under Delaney's tender gaze he was "forced to know that I was valued," as he acknowledged "The Price of the Ticket." Years after his mentor's death, he recalled in that essay, "Beauford never gave me any lectures . . . but he didn't have to—he expected me to accept and respect the value placed upon me." Under Delaney's encouragement, his self-esteem grew, and with it, a bit of a narcissistic ego. He was finally glimpsing what well-adjusted children take for granted: he was unique, endowed with singular qualities, talents, needs, and desires. He was whole, he was enough—part of the greater artistic world where all human beings belonged equally.

Delaney and his creative friends helped Baldwin accept his individuality but, as he soon learned, that individuality required that he make his peace with his violent ancestral history. As he wrote in "The Price of the Ticket," drawing on lessons learned at Delaney's studio, "Not only was I not born to be a slave: I was not born to hope to become the equal of the slave-master. They had, the masters, incontestably, the rope—in time, with enough, they would hang themselves with it. They were not to hang *me*: I was to see to that. If Beauford and Miss Anderson were a part of my inheritance, I was a part of their hope." This empowering, humanistic reasoning encapsulates the decades of wrangling with race, gender, class, and national and personal history that began with Delaney and led to what Baldwin remembers about his apprenticeship with him in the later essay.

Beauford's Black queer fatherhood, as we might call it today, guided Baldwin toward adulthood and a novel understanding of manhood and masculinity. Delaney's second work featuring his protégé, *Portrait of James Baldwin, 1944,* reflects the teen's progression toward self-confidence. Painted just three years after *Dark Rapture,* this pastel on paper bursts with an inner light that fights its way through dark blues surrounding the writer's face, shown from the neck up. Baldwin's serene face looks out of a halolike silhouette of white edged with blue and streaked here and there with a pale orange that shimmers at the edges and in corners. Baldwin's expressive eyes, flecked with sunlight, arrest us; his full lips are half-smiling, and the slight asymmetries of his ears, cheeks, chin, and nose are brimming with rich hues of sunshine reflected in water—yellow, red, orange, pinkish gray, purple, green, and brown. Here he appears as the beatific Prince fully and unequivocally, his face blossoming into the fullness of keen intelligence and enlightened presence. This portrait demands to be retitled "Blue Prince."

Delaney's later paintings of Baldwin, in black and yellow, blue, and green, and indigo, white, and lime, make his facial features clear. He appears as a witness and unwavering interlocutor in *Portrait of James Baldwin, 1965, Portrait of James Baldwin, 1966,* and *Portrait of James Baldwin, 1971.* These three works capture his penetrating gaze almost insistently, as does a sketch-like, yellow-and-black 1966 portrait that is nearly monochromatic in its stunning, yellow-gold saturation. Unlike these, however, *James Baldwin, circa 1957* is a riveting echo and radical reworking of *Dark Rapture*. It seems to capture a difficult moment in the writer's life, extending Delaney's painterly commentary on his surrogate son as he became a successful author.

By 1957, Baldwin's first two novels, a play, and his first essay collection had been published. In the wake of his controversial second novel, the homosexual romance *Giovanni's Room,* he was publicly known as a man who loved other men. He had examined his relationship with his stepfather in "Me and My House," which appeared in *Harper's* in 1955 and became one of his best-known pieces after it was retitled "Notes of a Native Son" and published in his first essay volume in 1956. He had lived intermittently in France since 1948 and traveled in the American South for the first time. The man Delaney captured in *James Baldwin, circa 1957* had arrived, in every sense of the word, as a writer and intellectual; in a few years, he would also become a lucrative speaker in support of the Civil Rights Movement.

In this portrait, the young man's entire body is visible, seated, even enthroned, with arms relaxing on invisible rests, broad shoulders clad in a blue top that seems fluid like water, while his strong legs in brown pants—whose color arises from a crimson-and-gold mix—rest crossed at the knee. In this portrait the sitter's body is not only seated but levitating, as if Baldwin might be floating both backward and forward through a tunnel of colorful lines and shapes that frame his body. Delaney's composition pulls together competing abstract lines and geometric shapes in the pastel background to meet where James's abdomen, hips, and legs suggest a center of gravity, a perspectival point. Like the 1944 "Blue Prince," whose coloring it faintly echoes, this painting shows us a Baldwin who was adored. But that is not all we can see.

Delaney's portrait deepens in meaning as our gaze lingers. Its dynamism suggests that its subject's journey is ongoing. We notice that Baldwin's eyes are not as prominent and focused as they are in the other portraits; he appears to be looking inward rather than at us. His eyes look bloodshot; his hair is red, flaming at the top and streaked with white. A slightly greenish hue to his cheeks gives him a haggard look. This is the man who will soon leave the United States again, this time for Turkey, to write the explosive *Fire Next Time* and *Blues for Mister Charlie*. Up close, Delaney's Prince is not as regal and powerful as he might have seemed at first gaze. The propulsive movements of his levitating body might not be entirely comfortable; he might be gripping his crossed legs; his slightly ajar lips are blood-red on top and drained white on the bottom. No longer protected by his spiritual father, this prince lived with the conflicting demands of his art, life, duties, and fears.

The Baldwin in that canvas had weathered international travel, bouts of depression, and two suicide attempts, one following his first trip to the South, which he found so distressing that he was unable to describe it until years later, in *No Name in the Street*. He was also increasingly aware of his mentor's depressive states, and that his own absences contributed to these; worries about Delaney became a fixture in his letters to friends like the economist Mary Painter, whom he met in Paris in 1948, and David Leeming. Baldwin and Delaney's summer holiday on the islands of Ibiza and Majorca in 1956, accompanied by their lovers, made a welcome respite. The Mediterranean hues, architecture, and brightness infused Delaney's art, and may have lent his 1957 portrait of Baldwin some of their power.

At a 2020 symposium on the two artists, D. Quentin Miller described Baldwin as a "painterly writer." We can read his cyclical syntax and remixed plots as textured compositions, both painterly and musical in the way Delaney's paintings can themselves be read as textual and syncopated—as stories that are as much painted as told, shouted, and sung. Given its date, Delaney's 1957 portrait contextualizes Baldwin's "Notes of a Native Son," while his New York City canvases float through Baldwin's novels *Another Country* and *If Beale Street Could Talk*.

"Notes of a Native Son" (originally published as "Me and My House") opens with the funeral of Baldwin's father, which took place just days after the 1943 Harlem riots. Caused by the shooting of an African American soldier by a white police officer, the uprising anchors this essay, though the author waited a dozen years to write it, as if needing distance to come to terms with its deeply personal story, rooted in complexities of national Black discontent. Baldwin paints his neighborhood as both a wasteland of destruction and his primary literary inspiration. In broad strokes, the first two paragraphs sketch out his life, entangled with his neighborhood, city, and country. The text moves back and forth through space, time, and history, flashing colors, sounds, and textures:

> On the twenty-ninth of July, in 1943, my father died. On the same day, a few hours later, his last child was born. Over a month before this, while all our energies were concentrated in waiting for these events, there had been, in Detroit, one of the bloodiest race riots of the century. A few hours after my father's funeral, while he lay in state in the undertaker's chapel, a race riot broke out in Harlem. On the morning of the third of August, we drove my father to the graveyard through a wilderness of smashed plate glass. . . . The day of my father's funeral had also been my nineteenth birthday. As we drove into the graveyard, the spoils of injustice, anarchy, discontent, and hatred were

all around us. It seemed to me that God himself had devised, to mark my father's end, the most sustained and brutally dissonant of codas.

The Old Testament father and God are still firmly in the son's head, pounding out a guilty message: "the violence which rose all about us as my father left the world had been devised as a corrective for the pride of his eldest son."

Like Baldwin's text, Delaney's 1957 portrait of Baldwin reflects, refracts, and indeed moves with its subject's authorial powers. It also reveals the fears and traumatic memories that Baldwin describes in the essay and that shade Delaney's canvas. There, the adult Baldwin's veins seem "pumped full of poison," as if he were deathly ill with the effects of racism he describes in the essay that killed his father—that "dread, chronic disease, the unfailing symptoms of which are a kind of blind fever, a pounding in the skull, and fire in the bowels."

This sense of refraction, of reflection through shattered glass, occurs frequently throughout Baldwin's work. One example is the rearticulation of an event that took place when he was working in New Jersey. After a waitress had refused him service in a restaurant, he hurled a pitcher of water at her. Missing her narrowly, the pitcher smashed a mirror on the wall behind her. Thanks to a white friend's presence of mind, Baldwin escaped the ensuing mob and police. He could not escape the shattering memory: "I lived it over and over and over again," he recalled in "Notes of a Native Son": "I could not get over two facts, both equally difficult for the imagination to grasp, and one was that I could have been murdered. But the other was that I had been ready to commit murder." Years after his father's death, he realized something about hatred that their tormented relationship taught him: "I did see this: that my life, my *real* life, was in danger, and not from anything other people might do but from the hatred I carried in my own heart."

Baldwin learned from his spiritual father that writing and art offered salvation from rage and danger. Both men tended to turn against themselves in times of trouble, though Delaney hid his anguish more effectively than his protégé. As Baldwin wrote to Leeming in 1966 from Turkey, he observed that Delaney's mental unrest was usually "healed" by his work. Having been diagnosed with "acute paranoid delusions" a few years earlier, the painter increasingly needed Baldwin to become his caregiver as the voices plaguing him grew louder and more menacing, knocking the brush out of his hand.

In 1965, in an unpublished letter Baldwin recommended Delaney to the Guggenheim Foundation for a fellowship with these words: "I have known Mr. Beauford Delaney for many years and I have the greatest respect for him, as a man and as an artist. Such a statement, springing from experience and conviction, cannot be documented—not even if I were in possession of the vocabulary of the art critic." He explains that "more than twenty years of watching Delaney's development have taught me" how to relate to "the physical world around me in a way that I could not have done if I had never known him."

And yet, as he told Leeming in 1986, he could not bring himself to attend Delaney's funeral on April 6, 1979, in Paris, his "worst moment." This act of belated, pathetic rebellion was also somewhat in character for a surrogate child prodigy. The Prince who acted "like a spoiled son somehow angry at his father for dying without his permission," as Leeming notes, locked himself away in grief, fear, shame, and solitude.

TRACK 3

Letters to Jewish Editors

"MY FATHER WAS a tremendous anti-Semite. I understand it now, but I didn't understand it then," Baldwin recalled in a 1986 unpublished transcript of an interview with Arthur Crossman. At DeWitt Clinton High School, he shared classrooms with Jews, communists, and atheists, and the friendships he made there marked the beginning of "a certain kind of liberation" from the racial categories that obsessed his father. "They were not white for me anymore, they were my friends," he realized about the Jewish peers his father despised. With the help of his teachers, he discovered that his impoverished childhood experience was shared by many, that intelligence had nothing to do with skin color, parentage, or birthplace. Of all the aspects of American identity, the fiction of race was both the simplest and the hardest to understand. The rich mix of his white, Black, Jewish, leftist, southern, and queer teachers and mentors helped him craft the sophisticated literary tools he used to reach that understanding.

Along with Delaney's profound Black queer artist influence, Baldwin's mentorship by New York's Jewish editors helped him understand race as a brutal invention serving those in power. Grappling with this important theme as he matured went hand in hand with the literary apprenticeships that produced his first publications. In "The Price of the Ticket" he recalls his first meeting with Sol Levitas, editor of the *New Leader*, who tasked him with producing a book review per week, standard fare for beginning columnists. This assignment created for young Baldwin a novel routine of reading, writing, and submitting pages by a deadline, helping him devise his authorial practice later.

Baldwin was grateful for these assignments for he was unable to find writing jobs in Harlem. No one wanted a too-young-looking "shoeshine boy" with no university diploma: "I . . . had simply been laughed out of the office: . . . I don't blame these people, God knows that I was an unlikely cub reporter: yet, I still remember how deeply I was hurt." His first published essay, "The Harlem Ghetto: Winter 1948," which appeared in the Jewish leftist magazine *Commentary*, details his stance on the class-and-color regime of Black establishments then: "Negro leaders . . . [were] created by the American scene, which thereafter works against them at every point." In such a context, the "Negro press . . . supports any man, provided he is sufficiently dark and well-known—with the exception of certain Negro novelists accused of drawing portraits unflattering to the race." Written when he was just twenty-four years old, this sophisticated essay introduced Baldwin's early nonfiction style, and marked him as the odd man out in the Black literary world, a position he would hold throughout his career.

Beginning with that essay, Baldwin's thinking on Blacks, Jews, and race relations in the United States evolved into another important theme, one that suffused interviews and works, influenced the creation of characters in *Another Country* and *If Beale Street Could Talk,* and prompted him to write to the imprisoned Black Power activist Angela Davis on November 19, 1970, "You look exceedingly alone—as alone, say, as the Jewish housewife in the boxcar headed for Dachau, or as any one of our ancestors, chained together in the name of Jesus, headed for a Christian land." Baldwin published these words in "An Open Letter to My Sister Angela Y. Davis" after he saw her photograph on the October 26, 1970, cover of *Newsweek* magazine. Davis appears frail and vulnerable, more a schoolgirl than a housewife. She is bespectacled, wearing a short dark skirt and button-down blue shirt, her hair slicked back, hands in handcuffs hanging limply, head averted as if avoiding gawking eyes. This photograph contextualizes Baldwin's ideas concerning Black-Jewish interconnectedness, his reading of it confirming the staying power of his "Harlem Ghetto" essay. More than two decades after that essay, Baldwin's words to Davis succinctly sum up transatlantic oppression chronologically and achronologically—from transatlantic slavery through the Holocaust to his own present, with the murders of Martin Luther King, Jr., and Bobby Hutton in 1968 still fresh in national memory.

In late-1940s New York, the young Baldwin was moving into the predominantly leftist and secular circle of outspoken Jewish scholars, editors, and writers, the group known as the New York intellectuals. He soon learned about internationalism, Marxism, political activism, and the intricacies of the literary imagination. Shaped by those debates, Baldwin's voice in the decades-long discussion of Black-Jewish relations during the Cold War remains one of the most insightful, and the kindest. His engagement with Jewish writers in essays and interviews—for example, Norman Mailer in "The Black Boy Looks at the White Boy" (*Esquire,* May 1961), Budd Schulberg in "Dialog in Black and White" (*Playboy,* December 1966), and Julius Lester, as described in "James Baldwin—Reflections of a Maverick" (*New York Times Book Review,* May 27, 1984)—all remix themes he first explored in "The Harlem Ghetto."

"The Harlem Ghetto" proceeds from a gripping opening describing the neighborhood's architecture—"the buildings are old and in desperate need of repair, the streets are crowded and dirty, and there are too many human beings per square block"—through sections on its Black churches and strained Black-Jewish relations. It is here that Baldwin first accuses Black Christianity of serving as "a complete and exquisite fantasy revenge: white people own the earth and commit all manner of abomination and injustice on it; the bad will be punished and the good rewarded." His indictment of Harlem's religious institutions for perpetuating poverty and ignorance among their followers anticipates his growing awareness of how ethnic and religious traditions worldwide serve those in power. He revisited these themes in *The Fire Next Time*.

The most impressive aspect of this first essay is its frank examination of what Baldwin calls the "Negro's ambivalent relation to the Jew," for it sets up his lifelong explorations of the myth of race. Bringing up this divisive issue at a time when Americans were finally beginning to combat anti-Semitism in the wake of the Holocaust confirms his place as a disorderly figure among aspiring "Negro novelists." In pointing an accusing finger at his fellow African Americans for their hatred of the Jews in Harlem, he invited hostility from some readers by drawing a portrait "unflattering to the race." (The Schomburg Center archive contains a letter in which he responds, patiently and graciously, to such criticism.) Baldwin knew that Black people saw white Jews, who were often Harlem's landlords and shopkeepers, as the "Man." Feeling exploited themselves, Black people were unwilling to see anti-Semitism as in any way related to their own experience of racism. The "Jew in Harlem," Baldwin explains insightfully, is a paradoxical invention, a figure of speech whose roots are both religious and secular.

Infused with the Old Testament imaginary of the Exodus, in the Black church the Jew is a fellow slave and survivor; "the wandering, exiled Jew . . . [is] a fairly obvious reminder of the trials of the Negro." In Harlem streets, though, Jews are understood to "include all infidels of white skin who have failed to accept the Savior." Baldwin is aware of racism on the part of Jews, too; but his focus is less on individuals than on how both the Jewish and the Black American are exploited. Pitting racial minorities against each other helped the U.S. power structure maintain a status quo of racial conflict that boosted the economy by creating an oppressed, laboring underclass: "Georgia has the Negro and Harlem has the Jew." This essay bears Baldwin's trademark style in its descriptions: long, sinewy, elegant sentences; wry, witty commentary.

As he worked and reworked its many drafts, "The Harlem Ghetto" introduced Baldwin to an important new mentor, Robert Samuel Warshow, the editor at *Commentary* who had assigned him the essay. A New York native, Jewish intellectual, and accomplished writer himself, Warshow remained Baldwin's adviser at the magazine until his sudden death in 1955. He was an award-winning poet and talented prose writer whose style and philosophy of culture influenced Baldwin in more ways than has been acknowledged. A graduate of the same high school as Baldwin, Warshow was born in New York City in 1917. Only seven years Baldwin's senior, the University of Michigan–educated English major was already an experienced writer and editor when they met.

Warshow published in the literary magazines *Inland Review* and *Contemporary: Michigan Literary Quarterly,* the latter of which he also coedited. His essay "The Worship of Art" (1934), for example, discusses pretentiousness in literary circles with an ironic wit and eloquence that informs Baldwin's own style. As Baldwin later would, Warshow published in the left-leaning magazines that promoted cultural and intellectual exchanges among diverse writers: the *New Leader, Commentary,* and *Partisan Review.* His interests were nearly as eclectic as Baldwin's, ranging from literature and Russian and Soviet art, movies, and politics to comic strips, theater, and the Ethel and Julius Rosenberg Soviet spy trial. Warshow was entrenched in the New York circles Baldwin later joined, and his mentorship helped the younger man achieve success. In a 1986 interview with David C. Estes for *New Orleans Review,* Baldwin called Warshow "my first real editor," describing their relationship as "marvelous."

Saying he was in Warshow's "debt forever," Baldwin recalled memories of the painstaking process of editing and revising his first essay. He liked Warshow, a tough taskmaster who took Baldwin seriously, and pushed him, saying, "Do it over" or "You know more than that." Uninterested in having Baldwin's essay please him, Warshow encouraged him to find his own voice by confronting big ideas: "When he saw me come close to what I was afraid of, he circled it and said, 'tell me more about that.'" Baldwin's key fear as a budding writer concerned writing about race. He had never thought about "the relationship between Negroes and Jews in Harlem," and wrestling with his fear allowed him to sound out what he had learned from his teachers and classmates. Under Warshow's watchful editorial eye, he juxtaposed that knowledge with memories of his father's prejudice and the stereotypes he encountered as a child, blending them into his own vision.

As Baldwin noted in the interview, the anti-Semitism of Harlem "began to hit me on a profound and private level because many of my friends were Jews, although they had nothing to do with the Jewish landlords and pawnbrokers in the ghetto." His realization of the gulf between the Jewish people he knew and loved and the despised ghetto managers of Harlem made him consider that he "had been blotting it out" because of his own racial prejudice. It "was a kind of liberation," he explained: "I suddenly realized that perhaps I had been afraid to talk about it because I was a closet anti-Semite myself. One always has that terror. And then I realized that I wasn't. So something else was opened." That "something" was a moment of enlightenment, an impetus to reinvent himself. He did not want to become an imitation of other Black writers, such as Langston Hughes, Richard Wright, and Countee Cullen, but rather a new quantity, a writer who was Black and also a New York intellectual like Philip Rahv, Lionel Trilling, Irving Howe, Leslie Fiedler, Nathan Glazer, Sol Stein (his school friend), Stan Weir, and Saul Bellow. As evidenced in copious correspondence with editors, agents, and friends, Baldwin's self-invention began in the company of Jewish mentors.

In a letter dated August 6, 1947, written on *Commentary* stationary, Warshow advised Baldwin about revisions of his first essay, at that time titled "The Harlem Letter": "I think you have succeeded quite well in adopting the proper tone—a mixture of informality, careful observation, and insight—but it still leaves me very hungry for more information. In a way you have kept yourself too far outside the subject." He elaborates that the piece might be "more exciting for you and more interesting for the reader if you would try to think of the matter a little more in terms of your own feelings and if you would go into the problem of anti-Semitism as it exists for the more sophisticated Negro." Warshow's instructions are as clear and persuasive as he is humble and helpful as an editor: "I feel that you are too good a writer and that I am too little informed on this subject for me to be able to make very specific suggestions, beyond the few questions that I wrote down after reading the first manuscript."

Importantly, Warshow was unafraid of directing Baldwin to focus on his "own feelings," urging him to value and trust his own insights, a practice Baldwin would later embrace when mentoring others. As Warshow wrote, "See whether you yourself do not feel that in a way you have failed to come to grips with the matter. I certainly hope you will not give up on this, because I have a feeling that this could eventually become a first-rate piece of writing . . . of even greater value to you as a writer." The letter closes with good luck wishes on Baldwin's novel and asks him to consider submitting excerpts as a short story. In another letter from January 29, 1948, addressing Baldwin as "Jim," Warshow, who signs his name as "Bob," informs him that "your Harlem piece will be in the February issue," noting, "Now I can with good conscience begin to bother you about some of the other work you promised us."

Warshow soon became a friend, one who understood the complications of Baldwin's genius, especially his hypersensitivity as it both benefited his work and impacted his health. In a brief letter of September 9, 1949, addressed to the Hôtel Verneuil in Paris, where Baldwin was staying, laid low by a depressive episode, Warshow wrote, "I am sorry not to have heard from you for so long. What are you doing, and what are you writing? Send us something for COMMENTARY and write and tell me all about Paris." A kind friend and consummate professional, Warshow thrived on and celebrated Baldwin's success, writing on March 28, 1950, "Only the other night one of our more sensitive readers told me that you had written the two best stories we ever published." The reader in question was unknown, though the letter was probably written by Alain Locke, the celebrated "Dean" of the Harlem Renaissance and a professor at Howard University. *Commentary* introduced Baldwin's fiction debut on its cover in October 1948: "'Previous Condition,' his first published short story, is a . . . powerful study of the life of a young Negro artist in present-day American society. It heralds, we think, an important new talent on the literary scene."

The second short story Baldwin developed under Warshow's guidance was "The Death of the Prophet," published in *Commentary*'s March 1950 issue (see Side A, Track 3). It is an early example of Baldwin's auto-theoretical, achronological narrative style. The story concerns a young Black man, Johnnie, who is walking to the hospital to visit his estranged, dying father at his mother's request.

Baldwin's first attempt at critiquing manhood and masculinity, this story entwined the theme of father-son conflict with race and religion—Blackness and Jewishness—a complex topic he circled around often. In a culture and state run by men, being male mattered. But what kind of man or masculinity was acceptable? Written with the cadences of the King James Bible, based on an actual event from Baldwin's life, this important story includes the father-son disagreement after the visit of a Jewish friend.

Cycling in and out of the memory of that event as he walks to the hospital, Johnnie then witnesses his father's dying moments, and passes out from shock. The Jewish friend who inadvertently caused the disagreement is David, possibly modeled on one of Baldwin's high school friends. David comes to Harlem one day to pick up Johnnie from the apartment where he lives with his fanatical preacher father. As the situation develops, it becomes clear to Johnnie that he must never become like his father. He hates and fears the man, as well as his unforgiving church. The scene depicts the preacher refusing to shake a Jew's hand, which provokes Johnnie's shame and rage, followed by the father's castigation of his son. Somewhat obliquely, it also references the forbidden world of books, movies, and secular ideas of the street that were the preserve of the Jewish friend, and that helped lead Baldwin on his own path as a writer.

After David leaves, Johnnie's "father looked on him with that distant hatred with which one considers Judas; . . . his father's eyes told him, he was henceforth damned by his own wish, having forsaken the few righteous to make his home in the populous Sodom and entered into an alliance with his father's enemies and the enemies of the Lord." David and the Old Testament vision of the condemned city of Sodom cohabit uneasily, for "making home" there hints at Johnnie's potential homosexuality—yet another mortal sin against the Lord that so plagued Baldwin's teenage imagination. Like fraternizing with Jews, attraction to men led to damnation. The reverend's further association of secularity, Jewishness, and homosexuality with whiteness positions his Black masculinity as righteous, heterosexual, and consecrated. Historically sexualized as much as Black bodies, racialized Jewish bodies were represented as dangerous, dirty, and abnormal, but the father's rage blinds him to the reality of anti-Semitism and its affinity with anti-Black racism.

The frustrated narrator in "The Death of the Prophet" is eventually led away from Harlem and his father by those white Sodomite forces "to backslide as an angel falls: headlong, furious, anxious to discover the utmost joys of hell." The story's titular death suggests multiple demises: those of Johnnie's father and the son's childhood, a symbolic death of the son at the hands of the abusive father, the death of filial love and cross-religious solidarity. There is also the death of Johnnie's faith at the hands of God the Man, and the passing of his hope for love as a young Black man with homoerotic desires. Shaped by Warshow's editorial support, "The Death of the Prophet" became a powerful advertisement for the magazine's young talent.

Baldwin was fortunate to work with a mentor who steadied his hand, believed in his ability to improve, pushed him when needed, and taught him how to read his own work critically. In a letter dated September 28, 1950, for example, Warshow admonishes Baldwin for being too personal, instructing him on the need to balance perspectives: "I'm afraid that the consensus here is that this article doesn't come off. You have somehow become too involved on the emotional level to achieve any clarity in the expression of your ideas. And so, although much of it is interesting and provocative, I think when you read it over yourself you will see some of the difficulties we find in it." An important lesson in how to balance personal experience with the expression of ideas came from an essay Warshow wrote upon his own father's death, "An Old Man Gone" (1951). It clearly echoes in Baldwin's "Notes of a Native Son," about the Reverend Baldwin's funeral, which was published four years later. In "An Old Man Gone," the first-person narrator's humbling self-awareness creates an ironic distance from himself as part of the story, from his subject, and from his surroundings. The in medias res beginning, parenthetical asides, and long, elegant sentences were all features that attracted Baldwin and influenced his nonfiction style. They are all on display in Baldwin's essay, which reflects Warshow's editorial lessons as well as their literary discussions and friendship.

Warshow opens "An Old Man Gone" with an epigraph from Christopher Marlowe's play *The Jew of Malta* that Baldwin later used in *Another Country*, whose long gestation as a novel was then beginning. In addition, Warshow's piece mixes introspection and personal detail with humanistic philosophical pronouncements, concluding with an evaluation of his father's life: "There is no doubt that he wanted more than he got." The two writers' relationships with their fathers could hardly have been more different, but their essays engage in a fascinating dialogue on Jewish and Black families, loss, gender, and creative expression. Drawing on their disparate origins and cultivating a strong sense of ethics they further confirmed their affinity.

Although he was happy to praise Baldwin's successes, Warshow never hesitated to remind him of the importance of discipline to writing. In reference to a piece by Alston Anderson, a Panama-born Jamaican author best known for *Lover Man* (1959), which Baldwin asked Warshow to help place with a publisher, the editor writes, "Some of Mr. Anderson's prose . . . reminds me of a tendency I have observed before in what I am forced to call Negro writing: a tendency to make use of language itself—especially a kind of elaborate heaviness of language and also sometimes a habitual and purely verbal irony—as a means of escape from the difficult problem of dealing with a very painful question." Warshow makes his rejection of Anderson an occasion to advise Baldwin: "If you should write any more criticism of the writing of Negroes, this is the point you might consider. (The content of this paragraph, I should imagine, is not for Mr. Anderson; but I leave it to you to judge)." Baldwin took Warshow's words to heart, later producing similar advice for writers he mentored. He and Warshow understood each other as thinkers and radicals who wanted to explore new genres, approaches, and styles. Diametrically different as personalities—Warshow calm and methodical, Baldwin dramatic and scattered—they were alike in their attention to intimate experience and the desire to convey that experience in a clear and disciplined way on the page.

Their correspondence includes an awkward exchange from November 3, 1950, concerning Baldwin's request for money. Baldwin had been in Paris since 1948, and he was often financially strapped. He would "borrow" sums from friends and acquaintances, frequently never returning the loan, a habit for which he soon became infamous. His letter requesting funds is not included among his papers, but Warshow's response clarifies that Baldwin wanted an advance from *Commentary* and a personal loan from Warshow as a friend. The request is apparently not the first of this kind. As Warshow explains, "I am terribly sorry to hear of your difficulties, but I am afraid I myself have no more money to spare. I did bring up the question of getting you a small advance from the magazine, but even there our budget has been cut so sharply that we are no longer permitted to make open advances." Baldwin's "very distressing" letter pushed Warshow to mention "an element of self-protection in my decision that I cannot spare any money, but I hope things will straighten themselves out. Above all, I hope you can send us something publishable." Gently reminding Baldwin that publishable work yielded income, Warshow refused him kindly but firmly, in a fatherly way. Unlike white benefactors who sponsored Black artists in Paris, of whom Baldwin had several, Warshow was not wealthy, and his job did not pay well. Their last exchange took place while Baldwin was still living in France. Soon afterward the editor died suddenly of a heart attack at age thirty-seven.

Following Warshow's death, Baldwin worked with other leftist liberal intellectuals, many of them Jews. Their appeal to Baldwin rested, as Warshow's had, not only in how open they were to his ideas, writing style, and personality, but also in their embrace of secular culture, creativity, and atheism. Baldwin had limited interest in the organized left, though he briefly joined the Young People's Socialist League (YPSL) and became a Trotskyite, allegedly because of his attraction to a young man. (His time in the league also inspired an unpublished draft on sex and Marxism that will appear briefly on the next track.) And while Baldwin retained deep fondness for the complex culture and atmosphere of the Black church—particularly its music and drama, which frequently resound through his fiction—he rejected Christianity and organized religion, committing himself to secular humanism.

When it came to publishing fiction, Baldwin, like many writers, had first to cut his teeth on book reviews, writing about others' novels. His first review appeared in the April 12, 1947, issue of the *Nation*. In "Maxim Gorki as Artist," he reviewed the translation of the Soviet writer's *Best Short Stories*. To him, Gorky read as "tender, ironic and observant [but] it must also be admitted that he is also quite frequently sentimental," and thus "incomplete" as an artist; some of these phrases would return in "Everybody's Protest Novel" two years later. The book reviews helped Baldwin identify qualities he learned to emulate or avoid in his own writing. Sometimes this apprenticeship would produce slightly humorous results as he moved through phases of youthful posturing. In the Gorky review for example, he remarks on the quality of the translation, finding it "most uneven." Though he could not have read the Russian original, or known much about Soviet letters, he was able to assess the fluidity of the English version, alliteratively assessing Gorky as "almost always painfully verbose" and as threatening "frequently to degenerate into simple propaganda." At the *Nation,* where he published several more pieces over the years, Baldwin worked closely with the magazine's editor Randall Jarrell. Baldwin later served on the *Nation*'s editorial board from 1978 until his death in 1987.

The book reviews and essays that began his literary career pushed Baldwin's writing in an unexpected direction: "I had never intended to become an essayist," he noted in "The Price of the Ticket." "But it came about because of Saul [*sic*]." Recalling his *New Leader* days with Sol Levitas as "a very great apprenticeship," Baldwin admitted that he came to love the "old man" who made him work so hard, for trusting his beginner's abilities—he "was proud of me, and . . . he loved me, too." Baldwin received ten to twenty dollars per review, and Levitas's assistant Mary Greene often asked the editor to pay him a few dollars extra. The many books Baldwin reviewed, he recalled, seemed never to be worth reading again: "It was after the war, and the Americans were on one of their monotonous conscience 'trips': be kind to n[–]s, for Christ's sake, be kind to Jews!" The book reviews nevertheless turned Baldwin into a superb essayist. Though determined to write fiction, it was through nonfiction that he discovered the powerful theorist inside himself, and he applied that lesson to becoming a novelist.

The major challenge he faced while working with Warshow and Levitas, he recalled there, was to be more than a "mere Negro writer." In his 1986 interview with Estes, he explained his disdain for racial writing as a vehicle for victimhood:

I was a black kid and was expected to write from that perspective.
Yet I had to realize the black perspective was dictated by the white
imagination. Since I wouldn't write from the perspective, essentially,
of the victim, I had to find what my own perspective was and then use
it. I couldn't talk about "them" and "us." So I had to use "we" and let
the reader figure out who "we" is. That was the only possible choice
of pronoun. It had to be "we." And we had to figure out who "we" was,
or who "we" is. That was very liberating for me.

Baldwin's *we* encompasses himself and all the humanity he ex-
pansively claims as a writer. His investment in the reader's active
participation in literature communicates the certainty that his
works would inspire, perhaps even must elicit, similar efforts.

Racial attitudes between Blacks and Jews in the United States
remained an important theme that Baldwin probed throughout
his work. Some three decades after "The Harlem Ghetto" was published, Baldwin's integrity on matters of race and politics was
questioned in a book written by a fellow Black writer who also was
Jewish. The public context of this event and its impact on Baldwin's legacy as an antiracist might give us pause today. In the early
1980s, one of Baldwin's colleagues at the University of Massachusetts, Amherst, the Black Jewish writer Julius Lester accused Baldwin of anti-Semitism. The accusation, apparently never spoken to
Baldwin's face, reappeared in Lester's memoir, *Lovesong: Becoming
a Jew* (1988), published a year after Baldwin's death. Lester, who
grew up Methodist in the South and converted to Judaism, claimed
that a lecture Baldwin delivered on the UMass campus on February
28, 1984, "blamed" Jews and gave students "permission" to express
anti-Semitic comments. The sixty-year-old Baldwin had agreed to
give that lecture in the aftermath of the so-called "Hymietown"
scandal that had made headlines two weeks earlier concerning the
Reverend Jesse L. Jackson's anti-Semitic comments to an inter-

viewer during his campaign to become the Democratic Party's presidential candidate.

Jackson's slurs came in a chat with a Black reporter, Milton Coleman, whose racial loyalty Jackson apparently counted on to keep his remarks out of the media. But Coleman took his job seriously and published the comments, incurring the wrath of the Nation of Islam's leader, and Jackson's ally, Louis Farrakhan, a militant, virulently anti-white anti-Semite. As the *Washington Post* reported, Farrakhan threatened Coleman on the radio, issuing a warning to Jews in Jackson's presence: "If you harm this brother [Jackson], it will be the last one you harm." The scandal undermined Jackson's campaign and his social justice nonprofit PUSH/ Rainbow Coalition. In the wake of the ensuing uproar, the UMass students wanted to hear Baldwin's opinion and discuss the issue openly.

Baldwin's lecture, whose transcript suggests that he had not followed the Jackson scandal very closely, opened with a familiar recapitulation of his childhood memories of learning to racialize others: "He comes to collect the rent, so you know him in that role. He runs the grocery store and he gives you credit. . . . He runs the drug store and he bandages your wounds. . . . You don't really know him from anybody else, but your father says, and your aunt says, and the neighbors say . . . whatever at that moment in your life a Jew is." In his analysis Baldwin explained the ties between two racial minorities: "The black American singles out the American Jew because so much of the black inheritance comes from the Old and New Testament. . . . A black person tends to expect more from a Jewish person than he expects from anybody else."

He also contextualized the politics of what he called the "American inheritance" controlling the United States and its international policy as much as its representations of national identity. Supporting the economic struts of power, it is "essentially an inheritance which is called opportunity; and in execution of this opportunity, it doesn't matter what principle or what human being is in the way." His analysis included identifying the founding of "the state of Israel" as a similarly opportunistic process, "a means of protecting western interests at the gate of the Middle East." He offered the listening students what he considered to be the truth about the overall Western post–World War II geopolitics: that not one of the Allies "really cared what happened to the Jews," and he singled out the British as "the authors of 20th century racism."

Never an ideologue to toe a party line, Baldwin believed that humanist ethics meant that no states or groups had the right to discriminate, no matter what competing histories of victimization they might use to plead their case. He rejected censorship that suppressed knowledge of oppression—including the silence the Black reporter had been expected to keep for Jackson. "I'm putting it to you this way in the attempt to clarify something which is happening all around us," Baldwin explained, moving a local issue into a national and global context to speak ominously about "something else which no one ever wishes to discuss." By referencing Israel and Western guilt vis-à-vis the racist historic roots and consequences of the Holocaust, he argued against the use of victimization as a justification by those in power to withhold the truth of history from its victims, and to cover up or emphasize other forms of victimization for political purposes. Lies, even lies used to "protect" the victims, serve to silence the victimized and further exploit them. "Whenever Israel is mentioned, one is required, it appears sometimes to me, to maintain a kind of pious silence. Well, why? It is a state like other states. It has come into existence in a peculiar way," he expounded. In his conclusion, Baldwin declared adamantly that Jackson's remark was anti-Semitic.

Because of his choice of words, Jackson bore responsibility, and thus "one has the right to question everything" concerning that "very serious event, maybe a disastrous event."

After Lester's allegations appeared in 1988, the W. E. B. Du Bois Department of Afro-American Studies at the university came to Baldwin's posthumous defense, self-publishing "James Baldwin on Blacks and Jews," a pamphlet with a transcript of his talk and Q&A session with the students, supplemented by appendixes with statements from faculty repudiating Lester's accusations.

Had he lived, Baldwin might have asked Lester to read "The Harlem Ghetto" alongside his transcribed lecture and invited him to an honest discussion. Like a patient editor, he could have explained where Lester's *Lovesong* had come up short. For Lester's racial-cum-religious transformation comes off as an unequivocal shedding of Blackness: "I am no longer deceived by the black face which stares at me from the mirror. I am a Jew," his book opens. Like Baldwin's John Grimes confronting his reflection in *Go Tell It on the Mountain*, like David in *Giovanni's Room*, Lester signals through his confusion about his racial identity an absence of a self that should be free to contain all of him. Rather than reconciling Jewishness and Blackness, Lester let what Baldwin called his "American inheritance" enforce definitions of both.

The 1984 lecture touched on a deep nerve in Baldwin and confirmed that the path he had chosen in "The Harlem Ghetto" would never be easy. His complex and frequently misunderstood *New York Times* essay on the same theme, "Negroes Are Anti-Semitic Because They're Anti-White" (1967), is a good example. There, Baldwin explains that "anti-Semitism among Negroes is, ironically, the relationship of colored peoples—all over the globe—to the Christian world." Decades later, his ideas reverberate online, where his words flash alongside newly formulated concepts like "Christofascism" and "civilizational apparatus of inequality." No society will rid itself of racial discrimination, Baldwin cautioned, both in "Negroes Are Anti-Semitic" and in his lecture to the students at UMass in 1984, until its members relinquish being solely defined by victimization. As he wrote in that essay, about growing up Black among Jewish landlords and shopkeepers in Harlem, "I know that my own oppression did not ennoble me, not even when I thought of myself as a practicing Christian. I also know that if today I refuse to hate Jews, or anybody else, it is because I know how it feels to be hated. I learned this from Christians, and I ceased to practice what the Christians practiced."

The twenty-four-year-old Baldwin wrestled with such ideas in "The Harlem Ghetto," while revising the never-ending drafts of his first novel, at that time titled "In My Father's House." While nonfiction brought income, he saw novels as a more important artistic vocation. He began working on what would become *Go Tell It on the Mountain* around 1938. Then, in 1945, a female friend introduced him to the novelist Richard Wright, who was sixteen years his senior. They took to each other, and Baldwin, nervous and overawed but still eloquent, told Wright about his authorial aspirations. Wright read parts of "In My Father's House" and recommended Baldwin for a fellowship to his publishers at Harper and Brothers. The novel Baldwin had hoped to publish was not ready, however, and his first business lunch, though a social success, did not lead to a contract. Baldwin met with Wright a few more times before the older writer left for Paris in 1946. The Eugene F. Saxton Foundation Fellowship, which Baldwin did receive thanks to Wright's recommendation, brought him five hundred dollars and helped support his family (a Rosenwald Fellowship three years later would help pay for his trip to France in 1948). Disappointed, perhaps feeling as if he had failed yet another father figure, Baldwin resolved to find his own writing style, a counter to that of his idol.

The liberatory writing style Baldwin was honing aimed to challenge the idea of a single racial identity; it was to be his American inheritance. Many years after his anti-sentimental proclamations in "Everybody's Protest Novel," he returned to this important theme in the retrospective essay "Every Good-Bye Ain't Gone," published in *New York* magazine in 1977. Writing it "just twenty-nine years after my first departure from America," he drew a "demarcation line" in it between the things that "happened to me because I was black . . . and . . . things [that] had happened to me because I was me." Like the famous demarcation line with which he ended "Notes of a Native Son"—and his mission to keep his "own heart free from hatred and despair"—the demarcation line of "Every Good-Bye Ain't Gone" led toward his Black queer humanism and later essays like "Here Be Dragons" and "The Cross of Redemption" (1985–87).

Before he could write those, however, Baldwin the author of "The Harlem Ghetto" had to wrestle with another kind of self-liberation, one that placed "Blackness and me" in confrontation with both the fictions and the materiality of his gender and sexuality as a young man. A self-described late bloomer, he met men and women, fell in and out of love, and experienced sex and much confusion about who and why he desired, lusted, and hated. Shored up by Delaney, Warshow, and other mentors, Baldwin entered sexual adulthood as a budding, passionate writer, treating every experience as potential material.

TRACK 4

A Lover's Kiss Is a
Very Strange Event

I N 1944, while working for the Post Office, the twenty-year-old Baldwin penned a poem about a boxer in "red satin trunks." He dedicated it to Arthur Moore, the unrequited love of his church childhood, and sent it to Moore enclosed in a letter he wrote at work. In his response, sent on May 13 from the Goodman Field, Kentucky, military base, Corporal Moore, addressing Baldwin by his nickname "Boon," wrote of Baldwin's "philosophical thesis on religion, sex, and life." Moore was surprised by his friend's views, wondering, "what goes on under your skin." In his eyes, Baldwin's "attitude about sex [had] revolutionized itself," while Moore reaffirmed that his own held fast: sex was "a sin and a shame" causing "woeful damage." Concluding, he chastised Baldwin for being reticent about "your lady fair that you told me about . . . Kay." That Baldwin's handsome boxer occupied his thoughts is unsurprising, for it was boy crushes on friends like Moore that made him doubt early in life that he was heterosexual. Moore's expectation of hearing about Baldwin's alleged girlfriend, "Kay," though, points to another way in which the young writer used his sexual awakening and spun its confusions into literary material.

In his essay "Family Secrets" Hilton Als situates Baldwin's sexuality and style within a spectrum of Black queer identities. As "uneasy members of the same tribe," Black queer writers must face the conservatism and homophobia of their communities. They can either pretend to be straight or hide behind smokescreens of overinflated rhetoric. Als, an admirer and literary descendant of Baldwin, terms Baldwin's style "high faggot." Growing up with the fanatical Reverend Baldwin, passing under the watchful-wrathful eye of Sister McCandless, young James had no choice but to embrace both tactics—pretensions of heterosexuality and "high faggot" style. Delayed by years in the pulpit, his erotic flowering took place in Greenwich Village. There, managing heterosexual pretense and laboring over rhetoric, he taught himself how to write about sexuality by sampling his new experiences in various mixes. These early attempts were foundational to his emerging humanism, which, in turn, would allow him to push his approach to sex and gender beyond the initial constraints.

Bathed in the glow of his mentor Beauford Delaney's first portrait of him, *Dark Rapture*, and guided by his Jewish editors, Baldwin would gather, remix, and replay memories of that period in the novels to come, *Another Country*, *Tell Me How Long the Train's Been Gone*, *If Beale Street Could Talk*, and *Just above My Head*. First, though, he worked on several pieces about his entrance into New York's gay world. Mostly never published, these drafts show, for example, that Baldwin usually fell for men who were or seemed to be straight or bisexual, or who showed only a passing interest in him. He liked them manly and strong, regardless of race, a description that fit the handsome Swiss painter Lucien Happersberger, whom he met in Paris around 1950, and Engin Cezzar, who hosted him in Turkey in the 1960s.

In the Village of the 1940s, the most important young man in Baldwin's life aside from Emile Capouya was his best friend, Eugene Worth. A member of the Young People's Socialist League and partially responsible for Baldwin's brief flirtation with the left, Worth was light-skinned, straight, and in love with a white woman whose parents disapproved of the match and of him. Baldwin was secretly in love with him; Worth hinted once that he might be in love with Baldwin, too. Trapped in the double bind of homophobia and faked heterosexuality noted by Als, they missed their chance to connect romantically. Baldwin later wished he could have heard Worth's "oblique confession" as a "plea" and acted upon it. Their unconsummated relationship lasted about three years, ending tragically with Worth's suicide in 1946. It remained an ideal of unconsummated, young homosexual love and a frequent motif in Baldwin's work.

An unpublished story, "That Evening Train May Be Too Late," written in Saint-Paul-de-Vence in the 1970s–80s, offers what may be a fictional rendering of their friendship, venturing where the two men never could. The story recounts a love affair between "Luigi," who is white, and a nameless Black narrator. They meet at "a political meeting in the Village . . . during the Second World War." The narrator is smitten with Luigi, much more than with the political slogans that brought them together: "We were not Stalinists—we were Trotskyists; the root motive, therefore, of this meeting, though we certainly did not know it then, was self-congratulation." Aware of putting it "too brutally," he remarks, with a self-mocking chuckle the reader can easily imagine, "but we were young, we were earnest, and, in this particular context, anyway, we were right." Later, when asked about his leftist sympathies, Baldwin would admit that although he was interested in politics, he was not a joiner and could never toe a party line—in "The Price of the Ticket" he asserts that it was "impossible to indoctrinate me."

The nameless narrator of "That Evening Train May Be Too

Late" confronts his attraction to Luigi while in a café with friends following the meeting: "I could no longer avoid him—which means that I had been aware of him all the time. He had a smile, a grin, like no other; he reminded me of no one, but he was recognized by my soul." The rest of the story describes their "falling in love" while listening to a recording of the actor John Barrymore reading from Shakespeare's *Richard III*. Luigi, who "intended to become an opera singer," is reciting the text "behind Barrymore, and we read & declaimed to each other and we talked." The story, possibly inspired by Delaney's passionate friendship with the singer and voice coach Dante Pavone, details the young socialists' erotic-nerdy courtship and, later, a no less detailed first sexual encounter. Possibly an oblique autobiographical confession, it echoes in "The Price of the Ticket" when Baldwin describes his connection to Worth: "I was to hurt a great many people by being unable to imagine that anyone could possibly be in love with an ugly boy like me."

"That Evening Train May Be Too Late" also recalls the names of childhood crushes and the first adult man he recognized as a homosexual who reciprocated his desire: "I did not realize that I was falling in love with him because it simply could not have entered my mind that he was falling in love with me." Insecure about his looks, the narrator mentions a high school crush, Ned, an older lover, Billy, and Uncle Hank, an adult, married neighbor who he sensed was queer. (Uncle Hank would reemerge decades later, sans homoerotic leanings, in *Little Man, Little Man*.) Baldwin's narrator admires these men, as he does Luigi, for knowing "what it meant to be in love with a man," and for knowing "'what to do'—he was very cool about it." His writing is completely free here, with passages of purple prose at times, as well as tender, poetic sections worthy of comparison to some of his later work: "I still remember how beautiful and bright was his face that morning. I still taste that moment, that delight, still see his arms in the air, still see those black & brilliant eyes, the black hair, still hear that voice, and that laugh." The young men have great sex and fall in love in the narrator's first Village apartment. He has two beds, a kitchen, and a bathroom, and now he also has a lover.

The story describes the life-changing discoveries that occur in young people's lives: cherished attachments, first sexual contacts, and moments of enchantment, desire, release, and carnal joy with another person's body. To Baldwin, sexual longing and erotic attraction become entangled with romantic love and loyal friendships that can save one from the cruelties of the world. He writes, "For very young people . . . for whom everything is happening for the first time, the beginning of a friendship is a miraculous moment—incandescent: and, though the friendship may fail, or the friend be lost, this incandescence can never thereafter entirely vanish from one's life." Some moments, he insists, "accompany one to the grave, and, for all I know, beyond it. It is the light which makes the darkness heal and enables me to begin to move within the darkness, and against it."

Eugene Worth, who inspired Luigi, also fueled the character of Rufus Scott, a Black jazz musician, in *Another Country*, which took on interracial love and sex while placing queerness at its center. The book enraptured and scandalized readers, became an international best seller, and was banned by some libraries. Rufus internalizes the white racial hatred he encounters and ends up abusing his one-time male and long-term white female lovers, Eric and Leona. When the consequences of his actions hit him, he is filled with self-loathing. He cannot face his family in Harlem; a brief encounter with friends does not erase his anguish, and he ends his life by jumping off the George Washington Bridge, just as the real-life Worth had done. Baldwin positions Rufus's death as a choice, a kind of self-punishment. Rufus thus embodies the senseless loss of Black life in the racist United States, while also providing an important lesson in individual responsibility. In *Another Country,* men and women abused by the hyper-visible, beautiful, and talented men like Rufus seem to be collateral damage. But Baldwin forces us to pay attention as well to the white working-class rape victim, Leona, and the white homosexual actor, Eric, who are hurt by Rufus because they love him and he has the power to do them harm, even as he is a victim of a racist state himself.

After Worth's death, Lucien Happersberger, an aspiring Swiss painter Baldwin met in Paris around 1950, took center stage as his love interest. Happersberger was seventeen and running away from his bourgeois parents toward a bohemian life in the French capital. Although their sexual relationship was short-lived, the tall and handsome man became the love of Baldwin's life. Their stormy affair inspired *Giovanni's Room,* whose central homosexual romance was a radical literary move in 1956. In fact, Baldwin had trouble publishing the book in the United States. Knopf, which issued *Go Tell It on the Mountain,* turned it down, making Baldwin furious ("They told me to burn it!"). The book did better in England, where the publisher Michael Joseph took it gladly; soon after, a small house, Dial Press, picked it up, becoming Baldwin's U.S. publisher for years. In the decades since, *Giovanni's Room* has become an international gay classic.

Giovanni's Room and *Another Country* boldly linked race, sexuality, and masculinity in ways that were unprecedented in American literary history. Baldwin began plotting both while still living in Harlem. At first terrified by his sexuality, once settled in the Village he got to work sorting it out and turning his apprehension and experience into literary material. Like "That Evening Train May Be Too Late," unpublished drafts of these novels in his archives describe sexual encounters with men that may have been based on his own life. Usually undated, they can sometimes be linked to the works and events, even people, in Baldwin's life. For example, a description of a possible first sexual experience with an older male mentioned in "The Price of a Ticket" and "Here Be Dragons" appears in his handwritten autobiographical piece.

There, a man of about "thirty-eight, handsome in a Spanish, high-yellow kind of way, tall, and on the heavy side, with bright, black, mocking eyes, and a small mustache," follows the "frightened, pop eyed, fifteen-year-old boy I was" into a church, where they strike up a conversation. Though attracted to the man, the young narrator runs away after they enter the man's apartment, having realized that the man is trying to seduce him. Then, after he turns sixteen, the narrator runs into the man again. The man's name is Billy, and the boy is ready this time. In Billy's apartment, the two are pretending to be reading magazines: "After awhile, Billy said, I bet your mind is as much on that magazine as I am in Chicago. He put down *his* magazine, and smiled, and opened his arms and, after a moment, pulled me into his lap." Baldwin describes that first contact with another man's body in lyric detail as a homecoming: "A lover's kiss, especially for the first time, is a very strange event. It testifies to the strangest of biographies, one's own: everything that had ever happened to me was in that man's kiss that afternoon, my brother, my father, my mother, myself, my pain and pride—his arms held it all, and his mouth seemed to be seeking to kiss me, to seek me, to soak me up from the depths of my terrified solitude."

Baldwin's first novel began taking shape soon after this romance, when he was seventeen, and its homoerotic moments probably echoed that affair in multiple drafts as Baldwin traveled from Harlem to the Village to Paris. He typed its concluding "THE END" during a visit in the Swiss Alps, in the tiny, predominantly Catholic village of Loèche-les-Bains (Leukerbad). As he recalled in his unpublished autobiographical notes, "I had been carried to

Switzerland . . . by a Swiss friend I met in Paris. Those early Paris years were rough—so rough that my friend's decision to kidnap me was a literal attempt to save my life." The friend was Lucien Happersberger, whose parents owned a chalet in Loèche-les-Bains. Baldwin recounts how Happersberger "ruthlessly blackmailed" his father for lodging and food money, pleading that he would die of tuberculosis if he were not allowed to stay in the chalet. Baldwin's first experience of living with someone who took care of him was life changing. In Thorsen's 1989 documentary, Happersberger recalls what a sight they were in the village: "a strange couple." But they got their work done: Happersberger painted and cooked, while Baldwin wrote.

It took three trips to Loèche-les-Bains before Baldwin finished *Go Tell It on the Mountain.* On a black-and-white postcard of a glacier, Baldwin wrote to his friend Mary Painter in 1952, "I have *never* [triply underlined] seen so much snow, and I find it depressing." In addition to completing the novel, he began a play, *The Amen Corner,* and wrote the essay "Stranger in the Village" for *Harper's* (published in October 1953), in which he described being the first African American in those parts: "It did not occur to me—possibly because I am an American—that there could be people anywhere who had never seen a Negro." Filled with white people and snow, the village becomes in the essay a metaphor for Europe and the West, against which Baldwin measures himself. Loèche-les-Bains was so secluded it seemed to be stuck in the seventeenth century; Baldwin had never been anywhere as primitive. Its inhabitants were shocked not only by his skin color and hair but also by his typewriter, an invention they had never seen.

The villagers' parochialism leads Baldwin to muse on slavery and colonial history, including his situation as a Black man in "the West onto which I have been so strangely grafted," he wrote in the *Harper's* essay. Two pages later, though, he admits that it is "not quite true" that he was a perpetual stranger in Loèche-les-Bains. Some people had become friends, some remained indifferent, while others disliked him. The situation was much what it had been in Harlem, or Paris; he almost felt at home there. Decades later, he reprocessed this experience as formative in his unpublished notes: "The mountains, a long way from home—me, Bessie Smith, Fats Waller, and the Swiss—a kind of breath-taking historical conjunction. And I actually climbed a mountain, to the great wonder of the village (and mine)." Away from big-city distractions, he hit his writing stride in that unlikely place, as he recalled in 1984: "After ten years of carrying that book around, I finally finished it in Switzerland in three months." That trip was perhaps his most significant confrontation with a new location and his first taste of domestic life with a male lover.

After his breakup with Happersberger in 1952, the grief-stricken Baldwin tried to get him back. His heartbreak lasted long and helped him complete *Giovanni's Room* in record time. For many years, he hoped for a miraculous reunion; as he wrote to David Leeming in December 1966, "No one has ever loved him as much as I." Happersberger was bisexual and went on to marry women three times. He had two children with his first wife, Suzy, whom Baldwin also knew; their older son, Luc James, became Baldwin's godson. But Happersberger genuinely loved Baldwin. Unlike other former lovers, he never felt ashamed of their sexual relationship, as he explained in our 2007 interview. A tall, handsome man, he inspired the character of passionate, bisexual Italian Giovanni. In Allan Morrison's profile of Baldwin in the October 1961 *Ebony*, Happersberger appears in two photographs, identified only as "one of his few close friends."

In our interview in 2007, shortly before his death of cancer, Happersberger spoke about the importance of men understanding "homosensuality" as vital to a healthy masculinity. In his eighties then, he retained the charm, vitality, and good humor that must have entranced Baldwin. Though their lifelong friendship was stormy and often grievous to Baldwin, who complained about Happersberger bitterly in letters to Painter and Leeming, Happersberger remained part of Baldwin's circle. He was at Baldwin's bedside in Saint-Paul-de-Vence in 1987 to nurse him in his last weeks, keeping vigil alongside Baldwin's beloved younger brother David and Bernard Hassel, Baldwin's house manager and friend. Recalling those last days, Happersberger cried during our conversation, admitting that he felt anguished because he had not supported Baldwin better in his last years.

From the moment he left Harlem, Baldwin's artistic evolution went hand in hand with a search for authorial havens and alternative families. He never resettled in his home country again. As he explained in Sedat Pakay's 1973 art film *James Baldwin: From Another Place:* "I leave and I go back. I leave and I go back." His homosocial relationships in the Village, in France, and later in Turkey gave him a fascination for the divisive politics of racialized, toxic masculinity, which his later work, beginning with *No Name in the Street* in 1972, identifies as the most destructive element in the American national character. Like his stepfather, some of his lovers were violent with him; he was once brutalized so badly in Turkey that he had to be hospitalized. Baldwin's struggles with depression, his suicide attempts, and his attention to all forms of sexual violence eventually led him to an understanding that brutality against women was widespread and that it had taken him a long while to see it—but first, they helped him understand himself. As he wrote in an unpublished piece, the hatred he felt for his father was the first lesson he had in self-knowledge as a man: "Hatred is sentimentality raised to its highest, most suicidal pressure. Whatever else hatred may or may not reach or destroy, it most certainly destroys the self."

He realized that he did not hate his father, nor did his father truly hate him, he wrote in the same unpublished piece: "We just couldn't find a way to get along." Having learned from Beauford Delaney how to look deeply into others, he regretted that most of those others would never do the same for him. "People who can't get along with each other can't bear, simply, what they see in each other. Each, in truth, is paralyzed before a mirror. One can be released from this stasis only by confession. My Daddy didn't live to articulate his confession." In a 1963 letter to Harry Belafonte, Baldwin explains that his debt to Delaney as his spiritual father "can never be repaid," adding, "only my life and my work can do that."

The work Baldwin did in the 1940s–50s reflected that conviction, laying the foundation for his prolific period of the 1960s and 1970s. Baldwin's connection with Delaney, his spiritual father, and his painstaking work with Jewish editors and other intellectual interlocutors, his crushes and encounters with lovers all provided indispensable tools for his own wrestling with sexuality, his writing, and ultimately, his gender identity. As we will see, by the time he had rearticulated his understanding of race, gender, and sexuality, his thinking had evolved to include feminine self-presentation and androgyny as new, radical ways of being American.

Side C

———

Because My House Fell Down
and I Can't Live There No More

O N JULY 15, 1961, on his popular WFMT Chicago radio
program, Studs Terkel introduced Baldwin as "a brilliant
young Negro American writer . . . one of the rare men in
the world who seems to know who he is today." An increasingly
important voice in American letters, Baldwin was invited to discuss his new essay volume, *Nobody Knows My Name: More Notes
of a Native Son*, inspired by his European sojourn and first trip to
the American South. In that book's opening essay, "The Discovery
of What It Means to Be an American," Baldwin credits the music
of blues icon Bessie Smith with helping him write his first novel.

A recording of Smith's "Backwater Blues," which she wrote in
the aftermath of the Tennessee flood of 1926, opens the interview.
As the music fades, Terkel asks Baldwin to describe his feelings.
Prefacing his response with, "It's very hard," Baldwin explains:

> The first time I heard this record was in Europe, and under very
> different circumstances than I had ever listened to Bessie in New
> York. [And] what struck me was that fact that . . . she was singing . . .
> about a disaster . . . which had almost killed her, and she accepted it

and was going beyond it. . . . [There's a] fantastic kind of understatement in it. It's the way I want to write. . . . When she says "My house fell down and I can't live there no more"—it's a great . . . a great achievement.

As his slightly breathless explanation confirmed, Smith's performance inspired the tender narrator in Baldwin. This example of his "high faggot" style communicates Baldwin's aesthetic debt to Bessie Smith and his embrace of complex female influences in his works.

In "The Discovery of What It Means to Be an American," Baldwin claimed that Smith helped him "re-create the life that I had first known as a child and from which I had spent so many years in flight," also evoking narrative and metaphorical inspirations he first experienced in his mother's kitchen. Smith's music featured prominently in *Another Country*, where her songs "Backwater Blues," "Empty Bed Blues," and "Shipwreck Blues" play in the background as Rufus and Vivaldo discuss women, love, and sex, and as Eric meets Cass after returning from France. Complementing and infusing what Ed Pavlić terms Baldwin's "musical, angular poetics," Smith's songs run throughout his other works—*Nobody Knows My Name, Tell Me How Long the Train's Been Gone, No Name in the Street,* and speeches and essays such as "Theater: The Negro In and Out" (1961), which critiques Edward Albee's 1959 play *The Death of Bessie Smith.* Baldwin's essay "The Uses of the Blues" (1964) begins teasingly, "I don't know anything about music" and in "Of the Sorrow Songs: The Cross of Redemption" (1979), he mentions another Smith song, "Long Old Road," and returns to "Backwater Blues" when describing his sisters. Baldwin also cites lyrics from Smith's "Sing Sing Prison Blues" in *The Devil Finds Work.*

While the theme of artistic influence dominated Side B of this Life Album, on Side C, ushered along by Smith's blues, the focus shifts to a discussion of the women mentors, queer collaborators, interlocutors, in Baldwin's life, as well as his descendants. Bessie Smith's role as his muse also signals the return of the theme of women's influence that we first heard on Side A. Remixed here, as Baldwin applies blues aesthetics to his increasingly experimental style and journeys to France, Turkey, and elsewhere, we will track his struggles with gender identity and the lessons he takes from feminists and friends. All these things, too, became part of his humanist philosophy.

Baldwin's flight from his difficult childhood took him from Harlem churches to Delaney's studio in Greenwich Village. His departure for France in November 1948 marked his flight from two oppressive conceptions of identity—racism and homophobia—that permeated his home country. Straitjacketed by these prejudices, Black queer artists were made into misfits; their houses fell, making them spiritually homeless. Bessie Smith's blues helped Baldwin endure his own pain, to find his own voice and places that nourished him as a writer. The search for home and alternative families emerged as a major theme in his life abroad and the works he wrote during this period.

In "Notes for *The Amen Corner*" (1968), the introduction to his first play, Baldwin touched on another theme that is often ignored in discussions of his life: his loneliness and need of support while he was living abroad. "All I had . . . was me, and I was forced to insist on this me with all the energy I had," he writes. "I had my head broken, . . . people laughed when I said I was going to be a writer . . . I finally split the scene." Like Delaney's art and love, his mother, and his editors and teachers, music offered him a guide and inspiration, helping to shelter him in his solitude and sustain his writing.

When he finally proved himself as an author, Baldwin became alienated by another American stereotype and public role into which he was being pushed: "When I came back to sell my first novel, I realized that I was being corralled into another trap: now I was . . . a *Negro* writer," he complained in the play's introduction. Hard-working and ambitious, he was enraged by the expectation that he compose "diminishing versions of *Go Tell It on the Mountain* forever." He wanted to try writing in all genres, and he did just that, though with varying results. In 1968, with a comfortable financial outlook following the global success of *The Fire Next Time,* he enjoyed what the money could bring. Happy with the economic benefit that fame also brought his family, he was also facing the mixed blessings and demands of celebrity that spilled into their lives, too. The "Negro writer" had soon become a profitable spokesperson-activist, staunch supporter of the Civil Rights Movement, and in high demand as a commentator on the "Negro question." The themes of activism and fame and the toll both took resonate in several works, such as the short story "This Evening, This Morning, So Soon" (1960) and the novels *Tell Me How Long the Train's Been Gone* and, later, *Just above My Head.*

As Baldwin juggled work, popularity, and activism, he developed a thematic and generic division of labor. From the 1960s on, he dealt with political and contemporary topics mostly in essays, while pursuing artistic, self-referential, auto-thematic, and theoretical ambitions in novels, short stories, plays, and unrealized screenplays and musicals. Finding it difficult to write during his visits to the United States, he sought havens abroad, such as Switzerland, where he had finished his first novel. He loved the islands of Corsica, Ibiza, and Puerto Rico. He also favored writers' colonies such as MacDowell in New Hampshire and Yaddo in New York State, where he liked working. He spent a lot of time during the 1960s in Istanbul, and beginning in 1971 he settled down in his final residence in Saint-Paul-de-Vence.

Throughout his life abroad, Baldwin continued wrestling with issues of gender and sexuality. He boldly embraced risky imaginative gender identifications in early drafts of his fiction and two published essays, for example, yet characters in his published novels often came across as conflicted and vacillating, even male chauvinists. When confronted with outspoken women during interviews, he sometimes appeared defensive and self-contradictory. Perhaps he wanted to protect Black men from feminist criticism. Or he might have been yielding to his desire for acceptance by the younger Black men he admired, such as Stokely Carmichael (later Kwame Ture) and Huey Newton.

This side of the Baldwin Life Album revolves around these themes as I track the development of his philosophy of Black queer humanism between 1948 and 1987. Its tracks sound out both Baldwin's blues-infused sense of himself and his desire for Black freedom and a better world for all. Aided by new friends, especially women, and new locales, he created literature that urged readers to become generous enough to accept themselves fully, while extending compassion and understanding toward others—to become better than the world. Baldwin wished to leave a tangible legacy for the "children," whom he, as a self-acknowledged unfulfilled Black queer parent and a loving uncle to his nieces and nephews, saw as America's and the world's hope. For that reason, and to supplement his income when the popularity of his later works was fading at home, in the last years of his life he took on a new role as a teacher of writing and literature at various U.S. campuses.

I Am All Those Strangers
and a Woman, Too

D URING HIS FIRST DECADE in France (1948–57, inter-
spersed with returns to America), Baldwin made friends
and fit easily into the bohemian scene on the Left Bank
of Paris. Feeling free of the constraints of his Harlem upbringing
for the first time, he threw himself into a new life. The city offered
a heady mix of intellects and styles, and he thrived, despite the
poverty and hardship of the French capital, learning the language
to perfection, and bouncing among cheap hotels and the cafés—
Les Deux Magots, Café Tournon, Café Monaco, and the Café de
Flore on the Boulevard Saint-Germain—frequented by locals
and expatriates. He met and read French writers, including Jean-
Paul Sartre, Simone de Beauvoir, and Albert Camus. He admired
artists, actors, and film directors such as Jean Cocteau, Jeanne
Moreau, Yves Montand, and Simone Signoret, some of whom became close friends.

More permissive culturally and sexually than New York, Paris
allowed Baldwin to begin shedding his guilt over loving and lust-
ing after men's bodies. He frequented what were then called homosexual bars: the Reine Blanche, where he first met Lucien Hap-

persberger, and the upscale Fiacre, which inspired descriptions of similar establishments in *Giovanni's Room*. After a night of partying, he and friends would eat breakfast around the clamorous city center market Les Halles, which is another important location in that novel. He hopped from bed to bed and had his heart broken. He sang at Chez Inez, a club run by the popular African American jazz singer Inez Cavanaugh. He also frequented the Abbaye/Echelle de Jacob, the establishment of the Black gay actor and singer Gordon Heath. He sang at an Arab nightclub and hung out with Algerian and other African immigrants, describing the experience in the essays "Encounter on the Seine: Black Meets Brown" (1950), "A Question of Identity" (1954), and "The Discovery of What It Means to Be an American" (1959).

American GIs who stayed in Paris after the war fascinated him and inspired some of his writing. He also encountered American authors who had relocated there permanently or temporarily: Richard Wright, Norman Mailer, Mary Keen, Otto Friedrich, Herbert Gold, Marty Weissman, Chester Himes, Frank Yerby, Themistocles Hoetis, Mason Hoffenberg, Harold Kaplan, and Priscilla Boughton. He was a frequent guest in the home of Stanley and Eileen Geist, where he met Saul Bellow and Philip Roth. A literary historian, Stanley Geist introduced him to the novels of Henry James, which soon became Baldwin's favorites. James's books would inspire his essays and narrative points of view; James's preface to *Lady Barbarina* is the source for the epigraph to *Another Country*. Many of the characters in that novel, and even more in *Giovanni's Room*, were inspired by the rich mix of humanity Baldwin encountered while living in Paris and Greenwich Village, or while traveling to Corsica, Ibiza, and England, searching for temporary writing havens.

Baldwin's travels and life abroad expanded his world and shaped his writing. Perhaps the most important aspect of that experience was the profound impact of two close women friends whom he met around the same time, 1948–49: a Norwegian journalist named Gidske Anderson and the American economist Mary Painter. The novels they influenced, *Giovanni's Room* and *Another Country*, turned away from the themes of the Black family, Harlem, religion, and adolescent angst that had preoccupied him in *Go Tell It on the Mountain*, and toward adult love relationships, interracial sex, and class and gender issues. Anderson and Painter were smart, educated, emancipated women who loved Baldwin, though it is unlikely that either was sexually involved with him. As listeners and empathizers, they enabled him to unburden his soul, as few of his male friends had the patience for his elaborately worded woes. Anderson and Painter listened to him, read drafts of his work, and discussed complex ideas with him. Like the big sisters he never had, they helped him with the practicalities of lodging, travel, food, and money. They advised him on love affairs, providing a shoulder to cry on when he was heartbroken.

Most crucially, Anderson and Painter helped him confront his growing realization that his difficulties with the binaries of race, gender, and sexuality would not be resolved simply by living abroad. Discussions with the two made Baldwin recognize his repressed reliance on the stereotypes he was trying to escape. Male chauvinism and, at times, outright misogyny and transphobia appear in his second and third novels. Though his male characters—Rufus, Vivaldo, David, and Leo in *Giovanni's Room, Another Country,* and *Tell Me How Long the Train's Been Gone*—were literary creations and their views fictional, they were his responsibility. Like Gustave Flaubert, the author of the nineteenth-century French classic *Madame Bovary,* who reportedly proclaimed that he *was* his character—"Madame Bovary, c'est moi"—Baldwin felt that his own creations were organically linked to him.

These characters were expressing a part of him that was conflicted about gender and sexuality. David, Vivaldo, and Rufus, for example, are homophobic and consider women to be less human than men. Rufus and Vivaldo make fun of Jane, Vivaldo's butch white female lover, calling her names like "bulldagger" and "dyke." Though misogyny was as commonplace in American culture as homophobia and racism, these strongly drawn characters ushered into Baldwin's novels explorations of masculinity that he had already begun sketching, in early essays written between 1949 and 1954.

Gidske Anderson, whom Baldwin initially referred to as his fiancée, was "tall and blonde, Baldwin dark and diminutive, " in James Campbell's description of their striking appearance as a couple in his biography of Baldwin. She knew of Baldwin's homosexuality and did not mind acting as his "cover." She may have inspired the tomboyish, conflicted Hella in *Giovanni's Room;* a possible "sexless and manufactured" Hemingway heroine who echoed Lady Brett Ashley in *The Sun Also Rises*. Anderson worked in the Norwegian Resistance during World War II and came to Paris the same year as Baldwin. A reporter for the Oslo Labor Party newspaper *Arbeiderbladet,* she was an androgynous-looking bohemian, "with a Dutch-boy haircut and wonderfully bizarre and colorful clothes." As she writes in her 1964 memoir, *Mennesker i Paris* (People in Paris), Baldwin was the first Black person she had ever met. A resourceful companion, especially when they traveled in the south of France, she organized their trips and helped Baldwin through two hospitalizations that included surgery for a recurring gland problem. In a letter to his family, Baldwin described her as the "Norwegian girl who saved my life." They were close in age and wary of societal restrictions and the politics of respectability. They shared a gender and sexual ambivalence, bonding while "exploring each other's souls." As Campbell details their early travels, they were young friends who took care of each other while struggling with hunger, bad accommodations, and Baldwin's financial ineptitude.

A writer in her own right, Anderson was not afraid to ask Baldwin about his distinctly American way of understanding others primarily through racial categories. As with his Harlem teacher Bill Miller, Baldwin's friendship with Anderson made it impossible for him to hate white people. Though she was not open about it at the time, Gidske was a lesbian, and in the 1960s she became involved with the first Norwegian female ambassador, Kirsten Ohm. It is unclear whether Baldwin was aware of her sexuality, but it seems likely that he was, given their closeness. After her time in Paris, Anderson lived in the United States for a while, then served as a Nobel Prize official in Norway. She published a novel, several books of poetry, memoirs, and biographies. In one memoir, she describes a deep kinship with Baldwin: "I was fascinated by the journey he had embarked on. I had great sympathy for him. . . . I felt related to him. This search for an identity in a world that flees from identity, this having to fight to be accepted as you were and to break free from the myths others have created about you, this anxiety to look back at your own past . . . knowing that if you didn't do it, you would become one of the dead souls—all this I felt."

Anderson's words are an apt description of the issue Baldwin was then facing—self-identification as a Black queer American in Paris, a struggling author of an unfinished novel, whose American colony included racists; the novelist Ann Birstein, for example, described him as a savage and a clown: "Put a bone through his nose and it would've made sense. . . . But Jimmy was laughing all the time." In an unpublished piece, probably dating from 1949 (it has a note from Anderson scribbled on the back that helps to date it to one of their trips), Baldwin toys with the idea of mental instability that he, somewhat romantically, associates with being a writer-artist. The setting is a southern town, possibly Aix-en-

Provence, where he and Anderson spent some time. He writes: "I am mad. I walk the streets of the world and I imagine that I am someone else, someone beautiful and rich and proud, superbly at home everywhere, loved and admired and wise and good. And rich, rich—in worldly goods, books, clothes, a home, a car, someone who need never wonder if he can afford this meal or this jewel or this impulsive gift. . . . I know and not without pain what it means in the world to be poor and naked and hungry—to be, in short, at the mercy of the world and of one's own overwhelming need and vanity." This lyrical, impressionistic confession reveals Beauford Delaney's painterly influence, showcasing the intimate hues and textures of the southern French landscape: "The cobblestones are solid beneath you and the street curves surely down . . . to stop at the edge of the water." The narrator hears radios and people singing, "the voices of the children in the open air," and sees the "flaking walls of the houses. The rooftops . . . are in the light of evening purple and red, blue and gray, subtly misted and changing in the failing light."

Perhaps his discussions on gender fluidity with Anderson encouraged him to imagine himself as the other in this unpublished piece, which offered escape from the judging eyes around him: "not as I am . . . a rather odd looking black boy with a certain excess of nervous energy, with great uneasiness, a certain charm, and much panic and dishonesty and foolishness," but as "a woman," even a white one. This new motif in Baldwin's writing creates a narrator who longs to inhabit a female body as a conduit to a new place, "another world, another situation entirely. It is this world and this vision I continually attempt to force into the actual, with what disastrous results can be imagined." This female-centered version of the story superimposes itself, if only momentarily, onto the reality in which the narrator walks as an observer, providing a transgender alternative to that reality. Baldwin's new focus on duality and the fluidity of gender also signals a shifting, experimental play with genre that will shape his later works.

In this same piece, another figure emerges in the landscape: "the lone, nearly naked and olive-colored boy stands quietly on the wet rocks, his long fishing line arced before him and bending into the water." We can read this piece as an experiment in a process of creative literary character integration: the olive-colored boy exists in the world where the narrator is walking, while also existing in the narrator's alternative world where he imagines himself as a white woman. Simultaneously visible to the narrator-as-man and the narrator-as-woman, the beautiful boy is the catalyst uniting the narrator's male and female parts in their alternative, "other world," where they desire to dwell, escape, and coexist.

This piece demonstrates Baldwin's explorations of how literature works. Through an act of creative imagination, his narrator can desire to inhabit a differently sexed body and to become a doubly gendered, plural self. "They" can become not only more than one body in this story but also a hybrid. Like a mythic creature, they can hold every identity at once: a man and a woman, Black and white, and all of them together with the olive-colored boy. The world of writing is an alternative to "my own reality," Baldwin writes, for his literal world "is so faint that everything around me is reduced to shadow; or as though each town I walked through became then entirely populated by ghosts." This sense of not just duality but a multiplicity of selves and identities that defies chronology will return only much later in Baldwin's essay "Here Be Dragons."

Another unpublished, undated piece associated with Anderson is a stream-of-consciousness text that may have been written while Baldwin was drunk. Scribbled on a torn-up piece of brown paper, this slightly incoherent rant on gender and sexuality, erotic desire, and love muses on confusing feelings—"all this rage, trembling, indecision, the phantom forces of boys, and the mysterious bodies of women"—and how they have "been bequeathed us for some purpose." The narrator seems to be an early sketch for David in *Giovanni's Room*. Tormented by sexual need, perhaps struggling with bisexuality, the narrator in this hastily sketched vignette imagines male and female bodies as "so many gateways." This overabundance of flesh causes him suffering in the face of "the visible symbols—boys or women," for he seems unable to choose between them. The sexual imagery is paired with an existential perspective that recalls his childhood longings—"the invisible unsatiable desire—to be loved, to belong in the world—to contain, one might be enabled to discover a life beyond this life."

As in the unpublished story with the male-female narrator in the south of France, this speaker longs to live in a world unbounded by stifling binaries. Here, however, the narrator's sexual desire rings with shame, dredging up a frightening past that overshadows an uncertain present, as if David Baldwin's descriptions of his stepson as ugly, sinful, homosexual, and tainted by association with whites and Jews and their licentious ways have followed Baldwin across the Atlantic. "For when I searched my heart (*and* however incompletely) I could not find that *I* had ever been satisfied. And when I looked around me, *I* could not discover, in all that company, anyone who had not been betrayed—by the symbols of life, which they had all mistaken for life itself." This coming to consciousness of pain and betrayal sounds like a sermon about false identities and prophets he once found in scripture. It is also a rite of passage—"the last stage of this apprenticeship" that the "fledgling artist discovers." Baldwin calls that moment a "crisis" the artist must endure. If he survives it, "he is (consciously, passionately, committed to his life, which is to say that he has lived through, and accepted his death)"(*sic*). If he does not, he hyperbolizes, "his end is, I think, worse than the end of other men."

Scribbled on stationery from the Orrington Hotel in Evanston, Illinois, another piece links the themes of race, individuality, and artistic vocation to what Baldwin abhorred as much as labels and stereotypes: being a victim. This piece gives evidence of his early humanist thinking. Referencing "my dialogue with *Gidske* in Paris in 1949," his notes connect the "A, B, C's" of his scribbled argument: "Victims. A. *How to cease to be one. . . . B. What such a liberation can mean.*" He embraces the strength and joy that come from confronting "the forces which (A) have produced you [and] (B) which menace and nourish you; one has finally become responsible for one's own life." Point C leads to being "placed in contact with all the lives there are." He concludes, perhaps echoing existentialist approaches of Camus and Sartre, that we all, "in our various, and first of all private ways," share anguish and pain, and "such convulsion of the spirit."

Baldwin's struggle with gender and sexual identification as key to defining one's identity can be traced back to his high school years, when, as he writes in his journal, he "fell in love . . . with a white boy"—a high school romance that returns in his last essay "To Crush the Serpent" (1987). Having no models of queer love at that time, only traditional Hollywood romances, the teen thought that if two men were in love, one of them, somehow, had to become a woman. His later explorations of duality and the multiplicity of identities made him feel as if he were many people existing in the same body—a vision that came to him in dreams and that undergirds many unpublished drafts among his papers. But he rarely dealt with these complex issues in public.

Fascinated with both gender binaries and how a female persona could exist within the male, he began exploring these questions in earnest in discussions with Anderson. Their analyses were carried into two of his early essays, "The Preservation of Innocence," published in *Zero* in 1949, and "Gide as Husband and Homosexual," in the *New Leader*, 1954, retitled "The Male Prison" in *Nobody Knows My Name*. In both pieces Baldwin attacked negative aspects of the male-female polarization; he later elaborated on them in *Giovanni's Room, Another Country, Tell Me How Long the Train's Been Gone,* and *Just above My Head*. In these two early essays, Baldwin also probed the philosophical responsibilities of the novelist and the need for men to understand women and female sexuality better as a precondition for attaining full humanity. Just twenty-five years old when he wrote "The Preservation of Innocence," he was then reviewing "thousands" of postwar books in the "be kind to n[—]s . . . be kind to Jews!" category, as he remembered it decades later in "The Price of the Ticket." In "The Preservation of Innocence," the young writer who struggled with his first novel criticized popular fiction authors James M. Cain and Laura Z. Hobson for creating appalling stereotypes: "Men and women have all but disappeared from our popular culture, leaving only this disturbing series of effigies" that embody labels and categories in a "neat . . . one-dimensional . . . fashion." A real novel, Baldwin proclaims, "insistently demands the presence and passion of human beings, who cannot ever be labeled."

Several years later, in "The Male Prison," he accused André Gide of having no sense of himself either as the husband of his long-suffering wife, Madeleine, or as a homosexual. Because Gide has no "apprehension of what a woman [is]," he cannot appreciate "genuine human involvement." To the Baldwin of that piece, Gide's writing exists in a hell where misogyny is the flip side of "powerful masculinity," and where binary gender and sexual divisions imprison everyone, creating a culture that erases women as subjects. Importantly, Baldwin also argues that men cannot exist without closeness to women because denying female subjectivity means denying an integral part of themselves. Remarkably, this issue had been at the back of his mind from the beginning of his career, remaining one of the most difficult for him to explore. Perhaps he abandoned it, given the problems he had publishing *Giovanni's Room,* in whose intensely polemical narrative these pieces clearly reverberate.

In both essays, as in the earlier unpublished pieces on androgyny, the density of Baldwin's writing and complexity of his ideas are often dizzying. Famously intense and energetic, once he got into a discussion, he could wind himself up for hours; and then, while others slept, he would write. His close Turkish friend and Istanbul host and flat mate Engin Cezzar recalled, for example, that Baldwin kept typing and inventing new projects, often all night long with only alcohol and cigarettes as fuel. While this was a celebrated, even clichéd MO for an author, Cezzar also claimed that Baldwin seemed possessed by a species of literary workaholism that was somehow his own. And yet, for all his work on these daring subjects, much of this writing never made its way to publication.

Baldwin's other close friend in Paris, Mary Painter, was a hardworking consummate professional like him. A Minnesotan by origin and economist by training, Painter was educated at Swarthmore College and worked for the government as part of the Marshall Plan to rebuild Western Europe after World War II. At the Board of Economic Warfare and the Office of Strategic Services, she developed groundbreaking techniques for analyzing Nazi Germany's military abilities. Her obituary in the *Chicago Tribune* named her "an important innovator in the use of statistical techniques." Very different from flamboyant Anderson, Painter was no less enjoyable a companion. Unlike Anderson, who eventually drifted away, Painter remained a part of Baldwin's life until the end, even encouraging him to move to Saint-Paul-de-Vence in 1971. After she relocated to the south of France in her later years, they lived some sixty miles apart and visited often.

Painter arrived in Paris in 1948 and worked at the U.S. Mission to NATO until 1960. Baldwin met her at the Montana Bar, where he would often spend time with Lucien Happersberger. She cooked well and hosted Baldwin and Happersberger for many a dinner in her apartment. (She later married Georges Garin, a prominent French chef and owner of a Michelin-starred Paris restaurant.) Painter was a dependable friend and supported Baldwin's work by lending him money and helping him with his life's many permutations. He wrote her some of his most personal and probing letters. In one, penned after she returned to the United States, Baldwin writes, "You never miss the water till the well runs dry. . . . You, more than any other person, had made my life in Paris bearable." Confessing the complexities of his attachment to her, he explains that she was "the only person I knew to whom I could always tell the truth—or try to—or, for that matter, try not to—and whom I altogether trusted to do the same with me." (As we saw on Side A, there was one other such confidante, his mother, Berdis, but we do not know what he wrote to her; letters to Berdis and Painter are sealed at the Schomburg Center until 2036.)

Baldwin told Leeming that he would have married Painter had he not found himself confident of his primary sexual attraction to men when he met her. A rare, published photo of them together appears in Allan Morrison's October 1961 *Ebony* feature on Baldwin. Baldwin is wearing glasses, a white shirt, and dark pants while sitting on a window parapet; Painter, petite, blonde, and in a dark dress, is leaning close to him. Both are holding drinks, looking sideways, apparently listening to someone outside the frame. Baldwin dedicated *Another Country* to Painter, calling it "your novel," "our book," and "our baby" in letters documenting its prolonged gestation. She was an inspiration for two characters, Cass and Leona, and possibly for Barbara in *Tell Me How Long the Train's Been Gone*. As a hypothetical couple, Painter and Baldwin were perfect for each other. She was patient and a much-needed stabilizing influence; he admired her cool-headedness. He loved her with no qualifications, though he also needed her material support and saw no conflict in accepting it—his letters contain requests for money and other favors in between intimate discussions. Painter was also close to Beauford Delaney and David Baldwin, James's younger brother, as well as to David Leeming; the four friends formed his lifelong international family.

Some of Baldwin's letters to Painter are masterpieces of the epistolary genre, demonstrating its utility as one of the most intimate forms of communication. Some are unremarkable stylistically, perhaps composed hastily, or driven by alcohol and emotional need to share his jumbled thoughts with someone who would withhold criticism. On June 14, 1957, for example, he wrote her from Corsica, where he spent eight months, "I trust your love for me and I also trust your judgment." Wrestling with overall human "wickedness," as well as his own personal brand of it, he remarked, "I can, apparently, create convincing humans on paper; and never seem to be prepared for them in life." A recipient of deeply personal, often anguished, missives, Painter knew the most private details of Baldwin's life. In a fourteen-page letter dated February 5, 1957, also from Corsica, he confesses: "I wish I could say that all this has made me wiser. . . . But no . . . my suspicion that a person who is very lonely and very strong is very likely to become intolerably egocentric is quite sound; and my sense of an antidote to this, genuine human involvement[,]. . . love, reciprocity, someone who will make you less alone . . . is not the province of the will." His dream of love, "my desire to be saved from my own galloping egocentricity, has simply made me more egocentric than ever," he concludes, "going back, as I always do, to the Bible, that, as faith without works is dead, I have, simply (!) to keep the faith and do my work. I can do the first, oddly enough, only if I manage to do the second."

In 1956, his efforts brought two significant recognitions. *Giovanni's Room* became a finalist for the National Book Award, and though Baldwin suspected that its homosexual themes would keep it from winning, he took the nomination as a "triumph." He also celebrated a grant from the National Institute of Arts and Letters. The grant and sales from *Giovanni's Room* brought in a significant amount of money for the first time, and Baldwin felt that he had attained some stability. Later that year, however, he spiraled into a deep depression, swallowing all his sleeping pills in a suicide attempt. He called on Painter for help, and she came quickly, making him vomit up the medication and summoning a doctor, saving both the author and "her" novel, their "baby."

Painter's letters to Baldwin are not available, which makes it impossible to gauge how much he affected her life and how she regarded their relationship. Glimpses of what Baldwin imagined their friendship might have meant to her can be found in an unpublished piece, "Spring 1949." A short story fragment about a man and a woman meeting in a French café, the Flore, it features a woman identified as "B," who is certainly based on Painter. The narrator explains that he and B were strangers at first, and "never talked about America. Her America and mine were very far apart."

The narrator admits that he has a racial bias against whites, a theme I explored on Sides A and B, where we saw that his white and Jewish schoolfriends and teachers complicated his thinking about identity and its fictions. As he develops these ideas in the story: "It is true, that in my relationship with B I, for the first time, shook myself free of the notion that no white American could really comprehend my fears." B helps him realize that his defensive attitude is a kind of racial essentialism, for he "felt that no white American had ever been so tried beyond the limits of his strength." Thanks to "B's forth-righteousness and her refusal to allow me any easy out," he grows in his understanding of himself and others. B's ability to empathize with him surprises the narrator; her insistence that he challenge his racial thinking shows him that personalities matter more than skin color, and their personalities make them friends: "I am lazy, she is forceful, I am frightened, she is not. It is very hard to tell which of us stands in the greatest danger." In other ways, Baldwin's narrator sees himself as being like B, in fact, becoming more like her—more like a woman even—throughout their deepening friendship.

In "Spring 1949," the narrator also casts his and B's stories against the background of the Paris they inhabit as Americans: "This little world does not really contain any happy people. We have all fallen out of some travelling cloud. B and I would never had met had we not at some point, and with great pain been forced out of the lives we would ordinarily have led." The implication that she is listening to his woes while hiding her own is strengthened when the narrator concludes, "All of us are scarred and I am inclined to be a little distressed when I encounter anyone who hides their scars as well as this girl does; and this same forceful proud reaction causes one to tremble when one conjectures how ugly those scars may be." Baldwin's voice here aligns his story with the woman's—two "scarred/scared" displaced Americans—though in using her to tell of himself, he also ends up occluding B's right to a story of her own.

Baldwin's occasional self-absorption and neglect of his friend's feelings are implied in a letter he wrote Painter in the mid-1950s in which he pleads with her to reply and not be "mad" at him. He also sketches out a long reckoning with his continued, failing attempts to win Happersberger back. Diva-like, he accuses himself of being inauthentic, a "conglomeration of poses, most of them disasters." He has been wrong about "most things"; he would like to be married, but he cannot imagine two men who are lovers ever becoming spouses, for the institution requires that one of them "become a woman." This argument returns in *Giovanni's Room*, where David expresses similar opinions on gender binaries, abandoning Giovanni for his unloved white American fiancée, Hella. Feeling divided and self-destructive, gripped by the despondency he often battled, Baldwin explains in the letter, "you, and [Delaney], are the only two people I know before whom I feel released from this strange power I carry around with me like an atmosphere."

Baldwin's acknowledgment of his depression—"this strange power"—leads him to suspect that he is a "dangerous person." He confesses to not being really "gentle, retiring, meek, unhappy—which I somehow love to think of myself as being." He admits that he can be "dangerous because I can be wrong with such authority." His honesty strips him bare: "I am still, until today, one of the strongest and most arrogant people I have ever met." Echoing what he wrote in the letter to his mother, he notes that his strength is also his "most awful weakness"; he regrets that most people around him are unaware of it. He admits to using his friends to escape his shortcomings, and in so doing, failing them. This self-flagellation may be an apology of sorts to Painter, who must have withstood many a situation that taxed her generosity and patience.

In the same letter, Baldwin mentions persistent memories of the Reverend Baldwin's abuse: "that small voice [still] screaming *What are you doing with your life?*" He was busy writing *Another Country*, whose characters he calls "that wretched band of people," who "*are* a little more than I bargained for." He assures Painter, "It's your book, after all, [and] I may as well tell you that Ralph . . . has finally decided to be a son of an Irish immigrant and an Italian-Jewish factory girl." (Ralph later became Daniel, Vivaldo Moore in *Another Country*.) In a subsequent letter, he confesses that the book makes him feel heavy with anticipation, like a woman giving birth: "I'm really having that baby. . . . Something is moving in me. . . . I would like to know how a real woman feels." Haunted by his stepfather's judgmentalism, the "new depths in the black sea of my troubles," he recalls "the same wound . . . the everlasting father. . . . . never changing, ever present, my mountain, my tiger—ah," and finds that his escape lies in giving birth to books. Baldwin ends the letter by promising to complete *Another Country*, using words that must have made Painter's heart melt: "I will be back in September, with, if I may say so, our baby under my arm. . . . A lot of love's gone into it, including my love for you."

Baldwin truly loved Painter, and because of that he could fail her badly. In a letter from 1960 responding to one of hers, which is unavailable, he writes that something she had communicated "upset me very much." Baldwin is referring to a sexual assault committed against Painter by a mutual friend, the composer, arranger, and musician Alonzo (Lonnie) Levister. The letter is painful to read, for in it Baldwin tries to acknowledge the rape—as he unequivocally names Painter's violation in a January 20, 1960, letter to his Turkish friend Engin Cezzar—yet also fears antagonizing his important Black male friend Levister. He sounds cowardly and evasive while explaining to Painter, "I knew about his dramas with Lucille [Levister's wife], but it simply never entered my head that he would ever touch you. And I introduced you to him." The way Baldwin guiltily wriggles out of taking sides in his letter to Painter is disappointing. Afraid to make his friend "mad," he wonders whether to write to Levister, as if expecting her to help him solve this dilemma.

In contrast, he baldly narrates the events in his letter to Cezzar: "Lonnie . . . walked into her [Mary's] house (she now lives in NY, has quit the government) a couple of weeks ago, and beat her up and raped her. Mary wrote me a one page note which was terribly restrained and terribly disturbing; my brother, David, whom she called at once, wrote me about it at more length." Baldwin ends his account speechless: "I can't really talk about it because I don't know what to say." He solipsistically links this news to the "emotional climate, or pressure, under which I've been living for the last few months." His postscript shows that he has already moved on to mundane matters, requesting a "good dentist" referral from his friend.

Reading through both letters, one cannot help feeling that Levister seemed more important to Baldwin than Painter. Was it because Levister and he were both men? Baldwin explains his discomfort in the letter to Painter, in which he frames her rapist as a man he fears: "The notion that I *can* take someone else's side against him has never failed to fill him with the rage—followed by the tears—of someone who has been betrayed. And to take the side of a *woman* against him—! for there are so many things that Lonnie doesn't know and doesn't want to find out." Shockingly, Baldwin also discounts Levister's wife's suffering: "I thought that the way he treated Lucille was horrible—but I was looking at it, of course, from the point of view of the good of his soul; Lucille, after all, was not really a friend of mine. She was simply Lonnie's wife. But it's very different with you: I don't care what he does to his wife, but I certainly care what he does to you!" Could any rape survivor have been comforted by such words? Baldwin confesses that he "loves" and "trembles" for Lonnie. Then he coolly relates his own dramas, as if he feels he has sufficiently paid attention to Painter's.

In another undated letter, possibly the next one he wrote, Baldwin admits that he never confronted Levister. He wrote to his brother David instead, from whom he heard that Lonnie "has gone over the edge." As if this somehow resolved things, he sermonizes that "it is always the destroyer who, by his acts, is destroyed," mentioning "the evil that is in the world. . . . To say nothing of the evil in oneself. . . . There is no excuse for Lonnie, and . . . there seems to me to be no hope." Baldwin finally admits the evil of Lonnie's actions, yet seems confused about how much Painter, Lonnie's wife, Lucille, and he and Levister were caught up in the gender conundrum he describes in "The Preservation of Innocence" and "The Male Prison." Given that he held himself to a higher moral standard as a writer, and how attuned he felt to being singled out and victimized himself, his blindness to Painter's and Lucille's sufferings seems surprising, if not out of character.

Still, the rape committed by a man he called a friend made an impression, and it echoes in *Another Country, If Beale Street Could Talk,* and *Just above My Head,* whose narratives include descriptions of rough sex, and male-female and male-male rapes. The first time Rufus and Leona are having sex in *Another Country,* for example, on a balcony during a party, Rufus fantasizes about violating her: He "cursed the milk-white bitch and groaned and rode his weapon between her thighs." We never find out what Leona's view is. Though she tells him, "it was so wonderful," afterward, we never enter her mind the way we intensely inhabit his; her postcoital response jars with what we have seen in the episode from his point of view; seeing her foremost as white, he calls her "a funny little cracker," while their host describes her to him as "Little Eva" (a reference to *Uncle Tom's Cabin*) and advises Rufus to "blast her" with some pot to help her "get her kicks."

After their breakup following Rufus's severe abuse, Leona is removed to an asylum by the violent rapist husband she had fled by coming to New York. Rufus asks his best friend Vivaldo Moore (a composite Irish Italian American) what he thinks about Leona's end. "Do you blame me or don't you? Tell the truth," Rufus insists. Vivaldo answers, "Rufus, if I wasn't your friend, I think I'd blame you, sure. You acted like a bastard. But I understand that, I think I do, I'm trying to. . . . Let's face it, you mean much more to me than Leona ever did, well, I don't think I should put you down just because you acted like a bastard. We're *all* bastards. That's why we need our friends." Whether or not Painter's situation influenced this scene in the novel, whether or not Baldwin wrote it to expiate for his failure with her, *Another Country* exemplifies the stereotypical disregard of American men for women in the face of male camaraderie. It also shows its male characters struggling with their gender roles and violence as a badge of manhood. When Vivaldo removes the damaged Leona from Rufus's apartment, his act of compassion accompanies feelings of retrospective remorse about having beaten up and left for dead a queer man that he and his buddies once kidnapped and sexually abused "for fun."

In his fiction, Baldwin's male characters, regardless of skin color, are ultimately doomed by the violence they commit or cause, just as he writes in his letter to Painter. In *Another Country,* Rufus is so racked with guilt and self-hatred that he kills himself—an act that Vivaldo cannot imagine Rufus committing over a woman. On the night they see each other, blind to his friend's anguish, Vivaldo blithely abandons the vulnerable Rufus to hook up with his "bulldagger" girlfriend Jane. Rufus dies begging Leona's forgiveness, a detail that, like the complexity of his character, like Leona and her plight, is rarely noted in discussions of this novel. Although Baldwin explained repeatedly that Rufus's death was inspired by that of his friend Eugene Worth, he never mentioned Painter's violation, probably to protect her and Levister's privacy. He made it clear, however, that he did not want his readers to see Rufus as solely victimized by racism, but as fully human, thus powerful enough to become a perpetrator tormented by what he had done.

In *If Beale Street Could Talk,* where a Puerto Rican woman is raped by an unidentified Black man, we never find out if the rapist was caught and punished. But we witness the victim, the light-skinned Victoria Sanchez, destroyed by her violation much as Leona was in *Another Country*. In *Just above My Head*, the Black teenager Julia's violent rapist father is punished by the community; the white men who abduct a Black choirboy, Peanut, during a tour of the South, though, go unpunished. In these various accounts, Baldwin demonstrates the way sex, sexuality, and race are inextricably connected in the American heterosexist politics and culture of violence. Unchecked machismo breeds brutality against those who are seen as the other—weaker, defenseless, nonconforming, easy targets. It destroys the morality and humanity of its perpetrators, for without the vulnerability, softness, even femininity that Baldwin saw as essential to all human beings, they are reduced to monsters.

The best example of this unchecked machismo drives the titular story, "Going to Meet the Man" (1965) in his only short story collection. In it, a public lynching, castration, and rape become a formative event for the self-hating, sexually ambivalent, racist white narrator, who as a child is forced to witness this horror by his parents. As an adult Jesse becomes a policeman and a victimizer of Black bodies of both sexes. The story frames racial and sexual abuse as the necessary condition for both Jesse's whiteness and his heterosexuality, the building blocks of male power and the state. Baldwin presents this gripping story as a series of memories taking place in Jesse's head while he lies in his bed unable to have intercourse with his white, very religious wife. He cannot perform until, horrifically, he summons up the memories of a Black man's castration that he witnessed at a "picnic" as a boy. Jesse's story confirms that, like racists, monsters are made, not born.

Baldwin carried his own experiences of violence at other men's hands, and he had increasingly come to recognize the sexual abuse of women and children, misogyny, homophobia, and discrimination against nonnormative people as a civil rights issue. This inclusive and organic view of social justice grew alongside his activism as he felt more and more disconnected from his home country's traditional gender roles.

In his last volume of nonfiction, *The Evidence of Things Not Seen,* for example, he links the general "sorriness" of the Black American culture and its southern roots to how men and women operate in Black families. Taking on racial and gender stereotypes, he expounds that Black women are both "supple" and "subtle" and thus able to read and dismiss racist definitions of themselves, while Black men cannot do that, ruled as they are by fear of emasculation by women, the "White Republic," and each other, all of which lead to violence. In such a family landscape, men "dream" and fight, while women ensure their families' survival, he explains, as if channeling the racial and gender stereotypes of the Moynihan Report. Similar to his argument in the epilogue of *No Name in the Street,* he nevertheless insists that it is men who are weaker and must learn from women, who already have "the weapons" to be themselves. True warriors ruled kitchens, raised babies, and organized communities—that was all the fighting that was needed.

As his philosophy of Black queer humanism developed in 1970s–80s, Baldwin came close to embracing what many feminists were articulating then, and what students in my courses today see immediately upon first reading *Giovanni's Room* or *Another Country*—that misogyny underlies all forms of discrimination. Two copies of Andrea Dworkin's controversial feminist study *Intercourse* (1987) survived in his Saint-Paul-de-Vence library. A note, "Sent at the request of the Author," confirms that Dworkin considered the two of them to be in agreement about sexual violence. Her epigraph quotes Baldwin's words from *No Name in the Street*: "True rebels, after all, are as rare as true lovers, and in both cases, to mistake a fever for a passion can destroy one's life." Today's America, even the twenty-first-century West, is still not ready to embrace this rebel's message, though his work may help us do so.

TRACK 3

———

Traveling through the
Country of the Self

FIRST PUBLISHED in the *New Yorker* in 1962 and later included in *The Fire Next Time*, Baldwin's much-quoted essay "Down at the Cross: Letter from a Region in My Mind" skyrocketed him to international fame as the most important Black American spokesman on the so-called Negro question. Yet his position soon made him miserable, even as it made him famous and his books best sellers. Credited with "foretelling" the racial violence that came to Birmingham in April–May 1963 and continued in cities across the country during the summer of 1964 and for the rest of the decade, Baldwin was in such demand that an editor once had to hide him in his home so he could work undisturbed. Baldwin was not only a commentator, though. From the 1960s on, he was very much a part of the Civil Rights and, to a lesser degree, Black Power Movements, traveling throughout the South, meeting Martin Luther King, Jr., befriending activists Medgar Evers, Fannie Lou Hamer, Jerome Smith, and James Meredith, and talking with Malcolm X. His skeptical report of a meeting with the Honorable Elijah Muhammad of the Nation of Islam appeared in *The Fire Next Time;* by 1964, FBI informants were reporting that while in Berlin he had denounced the Nation of Islam as an extremist organization in the journal *The New Crusader,* stating, "I have nothing in common with them. . . . No race is superior to another."

A charismatic speaker, Baldwin was an attraction for donors at fundraisers held in theaters, schools, churches, and penthouses alike for such organizations as CORE and SNCC. At the height of his participation in the Civil Rights Movement in 1963, as Bill Mullen notes in his biography *James Baldwin: Living in Fire* (2019), he spoke in nine West Coast cities over ten days, part of a grueling travel circuit. He raised about five hundred dollars per speech, a large sum then, and paid all of it to CORE, earning the organization about twenty thousand dollars. All this activity took a toll on Baldwin's health and finances, leaving him little energy for writing and thus for earning the money he increasingly needed to continue his travels and fulfill family and social obligations.

Nonetheless, while in Turkey and in transit between many destinations during the 1960s and beyond, Baldwin produced a significant amount of what can be classified as antiviolence literature drawing on his talents as essayist, fiction writer, poet, and investigative journalist. He probed what could be seen as different war zones in terms of racial, social, political, cultural, and personal conflicts—in, for example, essays like "White Man's Guilt" (1965), "Negroes Are Anti-Semitic Because They Are Anti-White" (1967),"White Racism or World Community" (1968), "An Open Letter to Mr. Carter" (1977), "Notes on the House of Bondage" (1980), and "Dark Days" (1980); the short story "Going to Meet the Man" (1965); the poetry collection, *Jimmy's Blues* (1983); and the essay volumes *No Name in the Street, The Devil Finds Work,* and *The Evidence of Things Not Seen.* These diverse works combined literary aesthetics with Baldwin's public activism by bringing together oral histories and political and cultural commentary with his familiar brand of auto-theoretical storytelling.

Baldwin's participation in the Civil Rights Movement infused many of his letters to Mary Painter, frequently underlying their personal themes, and attesting to the continued importance of women confidantes to his thinking. In one letter, dated October 18, 1957, written on the stationery of the A. G. Gaston Motel in Birmingham, Alabama, he relays to Painter his psychosomatic response to his first trip in the American South: "Having reactions symptomatic of hysteria barely controlled; always on the edge of tears; can't sleep; headaches—have a touch of the flu or something. . . . Have spent my evening reading the Southern press, and White Citizen's and KKK hate literature." He was afraid to spend any more time there, frustrated, and desperate over the condition of their "poor country," about which nobody seemed to care. "I've never in my life been on a sadder journey or through a sadder country—not even Germany or Spain compare to it." He ends the letter with his assignment for the next day, a visit to "the boy who was castrated on these streets a few days ago," which he planned to make accompanied by the young man's friend, a dishwasher at Baldwin's hotel. In the essay "A Fly in Buttermilk," included in *Nobody Knows My Name,* he describes noticing the red in the Georgia dirt, as if "this earth had acquired its color from the blood that dripped down from these trees." He recalls his parents' tales about rape, lynching, and men in white sheets riding through the night and burning crosses in the name of God and country.

Baldwin's travels in the South revealed that as a native New Yorker and an expatriate he was a foreigner in what he called the Black Americans' "Old Country." In another letter to Painter, written two weeks earlier, for example, he mentions the "emotional climate of the place," reiterating his fear for his own safety. He gushes about meeting Martin Luther King, Jr., "a great man," who looks "rather like some of the snot-nosed kids I've watched grow up." The Reverend Ralph Abernathy, he says, "a ferociously patient, gentle, rock-like man," is as impressive as other Black southerners, whose patience, love, and resilience humble him. Worried about sounding chauvinistic, he observes that southern Blacks "are much brighter and certainly much stronger than the whites. Whites are beginning to suspect this, too, and it does nothing to sweeten their disposition." Full of detail and careful analysis, these letters are a superb resource for studying American history from a writer-activist's point of view.

One experience from his first visit to the South in 1957 frightened Baldwin so badly that he was unable to write about it until he was composing *No Name in the Street* years later in Turkey. He describes "my unbelieving shock when I realized that I was being groped by one of the most powerful men in one of the states I visited. He had got himself sweating drunk in order to arrive at this despairing titillation. With his wet eyes staring up at my face, and his wet hands groping for my cock, we were both, abruptly, in history's ass-pocket." His Black queer body was on the line yet again, his agency reduced to that of a child: "This man, with a phone call, could prevent or provoke a lynching. . . . Therefore, one had to be friendly: but the price of this was your cock."

Hypersensitive and anxious, Baldwin struggled with stress-related health issues his whole life. Profoundly shaken by the murders of Medgar Evers in 1963, Malcolm X in 1965, and Martin Luther King in 1968, he imagined himself to be the next target. He wrestled with increasing bouts of depression and fatigue, especially during travel, breakups with lovers, and periods of writer's block. He noticed that his ailments intensified during trips through the segregated South, whose racial codes he could not read. His inability to navigate racial divisions there, for example—the "territory absolutely hostile and exceedingly strange"—compounded his fear for his safety, feelings he explored in *Nobody Knows My Name* and *No Name in the Street.* In the latter, with exquisite, bitter humor, he describes the "Marx Brothers parody of horror," as he faces a barely human creature, a white woman "with a face like a rusty hatchet, and eyes like two rusty nails—nails left over from the Crucifixion," who "barks" at him to use the "colored entrance" to a burger joint.

Other sources of angst were his family's expectations back in Harlem concerning his career, safety, and lifestyle, as well as memories of his abuse, illegitimacy, and anguish over his sexuality. In an undated letter to Painter, he confessed that he feared his family was ashamed of him: "I see how helpless I am, how driven, & how lonely. . . . I cling to my family precisely because I am the bastard half-brother: and I guess I am trying to prove that, in spite of everything, my birth & my proclivities I can be loved—by them." His family may never have loved him, he suggests; he has been "waiting for that moment which would make me see what they really felt about me—have been waiting, in sum, in dread of the return of that moment from which this whole, bloody, tangled thing began: when my father's eyes, & the world's eyes, told me that I was despised." He realizes that "if one does not get over this in oneself, there is simply no hope of ever getting over it. I cannot reconcile myself to so black a thought, so ignoble a defeat. But neither do I see any way out—unless the way out is, in fact, the way in; to descend into the heart of my confusion, & make peace with it before I die." He admits that he can lose hope in "a split-second. Then terror takes over, & one's life can end—I refer to the life, the real life, which animates this clay tenement."

His darkness and propensity for self-destruction caused him to attempt suicide several times. The first time was in Paris in 1949, after he had been incarcerated in the Fresnes prison over Christmas. The so-called stolen-sheet (*drap de lit*) incident took place during the early, lean, desperate days he described in the essay "Equal in Paris" (1955). An American friend had brought a pilfered bedsheet—a joke trophy—from a hotel to Baldwin's room, and the French police arrested them both for theft. Baldwin described his confrontation with the Parisian legal system, the only time he was ever imprisoned. He got out with the help of an American lawyer friend; the authorities laughed his case out of the courtroom, but he had discovered that racism could be found across the Atlantic as well as at home.

As David Leeming relates it, this suicide attempt took place after Baldwin had returned to his cold hotel room. With a bedsheet tied around his neck and slung over a water pipe, he jumped from a chair or bed. The pipe broke, leaving him "rebaptized by the flood of water . . . [and] overcome by a kind of laughter that was more powerful than the laughter in the court." Another attempt took place in 1956, in New York, during a bout of writer's block while he was working on *Another Country* and experiencing an unraveling love affair. Several other attempts followed during periods of depression and love troubles, all of which he kept invisible to the media, and possibly to his family.

When he first arrived in France in 1948, Baldwin brought his blues with him. Revived by the newness of the place and people rebuilding themselves after France's wartime occupation, he wrote in "The New Lost Generation" (1961), "What Europe still gives an American . . . is the sanction, if one can accept it, to become oneself. No artist can survive without this acceptance." Embracing his "own vision of the world," against that world's judgment, he gathered experience rooted in his identity and perception as a Black queer man, for life was not about "*what* happens but to *who*." In 1970, he told the Turkish photographer and filmmaker

Sedat Pakay that living abroad taught him that one must leave home to see it better, "from a distance, from another country."

Yet what had first pushed him toward writing as a child and then compelled him to leave home made Baldwin into a stranger to those he left behind. Despite encountering exciting friends and lovers in faraway places, he never shook off his blues—"rare indeed is an American artist who achieved" becoming himself "without first becoming a wanderer, and then, upon his return to his own country, the loneliest and most blackly distrusted of men." His critics in the United States charged that he had changed under foreign influence; Richard Goldstein commented on Baldwin's "distracted look Europeans cultivate" when they met in Greenwich Village for an interview in 1984. In his conversation with the Black feminist poet Nikki Giovanni, later published as *James Baldwin/Nikki Giovanni: A Dialogue* (1973), he explained that it was his responsibility to tell the truth no matter how his audience felt about it: "Because the responsibility of a writer is to excavate the experience of the people who produced him, the act of writing is the intention of it; the root of it is liberation. Look, this is why no tyrant in history was able to read but every single one of them burned the books."

By the mid-1960s, he had become internationally famous, cameras and journalists following him at airports, his expensive, chic wardrobe his pride and joy. Dining in "Manhattan's notoriously expensive restaurants . . . [on] Russian caviar and vintage champagne," he attracted an "army of yea-sayers, fear-chasers and night-watchers he once dubbed his 'menagerie,'" gushed Fern Marja Eckman in a celebrity biography, *The Furious Passage of James Baldwin* (1966); the series of features on Baldwin that preceded her book drew the FBI's attention. He delivered an address, "The Negro Writer's Vision of America," on April 23, 1965, at a symposium held at the New School for Social Research in New York, wearing a hand-tailored suit from Fifth Avenue. As Eckman reported, he fancifully presented himself as uninspired by "any American writer," having instead modeled himself on "jazz musicians, dancers, a couple of whores and a few junkies." The event honored his late dear friend, the playwright Lorraine Hansberry, whom he called "sweet Lorraine" and who had died that January. The scintillating public Baldwin was on full display.

When asked about his fame, he advised his audience not to "take yourself too *seriously*," for "you're not a great man because other people *say* you're a great man." Though he was "ostentatiously inept at handling money," he was "a soft touch for the most inept of hard luck stories," Eckman marveled, mentioning acquaintances who "sponged on him shamelessly . . . one . . . absconding with most of his patron's wardrobe." In another Eckman interview, he admitted, "I didn't want any of this shit. I didn't *want* a Cadillac . . . I've had the Cadillac and I *know*. Those grapes *are* sour." Having earned the enjoyment of the limelight and finer things, he dreamt of a peaceful home to nurture him and his writing.

Baldwin found another writing haven in Turkey, where he made his first extended stay in 1961, returning to live there on and off throughout the decade. Istanbul became his new home, providing respite from the activism and busy social schedule that consumed him upon every return to the United States. Enjoying the remote location and break from public life, picking up some Turkish but never immersing himself in the language as he did with French, he wrote some of his most important works during 1961–70, when he was traveling widely, enumerating the various writing locations on each book's last page: *Another Country, The Fire Next Time, Blues for Mister Charlie, Tell Me How Long the Train's Been Gone,* and *No Name in the Street.*

Though there are dark-skinned people in Turkey, and Turks

are not considered white by Europeans, Baldwin stood out, and was often called "Arap," Arab, a Turkish term for a Black person. As he told the anthropologist Margaret Mead in 1970, "I was one of the very few black things in Istanbul, except for various soldiers and sailors, and certainly the most famous black American there." Sometimes people assumed he was a Black Panther when they realized he was American; at other times they incongruously mistook him for the internationally famous Brazilian soccer star Pelé. He continued to travel, appear on television, and give speeches and interviews. Though he thrived on changes of scenery and meeting new people, he constantly longed for a stable relationship with a partner and a steadier work routine. This paradoxical mix of desires would drive him to briefly entertain the idea of settling down in spectacular Istanbul; he toyed with that fantasy in *Just above My Head*, where the protagonist, Arthur, briefly considers buying a place there.

Although he was criticized in the United States for this choice of location—now the bad press came with homophobic undertones implying that he had gone for sex tourism in the "Turkish baths"—Istanbul, located on the breathtaking Bosporus Strait between Europe and Asia, "saved my life," as Baldwin's Turkish friends Sedat Pakay and Engin Cezzar told me. Asked by the *New York Post* and Turkish journal *Cep Dergisi* in 1968 why he had moved there, he explained that his exile from the United States was the source of his productivity. His work abroad did not mean he could abandon his U.S. responsibilities, though he believed that the civil rights struggle had been "buried with Martin Luther King." He continued to hold his country to unwaveringly high standards. As his friend Lorraine Hansberry once commented, he held equally high expectations for his artist friends: "Jimmy," she said, "makes you feel you've still got a little bit of Uncle Tom left in you."

Baldwin's critical views on America's role in the Cold War

were sharpened while he lived in Turkey, a country that was not well known as a haven for Black artists and expatriates, though many resided there. As a NATO member since 1952 and an important strategic location for the U.S. military in the region, Turkey was very much on the government's radar. Outspoken Baldwin quickly became a target for U.S. government surveillance, and he suspected that some in his circle might be informants; he "became a great threat to the American colony there," as he explained to Mead in 1970. He was right: his copious FBI file contains notes on his allegedly dangerous activities in Istanbul and other places he traveled—Italy, France, Germany, England—underscoring the Bureau's obsessive monitoring of targets because of both their politics and their sexuality. The FBI's mid-twentieth-century fixation on homosexuals—deemed national security risks and communist supporters—is now known as the "lavender scare." (The surveillance paranoia trickled into Richard Wright's 1949 poem "The FB Eye Blues"; homophobic imagery permeates its last verses.) As the historian William Maxwell explains, the FBI followed Baldwin's every move, as it did those of many other Black writers, monitoring flights, wiretapping calls, reporting on public appearances, book reviews, and private meetings, and thus becoming an unwitting "pioneering archivist of black internationalism."

The Bureau's reporting on Baldwin makes fascinating reading, its twists and contradictions reflecting the FBI's changing priorities during the 1960s. On its declassified website, in a memo dated June 7, 1963, addressed to "Mr. DLoach" by "M.A. Jones," for example, Baldwin is described as "an author who has been critical of the Bureau and has been connected with communist front and integration activities." Another memo, from January 15, 1964, enumerates his participation in "Communist Party front organizations" (e.g., the Fair Play for Cuba Committee, Monroe Defense Committee, and Emergency Civil Liberties Committee). A hand-printed note from "LOYAL CITIZEN" links Baldwin to "Negroid Jews resembling *Castro*" who organized "Harlem riots" alongside "Trotzkyites." A November 25, 1966, report notes his residency in Turkey and that he was "not known to be involved in any suspect activity." Another quotes a female informant's report from summer 1966, when Baldwin "rented an apartment in the Bebek Section of Istanbul . . . [and] was evicted by the landlord for having homosexual parties."

An internal FBI translation of an interview published in Istanbul's *Yeni Gazette* on December 6, 1966, "Looking at New York from Istanbul," includes Baldwin's statement that he could never abandon America and its "white-black conflict"; settling in Turkey would mean "running away which I cannot do." The subtitle of this translated piece locates Baldwin in the "Vefik Pasha Library," a sumptuous villa on the Bosphorus, where "The Negro Writer Pursues His People's Cause." Yet another FBI file, from December 23, 1969, includes a translation of a Turkish daily *Milliyet*, in which Baldwin, a grateful guest, confesses: "I cannot imagine a country in the world as beautiful as Turkey, a people as nice as the Turks, and another land where Negroes can live comfortably." The same piece highlights what Maxwell terms Baldwin's "feast-or-famine work habits," when he "writes continuously for 24 hours without food or drink . . . does not even notice if you shout at him or hit him on the shoulder. Afterwards, he lies down and sleeps . . . for 48 hours. If you are able to awaken him, how fortunate you are."

The FBI's Baldwin was very different from the private man captured in Turkey by Sedat Pakay's art film *James Baldwin: From Another Place*, shot in Istanbul in 1970. During preproduction, in an unpublished recorded interview, Baldwin noted the disconnect: "Perhaps only someone who is outside of the States realizes that it's impossible to get out. The American power follows one everywhere." Pakay's black-and-white cinema-verité film follows

Baldwin through Istanbul; the soundtrack is excerpted from their interview. Pakay wanted to capture the real man, who walks around slightly dazed, who worries "about getting my work done, getting on paper, which is the best way for me, a certain record, which hopefully would be of some value to somebody, some day." Baldwin wanders through a book bazaar, bumps into a woman, notices a Turkish translation of his *Another Country* and picks up a copy of the Pulitzer Prize–winning *The FBI Story: A Report to the People* (1956), with a foreword by J. Edgar Hoover. Back inside his apartment, we see an issue of *Life* magazine (February 6, 1970) spread open on a cot, with the photos of Black Panthers who had been murdered by police. In Pakay's film, we find ourselves inside Baldwin's restless mind, a place where U.S. power and cultural pressures are never far away. Invading Baldwin's privacy and workspace, the informer's eye (Wright's FBEye?) frames the writer, but Baldwin keeps on keeping on, as he was fond of saying.

Trained by the famous photographer Walker Evans at Yale, Pakay took thousands of superb photographs of Baldwin in Turkey and the United States. While still in high school he met Baldwin in Istanbul and began photographing him, soon becoming a protégé of sorts. As he told me on repeated occasions, Pakay found Baldwin to be a beautiful, fascinating subject. The writer helped him obtain a student visa and wrote an affidavit of support so Pakay could study in the United States. In a letter to Baldwin dated September 28, 1966, Pakay writes about his first days in "your glorious country." Housed and taken care of by Baldwin's family in Harlem when he first arrived, he soon began earning commissions for his work. Pakay's gorgeous black-and-white 1964 portrait of Baldwin in Istanbul catches his pensive face over a samovar and a glass of tea—a fleeting private moment in public—captures his personality like no other.

In that early letter to his muse and mentor, Pakay made an

interesting observation concerning American male behavior in public spaces. He writes, "The strangest thing I've observed here is lack of love among people. They are colder to each other and boys are afraid to touch each other. They looked on us absolutely astonished when a friend of mine embraced me—Turkish style." Baldwin had found this difference just as astounding during his own first days in Istanbul, for the public displays of affection common among men there were as stunning to him as the hostile, homophobic stares Pakay experienced in New York. Both men got over their initial culture shock: Baldwin cemented his belief in the possibility of tenderness between men while in Turkey, while Pakay became a consummate New Yorker, married an American woman, and settled into a brilliant international career.

In 1969, Pakay related an exciting development in another letter: "In the midst of cooler air, New York Film Festival and metaphysical panic, I am signing a distribution contract with Radim Films for the Walker Evans film." Informing Baldwin about the details of postproduction work and his plans to travel to Istanbul, he boasts of receiving his first professional cash advance. Upon his return to Istanbul in May 1970, Pakay showed up with his cameraman, Cengiz Tacer, at Baldwin's apartment near Taksim Square to start shooting a film about him. As he explained in our 2002 interview, he deliberately mixed cinema-verité and documentary genres to frame Baldwin's life in Turkey. Finding the writer, who forgot their appointment, still asleep in bed, Pakay and Tacer began spontaneously taking photos and filming. Baldwin, it seems, did not mind being caught emerging from bed wearing only his underwear.

Baldwin enjoyed his stint as an actor, playing himself in Pakay's film. Fascinated with the stage and screen since childhood, he tried his hand at writing for both throughout the 1960s and beyond. In 1964, he returned to New York to supervise the Broadway staging of his second play, *Blues for Mister Charlie*, in which he remixed themes of violent masculinity, racism, and misogyny. Written partially in Turkey, *Blues* was his response to Elia Kazan's suggestion that Baldwin use drama to commemorate the murder of Emmett Till, a Black teenager from Chicago, in Money, Mississippi, in 1955. The play centers on the killing of a young Black activist, Richard, by a small-town white racist, Lyle, in a symbolic place, "Plaguetown, U.S.A." It follows the citizens of Whitetown and Blacktown—Baldwin racially segregated the stage and all the actors—as they respond as individuals and racialized communities to the murder and ensuing trial, which ends with Lyle's acquittal by an all-white, all-male jury.

Dedicated to "the memory of MEDGAR EVERS and his widow and his children, and to the memory of the dead children of Birmingham," *Blues for Mister Charlie* takes place amid a national plague that is "race ... [that also] is our concept of Christianity ... [that] has the power to destroy every human relationship." The play extended Baldwin's thinking about racialized manhood while its characters expressed the blues that continued to grip Baldwin's own soul, no matter how far he traveled from home. The play's secondary characters, Mother Henry, Richard's grandmother, and his pregnant tomboy girlfriend, Juanita (a precursor to the slightly younger Tish of *If Beale Street Could Talk*), could be read as Baldwin's spokeswomen; they embody the blues aesthetic Baldwin learned from Bessie Smith, giving voice to the loving, humanistic, womanist message that none of the men of *Blues* can comprehend.

Performed by the Actors Studio, the play opened on April 23, 1964, at the Anta Theater, with Mary Painter at Baldwin's side to share this important achievement. Its production was contentious and full of emotional difficulties for Baldwin, who felt that Lee Strasberg and Cheryl Crawford, two of the Studio's directors, did not understand his motives and were afraid of shocking white theatergoers with the truth about racism in the United States. Baldwin insisted on a low admission price to attract Harlem audiences, and the theater management decided to close the play after a month because it was so unprofitable. *Blues* was saved by a donation from two Rockefeller sisters, Ann Pierson and Mary Strawbridge, as well as a petition of support signed by famous actors and artists—Marlon Brando, Sidney Poitier, Lena Horne, Richard Avedon, Harry Belafonte, Sammy Davis, Jr., and June Shagaloff— that succeeded in extending the run until late August. When a truncated production was later taken to London, Baldwin publicly protested about the Actors Studio's handling of his material.

His disagreement with the studio appears in sections of his fourth novel, *Tell Me How Long the Train's Been Gone*, written largely in Istanbul and completed in San Francisco, whose protagonist is a middle-aged Black actor. Typically, Baldwin's fiction works mirrored his busy itinerary, his novels sometimes listing several locations of writing. The last page of *Tell Me How Long the Train's Been Gone* has this notation, for example: "New York, Istanbul, San Francisco, 1965–1967"; *Another Country*, which he worked on in many locations, lists only: "Istanbul, Dec. 10, 1961"—the date David Leeming reports that he first met Baldwin. In *Tell Me How Long the Train's Been Gone*, San Francisco plays an important role for Leo Proudhammer and his entourage, including his younger Black Power activist lover, Christopher. Descriptions of the city echo in a documentary that Baldwin filmed there, *Take This Hammer* (1963).

In late 1969, Baldwin debuted as a theater director in Turkey. A chance to counter his U.S. experience with *Blues for Mister Charlie*, the play was the Canadian playwright John Herbert's *Fortune and Men's Eyes*, which had already become famous in the United States and Britain after its 1967 debut. Performed at the Gülriz Sururi–Engin Cezzar Theater in Istanbul in 1969–70, with a traveling run throughout the country, it was a groundbreaking production that revolutionized the Turkish stage. Retitled *Düşenin Dostu* (Friend of the Fallen) in Turkish, *Fortune and Men's Eyes* examines sexual power struggles and violence among juvenile male inmates in a Canadian prison. Translated by Oktay Balamir and Ali Poyrazoğlu, it engaged local issues of homelessness and the sexual exploitation of children, gaining notoriety overnight. Briefly shut down by the authorities, the play increased its audience and revenue when it reopened, turning Baldwin and the actors into celebrities. Allegedly, Baldwin made no money on it, however, donating his labor.

The play was a great success but was never filmed, and its original musical score by the jazz virtuoso Don Cherry was presumed lost until it was recovered in Sweden; a journalist, Magnus Nyren, who was researching Cherry's life and collaborated with his family, contacted me about this find in 2019. Reports of the production of *Düşenin Dostu* written by contemporaries survive. Charles Adelsen, a journalist who lived in Istanbul, wrote about the performance in a beautifully illustrated piece for *Ebony* magazine, describing a "love affair" and "a kind of attraction for each other" between the writer and the erotically charged city of Istanbul. Adelsen did not go into detail about the play's challenges to gender and sexual taboos, but he mentioned that it was a "very, very graphic and very stirring portrayal" of controversial issues in Turkey. The play's translator, Oktay Balamir, Baldwin's one-time roommate and partner, put it more directly in our interview: "The play was a success because it was a revolutionary play for the Turkish audience. Although they were aware of homosexuality in Turkish prisons, and in prisons all over the world, this was the first time homosexuality was vividly being shown [in the theater]." Baldwin's play participated in Turkish culture and pushed him to further explore the metaphor of the prison house, which he would employ extensively in *No Name in the Street* and later works: *If Beale Street Could Talk,* the essay "Notes on the House of Bondage," and *The Evidence of Things Not Seen.* (Baldwin's interest in incarceration first appeared in Richard's unjust jailing in *Go Tell It on the Mountain;* he included references to jails and prison time in *The Fire Next Time, Tell Me How Long the Train's Been Gone,* and *Just above My Head,* as well as in many essays and speeches.)

Baldwin's most important friend in Turkey, and one of key reasons he decided to stay there for so long, was the actor and theater director Engin Cezzar. A handsome and gifted performer of North African ancestry, Cezzar had been trained at the Yale School of Drama. A protégé of Elia Kazan, he met Baldwin in New York in 1958. He played Giovanni in the Actors Studio adaptation of *Giovanni's Room* dramatized by Baldwin. They formed a blood brotherhood, as they both referred to it, that lasted until Baldwin's death. Cezzar also met Beauford Delaney, who visited Turkey and stayed with Baldwin for extended periods, their fun times often captured by Pakay's camera. Delaney painted portraits of Baldwin and Gülriz Sururi, Cezzar's wife, also a celebrated actor. Delaney's gorgeous nighttime landscape of the Bosphorus adorned Cezzar's apartment in Taksim Square, where Baldwin first lived in 1961. Their correspondence between 1958 and 1981 offers much information about Baldwin's life in Turkey and other places he traveled, though the letters are available only in Turkish translation.

A luxurious villa known as "Pasha's Library" in the affluent Rumeli Hisarı neighborhood was Baldwin's most opulent quarters in Istanbul. It was there that a talented young feminist journalist and theater critic, Zeynep Oral, interviewed him for an article she was writing for the local magazine, *Yeni Gazete.* She later became Baldwin's assistant, interpreter, and close friend on the set of *Fortune and Men's Eyes,* and after that the critic who wrote most movingly and astutely about Baldwin's time and works in Turkey. Baldwin also became close with Engin Cezzar's wife, Gülriz Sururi, a co-owner of the theater where the play was staged. A photo published in *Ebony* shows Sururi, Baldwin, and Cezzar walking hand in hand, chic, attractive, and joyful, on the Galata Bridge.

Baldwin's correspondence with Cezzar is filled with impressions of places he visited, advice on acting, and proclamations of love for his Turkish brother. Addressing him as "M'boy," pleading that they not "lose each other," Baldwin yearned for Cezzar's confirmation that he still loved him. Like many men who knew Baldwin, Cezzar never admitted to having been Baldwin's lover, though these letters imply otherwise. On January 20, 1960, Baldwin wrote him, "I'm a true fuck-up but if I love you, I love you, and that's *all.*" Undeniably, the two were close, and each benefited greatly from their collaborative connection. Cezzar championed Baldwin's writing of *Tell Me How Long the Train's Been Gone*, whose main character is an actor, and sent him an enthusiastic telegram on its publication in 1968: "Thanks baby for Black Christopher STOP the Train is great but not for people who have no love for children or actors love engin." In the novel Black Christopher is Leo Proudhammer's younger lover, a handsome, charismatic radical who also serves as Leo's valet and bodyguard. The implication in Cezzar's telegram is that Christopher's relationship with Proudhammer has affinities with that of Baldwin and Cezzar. In a letter of September 27, 1974, Baldwin reassures Cezzar, "I'm still wearing the ring, baby: blood brothers don't grow on trees," yet again implying that their connection went beyond friendship.

Baldwin's success in Turkey and his engagement with Herbert's play on homosexuality in prisons brought welcome validation at a time when he felt especially wounded by his rejection by many Black Power activists in the United States. Perhaps the best example of the misogynist and homophobic strain in the Black left is the Black Panther Party leader Eldridge Cleaver's book *Soul on*

Ice, which brands Baldwin's sexuality a "racial death wish." A Black man whose male lovers included whites, Baldwin, in Cleaver's eyes, was equivalent to a raped Black woman having a white man's baby. A self-acknowledged rapist and bombastic misogynist driven by sexual ambivalence, Cleaver called sexual violation of white women a "revolutionary act," boasting of practicing it on "Sisters" in preparation for a race "revenge." He also admitted that he "lusted" after Baldwin's books, yet had to reduce Baldwin, a despised "fag," to his "little jive ass" to manage his desire in the aftermath of *Another Country,* which had offended Cleaver the most.

Cleaver's review of Baldwin's work, an essay titled "Notes on a Native Son" that was excerpted from *Soul on Ice,* appeared in the popular New Left literary magazine *Ramparts* in June 1966. Next to the title, a caricature of Baldwin depicts a dandy-like monkey standing knock-kneed, coyly raising a foot, and looking into an ornate handheld mirror, while applying (presumably white) paint to his face. In the book, which has remained popular to this day, Cleaver writes, "Homosexuality is a sickness just as baby rape," and accuses Baldwin of waging "a despicable underground guerrilla war against black masculinity." To Cleaver, Baldwin feared the "stud" in himself, was a self-hating sell-out, sick from the "intake of the white man's sperm," "bending over and touching . . . [his] toes for the white man."

Inexplicably, Baldwin chose not to take public revenge on Cleaver, instead calling him "rare" and "valuable" in *No Name in the Street.* In a May 1973 *Playboy* interview, however, Cleaver's fellow Black Panther Huey Newton recalled how Baldwin had guessed at the insecurity, fear, and self-delusion (if not self-loathing) behind Cleaver's bombastic public persona during a party in San Francisco, sometime in 1966–67. Upon meeting Cleaver, Baldwin, who had probably read Cleaver's *Ramparts* piece about himself, gave Cleaver a deep French kiss. "Baldwin is a very small man in stature . . . Eldridge is about six-four . . . 250 pounds," Newton reported. "They kissed each other on the mouth for a long time. When we left, Eldridge kept saying, 'Don't tell anyone.' . . . And I kept my word—until now." Cleaver, who experienced or witnessed homosexual acts between inmates while in prison, was terrified that this encounter might become public. Offended by Cleaver's treatment of Baldwin, Newton, who respected the older writer and supported sexual minority rights, labeled Cleaver a fantasist whose macho egotism undermined the Black Power movement. In this context, perhaps, Baldwin's reticence was a mark of maturity, a wise choice to pick his battles as well as worthy opponents.

Since 1948, Baldwin's travels and time away from the United States had given him acute and searing insights into the workings of American culture and enabled him to use his distance as a tool for self-interrogation as a "transatlantic commuter," especially in his later years. In his material from the later 1960s on, he incorporated themes of identity and selfhood, remixing childhood memories, and increasingly tracking vicissitudes of Black masculinity in the arts and entertainment industries. These analyses fueled several fictional characters, such as the Black bisexual actor-activist Leo Proudhammer in *Tell Me How Long the Train's Been Gone,* the young sculptor Fonny in *If Beale Street Could Talk,* and the international celebrity singer Arthur Montana in *Just above My Head*—all traceable to events and people in his life.

During the period he stayed intermittently in Turkey, Baldwin took on two projects that allowed him to develop his blues aesthetic further while delving deeper into his conflicting selves: an artistic collaboration with the photographer Richard Avedon on a photo essay, *Nothing Personal* (1964), and an assignment to write a screenplay on Malcolm X for Columbia Pictures, *One Day, When I Was Lost* (1972). In the former, he describes an inner turmoil he calls

"the terror within"—fear of self-recognition and self-awareness—
that all humans share when faced with racial, gender, sexual, and
other types of social and cultural prescriptions. He examined the
origins and workings of that terror in both projects. Both also
illustrate his fascination with visual cultures and technologies
under the lasting influence of Beauford Delaney and Robert Warshow. As Baldwin's *Commentary* mentor, Warshow saw movies,
television, and comic books as powerful tools shaping human
consciousness and imagination and, thus, how a writer wrote.
Delaney's art taught Baldwin how to look beyond surfaces and
excavate deeper meanings within opaque textures, disparate shapes,
and contexts.

Long intrigued by pairings of images with prose, Baldwin
brought what he learned from both men to his collaboration on
Nothing Personal with his high school friend from the *Magpie* magazine years, Richard Avedon. They worked on the book while in
Puerto Rico, beginning on June 23, 1963; Leeming reports that their
general theme was to be "despair, dishonesty . . . things that keep
people from knowing each other." The original book was designed
by Marvin Israel and published in a limited large-format album
edition. It provides an original, achronological context for understanding Baldwin's Hollywood experience, which came soon afterward. *Nothing Personal* combines lyrical vignettes by Baldwin
with sections of gorgeous black-and-white Avedon photographs
that feature people and scenes from across the country: couples
at the Marriage Bureau in New York's City Hall, an unposed group
portrait of the Daughters of the American Revolution, "Brother
Malcolm X, Black Nationalist Leader," artists and intellectuals
such as Dorothy Parker, unnamed patients in "a mental institution," families on a beach, and "Members of the Student Nonviolent Coordinating Committee." Baldwin's prose in this rarely
discussed text is intimate and lushly pictorial. He comments on

Americans' "striking addiction to irreality" and—what he sees as "unprecedented in the world"—"our desperate adulation of simplicity and youth." The book can also be read as a single essay divided into four parts, with Avedon's photos in between; its power lies in allowing readers to create their own photo-textual interpretation.

In *Nothing Personal*, Baldwin also considers the general impact of television as a popular medium, offering uncanny foresights on the future of what, in our time, has become the information age onslaught on imagination and creativity. The African American Studies scholar Imani Perry writes about his "breathtaking and prophetic witness" in the Foreword to the 2021 edition of *Nothing Personal*: "How . . . could Baldwin have known what . . . social media, and the marketization of everything . . . would do to us? How did he know how it would shape us?" The dialogue between words and images that *Nothing Personal* offers today's readers remains astonishingly relevant and revelatory. A paragraph from Baldwin's text seems to foreshadow his Hollywood experience to come, while incorporating his views on the personal roots of the U.S. racial divide:

It has always been much easier (because it has always seemed much safer) to give a name to the evil without than to locate the terror within. And yet, the terror within is far truer and far more powerful than any of our labels: the labels change, the terror is constant. And this terror has something to do with that irreducible gap between the self one invents—the self one takes oneself as being . . . a provisional self—and the undiscoverable self which always has the power to blow the provisional self to bits. It is perfectly possible . . . to go to bed one night, or wake up one morning, or simply walk through a door one has known all one's life, and discover, between inhaling and exhaling, that the self one has sewn together with such effort is all dirty rags, is unusable, is gone: and out of what raw material will one build a self again?

In December 1966, Baldwin wrote to Leeming about a related issue, noting that "the key to everything one does is always found in one's relation to one's private life." Directly linking erotic desire and sexuality to self-building, he claims, "One is always the same person, and the sense of reality that governs one in the bed-room also dictates one's behavior in the office." In a 1986 interview with Leeming for *The Henry James Review,* linking the personal and the political, he pointed out the intimate, even erotic nature of his own work: "Writing is a private endeavor—a little bit like making love."

Formed by "the terror within" he described in *Nothing Personal,* identity, Baldwin believed, was what most people performed in public ("provisional self"), as he learned with Bessie Smith's blues playing in the background and while wrestling to create his first published works. As he developed his philosophical understanding of humanity in the 1970s and 1980s, he insisted that maturity depended on how vividly the question "who am I?" lives in each person's mind, "a question which can paralyze the mind, of course; but if the question does not live in the mind, then one is simply condemned to eternal youth, which is a synonym for corruption." In Baldwin's understanding, "eternal youth" in America equaled ignorance, which equaled innocence, making one vulnerable to becoming a tool in the hands of power.

In the busy year of 1968, Baldwin was hired by Columbia Pictures to write a screenplay based on Alex Haley's *Autobiography of Malcolm X.* Baldwin and Haley had become friends, and it was a great opportunity for him to make connections in Hollywood. Baldwin responded to Malcolm X as a brother from an impoverished, violent city ghetto background like his own. After a stint at the glamorous Beverly Hills Hotel, Baldwin worked in a posh Palm Springs house with a swimming pool. As he labored, friends and lovers came to stay with him, including Sedat Pakay, who took many photographs commemorating both the writer's progress and moments of conviviality. While writing, Baldwin listened to Aretha Franklin's records. Like Malcolm, she was from Detroit and, as with Bessie Smith's influence on his first novel, Franklin's musical style and tough sensibility helped Baldwin shape the life story of Malcolm X.

But the studio objected to Baldwin's approach and resulting pages, complaining that his writing was too literary, and saddled him with a co-writer, Arnold Perl. Baldwin took the move personally, falling into a depression. Columbia wanted to tone down Baldwin's depictions of Malcolm's radical views on race, especially after his return from Mecca and break with the Nation of Islam. In addition, the country was in the throes of the violence that erupted following the assassination of Martin Luther King that April. Bruised by the criticism of his aesthetic, Baldwin bridled at being pressured to water down the message that he saw as central to Malcolm's legacy; he also resented being told how to write his "brother's" story. An altered version of the film, directed by Perl and co-produced by him and Marvin Worth, on which Malcolm's widow, Betty Shabazz, consulted, was released by Warner Bros. in 1972, *Malcolm X: His Own Story How It Really Happened*; it received an Academy Award nomination for Best Documentary Feature in 1973.

Malcolm's racial reconciliation message, as idealistically American as it is Pan African, echoes Baldwin's own in the final pages of his screenplay, *One Day, When I Was Lost*, which in his signature style remixes scenes of Malcolm writing a letter to Betty Shabazz from Mecca, of her reading it, and of speaking tours he made to Nigeria and Ghana. Malcolm's discovery of his kinship with all humanity is concurrent with the discovery of race as a fiction, in Baldwin's words: "We were truly the same—brothers!—because their belief in one God had removed the 'white' from their minds, the 'white' from their behavior.... In the past . . . I have made sweeping indictments of all white people. I never will be guilty of that again." In Baldwin's quarrel with the studio, he claimed, the portion on Mecca killed the project. As Baldwin told an interviewer from *Cinema* magazine, he intended to tell the story, "my way or not at all." To him, Malcolm's triumph over his racial inner terror was his profoundest legacy: "The American public . . . took him to be a racist, a fanatic, a hoodlum, a murderous man. And from my point of view that's a very useful cloak for the American people. It's a way of avoiding what he was really saying. He was one of this country's most spectacular tragic heroes who was destroyed because he told the truth about the plight of this country."

Before the screenplay debacle, Baldwin and Haley had planned to turn Haley's book into a play. Baldwin had been working on it while seeking the cooperation of Malcolm's widow before Columbia Pictures entered the scene. In a letter to Haley of February 13, 1967, he mentions his correspondence with Shabazz, and his "vow . . . that I would do the most truthful job I possibly could." He had met Malcolm and talked with him. He admired the transformation of Malcolm's views that had so displeased Elijah Muhammad and the Nation of Islam. He was ready to travel to Mecca, too, for "my third act pivots on it, and I think I have to see it." Standing by his promise to Shabazz, again, meant including Malcolm's abandonment of the Nation of Islam's racialist ideology that had prompted his Mecca pilgrimage. Baldwin's original screenplay was published in 1972 as *One Day, When I Was Lost: A Scenario Based on "The Autobiography of Malcolm X."* The director Spike Lee later rewrote the forgotten Perl-Baldwin screenplay for his award-winning biopic

Malcolm X (1992). At the request of Baldwin's estate, though, Lee did not give full credit to Baldwin, though there are clear imprints of the *One Day* screenplay on Lee's final product.

Baldwin's trademark strategy of linking individual and national predicaments, in which the lives of men and women reflect the lives of societies and cultures like mutually dependent organisms, spilled into *The Devil Finds Work*, a volume of pioneering cultural criticism. Propelled by his love of cinema and theater, the volume came out of the period that Baldwin spent in his beloved house in Saint-Paul-de-Vence. In his last sixteen years he oscillated between settling in that peaceful setting and traveling, teaching, and socializing. Away from prying eyes and puritanical U.S. culture, bolstered by the privacy of his household, Baldwin undertook further explorations of gender divisions, queer domesticity, and especially the somewhat fraught issue of an inner woman—the subject that preoccupied, and troubled, him until the end of his life.

TRACK 4

The Houses of Baldwin

*T*HE *DEVIL FINDS WORK,* a collection David Leeming calls "a fifty-year-old's evaluative reminiscence," offers a rich context for understanding Baldwin's continued struggles with gender and its representations and articulations during the 1970s and 1980s. The book also marks a return to discussions of masculinity in his nonfiction that he had abandoned in the late 1950s. In his work from this period, especially a series of interviews he did with Black and white feminists, we see Baldwin's complex reactions to the hostility he faced from fellow African American radicals, who disliked him for his sexuality—Huey Newton's proclamation of solidarity with homosexuals in August 1970 was a notable exception—and for his humanist politics, rather than the separatism they favored.

Longing to be a "man's man" and included among "race men," the writer masked his homosexuality in public, though he may privately have despaired at the likelihood of deceiving anyone by his actions. "Baldwin-bashing was almost a rite of initiation" among Black militants, recalls Henry Louis Gates, Jr., who as an aspiring journalist interviewed Baldwin in Saint-Paul-de-Vence. Gates observes that "national identity became sexualized in the sixties . . . engender[ing] a curious subterraneous connection between homophobia and nationalism." In such a context, the middle-aged Baldwin became an easy target.

Always deeply hurt by the rejection of Black men, in 1972 Baldwin juxtaposed "the odd and disreputable artist and the odd and disreputable revolutionary" as different types of Black male leaders who "seem to stand forever at an odd and rather uncomfortable angle to each other . . . and . . . to the people they both . . . hope to serve." His fear of alienating Black men, the Black Christophers whose acceptance he craved, sometimes also led him to defend them against well-deserved criticism. In such moments, we can see the disconnect between the private, feminine Baldwin ensconced in his house, free to embrace his flamboyant, queer persona, and the public, more stereotypically masculine (if not movie-made) performative incarnations of his provisionary self. Armored as the race man, shielded by manly images of Civil Rights Movement activists that filled newspapers and television screens, he worked to blend in.

The man whose youthful friendships with Gidske Anderson and Mary Painter encouraged him to embrace the "woman" inside "all those strangers" within his complex self was especially reluctant to criticize Black radicals' misogyny and homophobia in public debates with feminists, even later in his life. The two-sided, complex Baldwin in this track poses some troubling questions: Why did he act so defensively? Was his private life at Sant-Paul-de-Vence too painstakingly assembled, too precious for him to put at risk by speaking his mind publicly? Was he still ashamed of his origins, which—transformed into best-selling books—had financed a house for his mother, his international travel, his chic wardrobe, and his picturesque privacy in Provence? Conversations he had with three feminists—Margaret Mead, Nikki Giovanni, and Audre Lorde—will help uncover answers to these questions.

Baldwin's "sissy heroics" pioneered Black male queerness, as the scholar Marlon Ross notes in *Sissy Insurgencies* (2022), even though many insecure men defined their masculinity against Baldwin's vulnerable, complex figurations of gender, race, sexuality, class, and power. He was strange, he was an elder, and he forgave the gay bashing he experienced from the Black Arts Movement poet, playwright, and nationalist LeRoi Jones (later Amiri Baraka, who himself struggled with misogyny and sexual identification) even though Jones used the word *faggot* freely in his earlier works, some explicitly attacking Baldwin, such as "Brief Reflections on 2 Hot Shots" (1963). In the 1980s, Baldwin and Baraka became friends, and Baraka—a lucky beneficiary of Baldwin's fatherly lessons in humanity, tolerance, and acceptance—spoke movingly at Baldwin's funeral. Baldwin never reconciled with others who took aim at him, including the writers Ishmael Reed and Albert Murray; in his last interview with Quincy Troupe he recalled that the former called him a "cocksucker."

Though Baldwin could express and even master his fears and insecurities to some degree in his fiction, in his nonfiction and public utterances they often prevented him from denunciations of the violent assertions of masculinity he despised. His conflicted sexual sense of himself was a factor in his reticence, for he was strongly attracted to exactly the kind of macho, hyper-heterosexual men who had caused him so much pain in the past; the unpublished erotica pieces we explored on Side B reflect these desires. When Baldwin was teaching at Bowling Green University in 1978–79 and 1981, for example, his host, Ernest A. Champion, remembered that one such macho companion "did not endear himself by his behavior toward others and did cause Jimmy some embarrassment." In his biography David Leeming cites repeated incidents of physical abuse by violent lovers or pick-ups. Hélène and Pitou Roux, who with their mother, Yvonne, made up Baldwin's adopted family in Saint-Paul-de-Vence, recalled in our 2018 interview that he once barricaded himself in a room to escape a beating by a lover while his cook ran to their mother for help.

Baldwin put himself through excruciating self-analyses in his letters yet stuck to repeating well-known facts of his life in public interviews, hardly ever engaging in issues of gender or sexuality. Even in conversations with feminists he defended the behavior of aggressively "masculine" Black men. Two notable public conversations will illustrate this tendency. The first was an interview with the anthropologist Margaret Mead in August 1970 that was taped in New York and later published as *Margaret Mead/James Baldwin: A Rap on Race* (1971). The second was with the Black Arts poet Nikki Giovanni; videorecorded in London, it aired on the television program *Soul!* in December 1971, and was later published as *James Baldwin/Nikki Giovanni: A Dialogue* (1973). In both discussions, disagreements arise hinging on the fact that though Baldwin had considered sexuality and gender as important as race in his fiction, he avoided discussing them openly in public. In both he came across as conservative, even closeted.

Mead, a feminist and adjunct professor of anthropology at Columbia University who was twenty-three years his senior, invited Baldwin to participate in a conversation on race. They met in New York on August 25–27, 1970, and recorded some seven hours of dialogue, which was released as a two-disc LP audiobook in 1972. Their fascinating discussion on difference, mythologies of race, and the evils and violence of racism was open and honest, though its published transcript drew a negative review in the *New York Times* by Richard Ellmann for its rawness and loose structure. The occasional sharp moments between Baldwin and Mead confirmed their different styles and uses of rhetoric: a long-winded author who played with figurative language confronted a social scientist focused on logic, facts, and data.

The discussion covered a wide field, including colonialism and imperialism, rape, slavery, religion, and Blackness in the United States and Great Britain during and after World War II. They agreed that Americans were afraid of touch and intimacy and were puritanical about sex; they also agreed about the universality of racism, and the oneness of humans "from New Guinea to Harlem . . . to New England," as Baldwin put it (claiming that it was his prophetic duty to redeem his misguided country), "and from Tokyo to London" as Mead had it. They touched on beauty and self-esteem: Mead described her white origins and research experience in Samoa and Baldwin his observations in Harlem and Europe, emphasizing that Black boys were menaced while developing their "sensuality" while surrounded by racist stereotypes of Black sexuality. Their conversation also revealed some of Baldwin's masculine anxieties that underlay his unease about gender and that reappeared in his conversation with Giovanni, as well as in a discussion with Audre Lorde, the Black lesbian author and activist that followed a decade later.

In the published transcript of Baldwin's conversation with Mead, for example, Baldwin talks about his experience of Christian hypocrisy. But his response to injustice should not be construed as feminine, he insists, with an awareness of his public persona and smarting at homophobic charges against his writing style: "I am not being as vehemently romantic and sentimental as I may sound." In response, Mead steers the conversation toward gender as a power structure and category of analysis parallel to race. Mentioning a psychological experiment in which "they asked the little white boys which they would rather be, little white girls or little Negro boys," she asks Baldwin what he thinks the response was. "I can't guess," he admits. Hearing Mead's answer that "they would rather be Negro boys," he responds, "Ha, that's encouraging. They had some sanity left." Was Berdis Baldwin's son agreeing that being a Black man was preferable to being a white woman? Or that being a man was better than being a woman, regardless of race? Did he mean that for any man to dream of being a woman of any race implied insanity?

Mead responds helpfully as a scientist: "You define people as human and inhuman in certain sorts of terms, and this is the kind of behavior you get." She takes evolution into consideration: "Twenty thousand years ago people weren't capable of thinking of more than thirty or forty people as human." Then she looks at class and caste differences: "And if you incorporate someone else's lower status as an element of who you are, then you're really trapped." While these remarks echo Baldwin's pronouncements on race, Mead's next words make it impossible for him to ignore gender: "You know, men do that about women, and they are un-manned because a woman gets a job of the sort they are doing." Using examples of gender discrimination in the U.S. Army and the faculty of political science at Columbia, who refused to hire a woman professor, she concludes: "American men become abso-lutely vulnerable, because what most American men have been taught is that the point of being a man is that you're not a woman." Baldwin stubbornly responds, "Which is exactly not the point. . . . The point of being a man is being a man."

This exchange leads to a fascinating segment on Americans' binary thinking. Mead focuses on the U.S. South, where "an essen-tial element in the identity of each race was they weren't the other. So if you change the position of the member of the other race you're threatening the other person's identity," her words again confirming Baldwin's own thinking on the matter. They agree on the inevitable movement toward a "world civilization" as the only solution to human divisions and exploitation. Baldwin mentions his conviction that education and individual self-improvement are key to this process. Mistakes are part of learning, he emphasizes, using Huey Newton as an example of someone who is "learning

all the time ... and ... can listen." He identifies with the younger
Newton, and dissociates himself from general Black nationalist
posturing in ways he would repeat the next year in his interview
with Giovanni: "I don't agree with all those people running around
with Afro wigs. . . . I'm tired of being told, by people who just got
out of the various white colleges and got a dashiki and let their
hair grow; I am terribly tired of those middle-class darkies telling
me what it means to be black. But I *understand* why they have to
do it!"

The public Baldwin here often seems baffled and self-contradictory, but he is also effective at demonstrating his interest in
constantly remixing ideas, learning new concepts, and modify-
ing his thinking. His auto-theoretical, nonlinear, emotionally and
metaphorically charged reasoning differs strongly from Mead's.
While both at various points in their dialogue identify themselves
as "rational," their distinct viewpoints demonstrate the fallacy of
the stereotype that women are governed by emotions and men
by reason. They consistently conduct their exchange as if to prove
this, Mead coming across as more hard-headedly logical and Baldwin as diva-like and passionate. They establish early in their conversation that race is a myth, an invented category, but one with
profound material consequences. If either speaker pulls rank on
the other, it is Baldwin, who in several instances swerves from
Mead's focus on gender and "Women's Lib" (the term then in use
for the largely white, middle-class second wave of feminism) to
race whenever he seems confounded or uncomfortable. Baldwin
and Mead articulate important notions—for example, that Black
men are seen primarily as oversexualized, phallic symbols. That
notion propelled Baldwin's critique of masculinity in *No Name in
the Street*, on which he was then working, and would spill into later
works as well. Still, neither with Mead nor with Giovanni a year
later was Baldwin able to explain precisely how masculinity fit

into the American system of race and sex he had been describing for decades (and began analyzing in his early essays, "The Preservation of Innocence" and "The Male Prison," explored on Track 2 of this side).

Nevertheless, in both conversations, Baldwin articulated some tenets of his Black queer humanistic thinking that are important for his writing. Discussing the "trap" of American discrimination, he offers the observation informed by his life abroad: "All the things you do to prove you're not inferior only really prove you are. They boomerang. . . . You're playing the game according to somebody else's rules, and you can't win until you understand the rules and step out of that particular game, which is not, after all, worth playing." Agreeing with Mead that race and sexuality are inextricably connected, though again avoiding making a clear statement on gender, he calls "the game" what today we term the politics of binary identity, or thinking of humans in terms of exclusion: I'm a man because I'm not a woman; Black because not white; straight because not gay, and so on. Baldwin expresses his ideas in beautiful language, calling himself a "poet" while Mead recognizes his prophetic role as a spokesman and artist, who by embracing feminism—could he bring himself to do so—could bring about tangible change in how men think of and communicate about gender in relation to themselves.

In one of the earlier cruxes of their long conversation, Mead claims that women need to forge a new language and create new images so they can see themselves as real, liberate themselves from the history of their subordination in all areas of life. Baldwin agrees, elaborating on how this is also true for him: "You've simply got to force the language to pay attention to you in order to exist in it, and you have no choice but to exist in it. . . . You need the English language to do all the things which have yet to be done in this terrifying country. The whole race-sex thing . . . is almost impossible to do, because both areas are so inaccessible to the memory and so wounding to the ego that you have to go through extraordinary excavations with your own shovel and your own guts to be able to come anywhere near the truth about the connection between your rage, for example, and your sexuality. You know, the proximity in your sexuality." The truth Baldwin rages about is manhood, and his Black queer version thereof, forged in these circumstances.

Mead responds by nudging him again back to gender, reminding him of the lessons he learned in his mother's kitchen. She is turning back to Baldwin's earlier reference to Berdis's influence, when he mentioned that his mother's lessons often clashed with what preachers taught him. Mead explains, "Since you're talking about what the mother gave the black boy, I wonder if it's worth saying that the women who are angry are the daughters of fathers who have destroyed their femininity, who have destroyed them as people by laughing at them as women." This evokes Baldwin's own childhood trauma—the abuse he suffered at the hands of his stepfather (see Side A, Track 3): the story of Mead's hypothetical little girl reflects his own. What becomes clear in this moment of their exchange is that it doesn't really matter that Baldwin was a boy whose masculinity was "destroyed" by his father; the damage done to the child is the same no matter the child's gender, and the results of that damage rage through families in innumerable neighborhoods, cities, and countries. What he misses or refuses to engage in Mead's comments throughout their encounter is the importance of gender to any writer bent on forcing a liberatory language to express "the whole race-sex thing" in any society, and especially in the United States.

A similar struggle with Baldwin's manly self-image was present in his conversations with Nikki Giovanni in 1971. The scintillatingly charismatic Giovanni, while respectful and deferential, danced circles around Baldwin, who was unable to shed his public persona of the race man in front of the camera and a studio audience. Yet, as in the extended discussion with Mead, there were moments of openness, in which Baldwin allowed his inner woman to peek through his armor. In both encounters, though, his public persona effectively obscured the radically imaginative writer. At the height of his friendship with Gidske Anderson he once dreamt of becoming simultaneously a woman and an olive-skinned boy; he later freely inhabited all kinds of bodies in his fiction, for example, telling Tish's story in her own teenage voice in *If Beale Street Could Talk* and becoming one with Julia Miller's violated body in *Just above My Head*.

Baldwin's televised interview with Giovanni filled two consecutive episodes, airing on December 15 and 22, 1971, of the popular Black arts and culture show *Soul!* (1968–73), hosted by Ellis Haizlip. The debonair Haizlip, himself queer, introduced them as "two brilliant members of the Black family," thus gently herding the queer Baldwin and the controversial, outspoken Black feminist single mother (now married to a woman) Giovanni into a position of familiar respectability. A frequent presence on *Soul!*, Giovanni was both a performer and a producer. It was her idea to invite Baldwin to discuss the "war of the sexes," and its racial entanglements. Their interaction—both interlocutors glamorously chic and effervescently eloquent—is a fascinating record of Black cross-generational dialogue on the topic. It also demonstrates Baldwin's difficulty embracing the lessons he learned from his mother, from his friends Gidske Anderson and Mary Painter, and from his muse Bessie Smith. Yet again, we can see inklings of his playful, freer inner self: at times, Baldwin sits back to listen and learn from Giovanni, his admiration palpable.

Faced with Giovanni's insistence that Black men shoulder burdens equally with Black women in couples, families, and communities and, most important, stop the cycle of family violence, for example, Baldwin demands that she show an understanding bordering on special treatment for Black men. When Giovanni tells him, "I don't understand how a black man can . . . be brutalized by some white person somewhere, and then come home and treat me or Mother the same way that he was being treated," Baldwin responds, "You and I say mistreated, but in the mind of the person who's doing it, he's not mistreating you." The feminist Giovanni does not accept this: "I'm not going to deal with the cracker who is mistreating him. I'm going to deal with him." She rejects Baldwin's claim that passing along violence is human nature, that given the destructive and violently rigid masculinity historically forced upon them, Black men have to find a way to blunt the pain of their victimization at the hands of whites by victimizing their wives and children. Disagreeing that the violence is impulse, not a matter of choice, Giovanni counters that such an illogic makes the Black woman the most alienated and endangered person in the United States: "I don't like white people and I'm afraid of black men. So what do you do?"

Baldwin's response? Race is a fiction—"the words 'white' and 'black' don't mean anything"—but a man is a "human being; it's got to come out somewhere." He pleads ignorance concerning "what happens to a woman," as opposed to his understanding of "what happens to a man," when "they've got you by the throat and the balls. And of course it comes out directed to the person closest to you." When Giovanni protests this line of thought and suggests that societal attitudes about gender are wrong and have to change, he retorts, "One cannot be romantic about human nature; one cannot be romantic about one's own nature." To which she responds with a succinct assessment of the position of Black women in the Civil Rights and Black Power Movements alike: "Even today . . . black men say, In order for me to be a man, you walk ten paces behind me."

In his encounter with an outspoken Black feminist, Baldwin's rhetoric on race is dully familiar. What is unusual in this context is his staunch refusal to see obvious parallels between his ideas and those on gender discrimination that Giovanni offers, though she clearly defers to him as her elder. Especially in the published version of the conversation (edited more carefully than *A Rap on Race*), he sounds as if he believes that men are more important than women because race is a more important marker than gender. But as always, once we feel we've "got him," and prepare to rest in our feminist outrage, Baldwin begins disagreeing with himself. He scrambles our expectations, bringing up anecdotes from his life, returning to race and its material consequences, then excoriating the political fictions that keep men and women fighting each other, enabling those in power to remain in control. (What a pity that no one talks this way on television anymore!)

Echoing his conversation with Mead, for example, Baldwin transitions from the theme of writing and semantics to the idea of fear as the impetus for men's self-destructive thinking: "People invent categories in order to feel safe. White people invented black people to give white people identity. . . . Straight cats invented faggots so they can sleep with them without becoming faggots themselves." Giovanni, naming other kinds of divisively deployed "hypes people go for"—"junkie hype, that whole war hype, that whole homosexual hype" during that decade of overdoses, the Vietnam War, and Stonewall—nudges their dialogue closer to gender. Angry at Black men's deafness to women's legitimate criticism, she complains that they refuse to listen. Seeming to wrestle with his own gender trouble, Baldwin tries to present the Black man's perspective: "He's not mad at you; he's mad because you told him the truth. . . . He's mad because he's trying to establish an illusion which you're breaking."

Truth-telling is risky, and Baldwin uses the power structure of the Black church to illustrate how it threatens men's power and sense of superiority: "He's mad the same way those terrible preachers in the church I grew up in were mad. You know, I began to ask them questions about what this really means. And I began to watch their lives. They were nothing but pimps and hustlers, really. Wrapped in a cloak, in the blood of Jesus and all that jazz. You ask them a real question and they hate you. They hate you." Baldwin's response brings back images of both the vengeful reverend and his own teenage self in the pulpit, where he caught himself beginning to enjoy the cloak-blood-Jesus-jazz manly strategies. Here, unlike in the exchange with Mead, the angry people are the power-hungry, greedy men who lord it over others, exploiting them for economic gain. Baldwin disidentifies from this kind of manhood, however momentarily, echoing the stance he took in his early essays "The Preservation of Innocence" and "The Male Prison."

This exchange with Giovanni illustrates not so much Baldwin's growing understanding of patriarchal power structures—he had already grasped these instinctively in the pulpit—as his willingness to articulate that understanding publicly. It provides a welcome corrective to an earlier segment in their conversation, in which they talked about the damaging effects of Baldwin's premature economic responsibility for his family. After he described his "parenting" of his younger sisters and brothers, Giovanni challenged him—perhaps the first interviewer to do so publicly— about how he was framing his role. Pointing out that he had been a child himself, not his siblings' parent, Giovanni, a single mother of a son, explained, "One cannot, and I'm not knocking your life, but one cannot be responsible for what one has not produced."

To which Baldwin responded, "I said we're not being rational."
And Giovanni, exasperated, retorted: "But I say we must."

> BALDWIN: No, no no.
>
> GIOVANNI: We must become rational.
>
> BALDWIN: Those are my brothers and sisters.
>
> GIOVANNI: They were your brothers and your sisters, not your
> children.

Giovanni is expressing again what she considers common sense:
only a parent can be responsible for parenting. Baldwin, the poet,
as he increasingly calls himself in 1970s, is after something else,
though he cannot fully articulate it.

In the conversations with Giovanni and Mead, it is the women
who are more clear-eyed and plainspoken than Baldwin can be
himself. But by insisting that rationality be abandoned, Baldwin
disidentifies from the typical masculinity he had to project in
public—he flips the gender script, as it were, seeming to indicate
that a state of rationality belongs to women. Like truth, being rational and possessing reason have traditionally been gendered
masculine in heteropatriarchal cultures. Baldwin seems to want
to have it both ways. This contradictory approach reveals Baldwin's complex relationship to his gender underlying the performance of his public persona. As in his early man-woman literary
fantasies from the Gidske Anderson period, he seems to want what
he can only make happen in writing: to be a mother while also
being a big brother; being unlimited in human experience.

In his conversations with both Mead and Giovanni, Baldwin
has trouble decoupling traumatic memories of his childhood and
their effect on his adult life from the "rational" facts of his situation. He tells Mead, for example, that he felt "penalized by history" and responsible for the deaths of the four young girls killed

in the Ku Klux Klan church bombing in Birmingham, Alabama, on September 15, 1963. His reason: he failed to stop it. Mead responds that although it was natural to feel affected by the murder, Baldwin is not responsible for the crime, for he could not have stopped the attack. He disagrees, saying, "I'm responsible for it. I didn't stop it."

MEAD: Why are you responsible? Didn't you try to stop it? Hadn't you been working?

BALDWIN: It doesn't make any difference what one's tried.

MEAD: Of course it makes a difference what one's tried.

BALDWIN: No, not really.

MEAD: This is the fundamental difference.

On the third day of their dialogue, Mead seems exasperated, "Everybody's suffering is mine but not everybody's murdering. . . . I do not believe in guilt by association." She suggests that Baldwin's position is "exactly like a Russian Orthodox. 'We are all guilty. Because some man suffers, we are all murderers.'" Baldwin's uncritical acceptance of guilt à la Dostoyevsky's *Crime and Punishment*, the writer and novel he loved, can be frustrating for the reader of the *Rap on Race*, too, as we follow his inconsistencies. At the conclusion of their first day, for example, he flatly rejects responsibility for the deeds of "the band of mediocrities which appear to rule this country," vowing to work for a better world for his two-year-old great-nephew.

Baldwin, Mead says, is now a man who lives in a nice house in France and is comfortable financially. He is a spokesman and an activist but is far from suffering in a literal sense and he is unable to intervene in historical events. She argues that "real suffering is when the iron is on your flesh. No matter how much you care about the people who have the iron on their flesh, if you don't have it on your own you don't suffer" in the same way. True victims exist in the moment, Mead explains, while those who have not experienced violence firsthand can only know that it is wrong, feel compassion for the victims, and take pains to stand up against it, as she does and as she thinks every American and human being with a conscience should do. But we should not equate the arduousness of our activism, or our depth of rage and pain at the victimization of others, with the iron on our own flesh. This is a perceptive critique: in his writing and speeches, Baldwin often used passionate rhetoric that made it sound as if he had personally suffered the auction block and lash of his enslaved forebears. Mead does not challenge Baldwin's artistry and ancestry, but she bristles when he patronizingly pulls rank on her in his performative public persona—his provisionary, representative, synecdochic self as "the Black man in America."

Baldwin's discomfort in his conversations with Giovanni and Mead reveals that his attachment to being seen as a man in public overpowers him, as if the Reverend Baldwin were watching, ready to punish his misbehavior; as if all those beautiful young men like Black Christopher would turn away from him if he shed his public race man persona; as if he still had to choose between loyalty to men and loyalty to the women in his life as he did in the case of Mary Painter's rape. This gender anxiety and affliction, which he had earlier diagnosed astutely in men like Norman Mailer and Eldridge Cleaver, or while he was reading André Gide and creating characters like Rufus in *Another Country* or David in *Giovanni's Room*, was something he was unable to overcome in conversations with women who were his intellectual equals. In the conversations with both Mead and Giovanni, there were moments when he seemed lost, contradicted himself, or became obstinate, yielding to his insecurities, as, for example, when Mead caught a geographical mistake he made, confusing La Guinea, in Panama, with

British Guiana (Guyana), in northeastern South America, to which she was referring. Instead of admitting his error, understandable to any reader, Baldwin goes on to attack Mead in such a chaotic manner that their exchange falls apart.

What explains Baldwin's insecurity in his conversations with Giovanni and Mead? Most likely, it was the tension between his public persona and his growing awareness of his conflicting selves, something he had hinted at in the earlier interview with Eve Auchincloss and Nancy Lynch published as "Disturber of the Peace." Recorded in May 1963 for *Mademoiselle* magazine, then reprinted in 1964 in *The Black American Writer,* this unusually intimate interview enumerated "all those strangers called Jimmy Baldwin": "the older brother with all the egotism and rigidity that implies" and "the self-pitying little boy. You know: 'I can't do it because I'm so ugly.'" When asked what other Jimmy Baldwins there were, he responds, "Lots of people. Some of them are unmentionable. There is a man. There is a woman, too." In publications and speeches during the later 1979s–80s, he began shunning labels and categories such as Black manhood, preferring "the power and the glory and the limitless potential of every human being in the world," as he wrote in 1986 in the introduction to the scholar and writer Michael Thelwell's *Duties, Pleasures, and Conflicts.*

The later Baldwin's Black queer humanist emphasis on the gender and racial complexities embedded within each human struck at the uselessness of fixed identities, labels, and representations. Yet his fears and anxieties—including that "eternal father" always breathing down his neck, as he wrote in the letter to Mary Painter we examined on Track 2 of this side—made him ashamed to explore his own gender and sexuality in public. In that shame, the former repressed teen preacher was joined by numerous other Black writers who felt pressured by the politics of respectability and the religiosity of their communities—even Nikki Giovanni, two decades his junior, remained reticent about her queerness. Boldly writing scenes of sex and gender confusion in his fiction, Baldwin found it much easier to explore such themes while sheltered in his study than under the hot lights of television cameras. He never felt comfortable expressing vulnerability publicly, the way his "dear Sister" Maya Angelou did, an uneasiness that suggests how greatly Baldwin still felt constrained by notions of masculinity, despite his embrace of the feminine.

A letter he wrote on November 20, 1970, to Maya Angelou, his "solid, loving, funky, no-shit friend," exemplifies some of his inner struggles with his fear of public self-disclosure. He writes about his conversation with Mead, for example, which he considered a somewhat satisfying, "daring experiment," yet painful, because "I've left myself wide open—I've never been so naked before." He sounds patronizing, though, when summing up "Dr. Mead," who refused to agree with him. He also complains of health issues— the "betrayal of my exceedingly inventive body"—and laments his alienation, sounding like a stereotypical middle-aged woman: "I've been very much alone, perhaps too much. I've been through so many changes that I have some difficulty recognizing me, though I don't think you will."

In the letter he mentions Lorraine Hansberry's death, and he expresses his grief and rage in words he never uttered in public: "I'll never forget that last look . . . a weariness unbelievable in those eyes and a disappointment and a fury with her body . . . death, for so many of us, is a matter of unbearable weariness. . . . Who the fuck really, after all, wants to write another book? What for? for whom? *to* whom?" His thirteenth work, then in progress, *No Name in the Street*, exacts painful labors. "I've spent my life shitting bricks," he complains, admitting what he could only tell his closest friends, that birthing books did not fulfill him: "No one will believe that I wanted children." In his conclusion he asks

Angelou to intercede with his family when they read his latest book, instructing her to carry the words of a stereotypical strong Black man to them: "Tell Gloria and David . . . that I think I know what I'm doing. I'm in a dangerous place, but I'm doing what I've always done: I've always fought back, and I'm fighting . . . for all of us."

Perhaps Baldwin's most vulnerable public moment came when he was in Turkey in 1970 taking part in Pakay's *James Baldwin: From Another Place* (1973). Baldwin is sitting in his study, smoking, fingering his Turkish tasbih beads, a drink on the desk nearby, responding to a question about his sexuality that we cannot hear. This private setting, like the bedroom shot opening the documentary, frames this film as an intimate encounter, and Baldwin's privacy as heavily guarded. He speaks of "a few men" and "a few women" whom he has loved, and of how the love of those "few people" saved his life. He speaks of himself as a man "without antecedents . . . as if I had no mother, no father," an orphan because of his Black queerness. This fleeting glimpse of vulnerability is captured beautifully by Cengiz Tacer's camera. Baldwin's guard usually rose when he was in front of his fellow Americans, but subsided when he was abroad, where he felt freer.

By the 1970s, Baldwin had published four novels featuring queer characters, committing to paper what he found debilitatingly hard to express in public. He had read Walt Whitman and liked his evocations of human multitudes, American homoeroticism, and nature. He must have read Geoff Brown's *I Want What I Want* (1966), an English novel about a trans woman that survived in a tattered copy in his library, alongside books on homosexuality and rape, such as Dennis Altman's *Homosexual: Oppression and Liberation* (1971) and, later, Andrea Dworkin's *Intercourse* (1987) an advance copy of which he also owned. Dworkin was a great fan of his, modeling herself on Baldwin in *Heartbreak: The Political Memoir of a Feminist Militant* (2002). In the late essay "Here Be Drag-

ons," he stated his position succinctly: "All of the American categories of male and female, straight or not, black or white, were
shattered, thank heaven, very early in my life." This essay articulated for public view at long last what some of his unpublished
papers—the Gidske-period writings in France and the two published essays "The Preservation of Innocence" and "The Male
Prison" that appeared on Track 1 of this side—had already probed.

As David Leeming and many of his close friends told me over
the years, Baldwin yearned to describe the woman within himself.
Yet something—childhood trauma, an old-fashioned sense of privacy and respectability, shame driven by the church's and then
the government's invigilation of his life, fear of even greater rejection from his Black peers—made him afraid to express this view
in public. Homophobia has been a faithful sidekick to misogyny
in American culture, no matter what the racial or ethnic group.
The internalized homophobia that Baldwin described movingly
through David and Hella in *Giovanni's Room* fed on policing socially acceptable gender roles—the topic he would have difficulty
addressing during his discussions with Mead and Giovanni. In
his other novels, *Another Country, Tell Me How Long the Train's
Been Gone,* and *Just above My Head,* misogyny is clearly linked to
homophobia and vice versa, while racialized gender and sexuality
attitudes spin into vicious circles of never-ending discrimination,
abuse, and recrimination in practically all his works. This dynamic
was not easy to decode in the 1960s–70s, before the concepts like
intersectionality were defined and disseminated, and queer people became more visible and vocal. It is impressive that Baldwin
took it on, despite how excruciating it was to him to openly discuss such issues; his letters let us glimpse most clearly how painful he found it to write about them.

Though *Giovanni's Room* has become a classic, the Australian
writer Dennis Altman critiqued it harshly in his pioneering 1971

book on homosexuality. Like many since then, Altman, a generation younger than Baldwin, saw him as shying away from a more
activist and vociferous stance. He appraised *Giovanni's Room* as
"weak . . . too pat in its melodrama" and appeared to miss its characters' honest grappling, however unsuccessful and unresolved,
with American notions of gender and sexuality. Their struggles
were, after all, Baldwin's key point in that novel, as was the shaded
and veiled discussion of race and Americanness in its pages. In
Altman's reading of Baldwin's later works, however—the 1970
letter to Angela Davis is a key example—he recognized Baldwin's
"refusal to accept the conventional definition of masculinity" in
the face of condemnation he received from Black nationalists like
Cleaver and Amiri Baraka.

Altman's difficulty understanding Baldwin's reasons for de-
fending the Black Panthers despite their mistreatment of him can
help further elucidate Baldwin's inner conflict. Altman misses the
fact that, like Black Christopher, in the author's eyes these younger
Black men were his "children," much as, early on, his own siblings
and, later, these siblings' children—his nieces and nephews—were
"children" to him. Baldwin felt responsible for them all, might have
even felt accountable for their actions, a tendency for self-blame
we have seen in the Mead and Giovanni conversations. Baldwin
felt that he was a father figure to younger men, as Beauford Delaney had been to him. He needed to protect and teach them as he
had taught his brothers and sisters in his mother's kitchen growing up. This may be why he gave Cleaver that French kiss rather
than punishing him for his homophobic attacks. Misguided by
his experience to see himself as more a parent than a brother in
his family of origin, as Giovanni pointed out, Baldwin made peace
with these men's shortcomings like an overindulgent "dad." Perhaps his judgment and self-image were more deeply affected by
his traumatic memories than he cared to admit, his bouts of de-

pression and suicide attempts proof of a deeper inner struggle he could never resolve on his own.

That struggle continued to fuel his work. Mixing and remixing those difficult memories, letting trauma resurface from time to time, made it possible for Baldwin to arrive at the shape of his Black queer humanism in the 1980s. The essay that best exemplifies this philosophy appeared as "Freaks and the American Ideal of Manhood" in the January 1985 issue of *Playboy*. Later retitled "Here Be Dragons" in *The Price of the Ticket*, it engages with the issue of nonbinary identity, concluding with a bold statement on what Baldwin called androgyny:

> We are rarely what we appear to be. We are, for the most part, visibly male or female, our social roles defined by our sexual equipment. But we are all androgynous, not only because we are all born of a woman impregnated by the seed of a man but because each of us, helplessly and forever, contains the other—male in female, female in male, white in black and black in white. We are a part of each other. Many of my countrymen appear to find this fact exceedingly inconvenient and even unfair, and so, very often, do I. But none of us can do anything about it.

"Here Be Dragons" is a no-holds-barred critique of racist, sexist, and homophobic violence as the basis of a manhood that was foundational to U.S. history and identity—and it was published, no less, in a mainstream straight men's magazine. (Baldwin often wrote for *Playboy* and similar outlets, which paid well and offered wide readerships.) These views made him vulnerable as his country was embracing evangelical "family values" in the Reagan-dominated 1980s, amid a rise in homophobia as the HIV/AIDS epidemic unfolded. Attracted to gender-bending pop-culture icons like Boy George and Michael Jackson, reading the works of Alice Walker,

Toni Morrison, and Maya Angelou, Baldwin advocated for both a female-within-male identity and a black-within-white one. His brilliant take on identity—that it repressed another inner self and was a disguise for fear—is still relevant in our time.

A decade earlier, he articulated similar ideas, though less directly, in *The Devil Finds Work:* "Identity would seem to be the garment with which one covers the nakedness of the self.... This trust in one's nakedness is all that gives one the power to change one's robes." Wearing characters like costumes, actors provided a helpful example for Baldwin of how we all perform and change identities, switch codes, and self-fashion our public, performative personae. In this important work, Baldwin critiques race and gender in Hollywood, recalling childhood impressions of films and plays, his female teacher Bill Miller, and how he fell in love as a child with a Black woman who looked exactly like Joan Crawford. The book is a tribute to his silver screen idols—Bette Davis, Sylvia Sidney, and Lena Horne. Baldwin loved stylish women and chic clothing, and in his later life in France he embraced his inner diva as he had done earlier in remote Turkey.

David Leeming recalls Baldwin's "love of silk, of the recklessly thrown scarf ... the large and exotic ring, bracelet, or neckpiece," and how "his movements assumed a more feminine character." (The collection of Leeming's photographs at the Schomburg Cetner contains many images of chic, trend-setting Baldwin.) Inspired by glamorous female friends and visitors, he embraced "nostalgia for a lost woman within his manhood," dreaming of "novels he could write about women who would convert the Jimmy Baldwin he still sadly thought of as an ugly little man into someone tall, confident, beautiful ... 'impeccably' dressed in silks and satins and bold colors," a "character" in whom "James Baldwin would be transformed into a Josephine Baker." Approaching his sixties, Baldwin was becoming a bit of "an old auntie," a derogatory term that some of his younger lovers would use. He usually laughed such slurs off, possibly recalling that not long ago he might have said the same himself to Beauford Delaney. A local mail carrier remembers Baldwin's affectionate greetings: "He was . . . like a grandmother to me, kissing me—and I'm not gay!"

Despite Baldwin's fears of becoming an old auntie in public, he finally spoke about his sexuality candidly with Richard Goldstein of the *Village Voice* in 1984. In their interview, "Go the Way Your Blood Beats," he linked his personal experience to a larger problem ailing American culture: "The discovery of one's sexual preference doesn't have to be a trauma. It's a trauma because it's such a traumatized society." He explained that "the word 'gay,'" which was all the rage in the 1980s, "always rubbed me the wrong way." When Goldstein probed farther, asking incredulously, "You never thought of yourself as being gay?" Baldwin was emphatic: "No. I didn't have a word for it. The only one I had was 'homosexual' and that didn't quite cover whatever it was I was beginning to feel. . . . It was . . . very personal, absolutely personal. It was really a matter between me and God." As we recall from Sides A and B, his involvement with religion and the church caused him to be a late bloomer sexually, though he had fallen in love with boys and felt erotic and sexual desires since childhood. This interview and Baldwin's essays "Here Be Dragons" and "To Crush the Serpent," his last essay (published in *Playboy* in 1987), show the culmination of Baldwin's thinking on sexual identity and identification.

His important exchange with Audre Lorde in 1984 also fueled the writing in his essay "Here Be Dragons." Black and queer, Lorde proved a relatable interlocutor, despite their age and other differences, such as her immigrant parents' roots in the Caribbean. Recorded at Hampshire College in Amherst, Massachusetts, their edited discussion appeared in the December 1984 issue of *Essence* as "Revolutionary Hope: A Conversation Between James Baldwin and Audre Lorde." Its full transcript lives among his papers at the Schomburg Center, marked with editorial comments of both writers; Baldwin's scribble in green ink, "conversation must be cut to begin on page 14," determined its beginning, which deals with his signature views on race. In both the transcript and the section published in *Essence*, Baldwin's loneliness, pain, and sense of fragmentation stand out in stark relief against Lorde's self-possession, openness, clarity of mission, and strength.

Lorde was ten years Baldwin's junior. Her ideas on the importance of gender, desire, and racialized sexuality, delivered in a 1978 address at the Berkshire Conference of Women Historians (later published as "Uses of the Erotic: The Erotic as Power" in her essay collection *Sister Outsider*) drive their exchange. She had read Baldwin, and his thoughts echo in hers when she describes sensuality as "creative energy . . . [and] knowledge [that] empowers us [and] becomes a lens through which we scrutinize all aspects of our existence." Lorde saw herself as a "warrior poet," and, as she spoke about it in 1980 at Amherst College, in a lecture titled "Age, Race, Class, and Sex: Women Redefining Difference," she was proudly herself, "a forty-nine-year-old Black lesbian feminist socialist mother of two, including one boy, and a member of an interracial couple." Legally blind since childhood, she grew up in Harlem and was part of the Village lesbian scene, working menial jobs before becoming an academic.

In their fully transcribed, archived conversation, the heavy line editing by Lorde sometimes focused on making her message milder. The pages excluded from *Essence* contain stories about their origins in Harlem (Lorde was raised a few blocks away from Baldwin's childhood home), sexual identity in public, and views on the importance of education. They discuss growing up with fathers who were terrified by their precocious children's early writing and ideas. Lorde's upbringing by her Caribbean parents offered more comfort and education, and yet she was beaten with a slipper by her father when she was fifteen because of a poem she wrote. Upon seizing Lorde's hidden poem, "Strange Gods," her father "saw the rebellion—that I could use my writing, which he had encouraged, in a different way," rather than to become a teacher, as he had wanted. This anecdote follows Baldwin's account of his own confrontation with the reverend, who tore up his early short story, "Holy City," about the plight of Jews in Nazi Berlin—"I was very, very young and I didn't know anything more than that the Jews were being exterminated in Germany"—and attested to the child's empathy to human suffering. Baldwin's father was unmoved and violated the privacy of the young writer's desk, "my territory. No one was supposed to touch that desk. Nobody. Not my momma and certainly not the kids and not my daddy." Lorde astutely concludes both these accounts, which were excluded from the *Essence* article, by marking their gender difference as children raised by strict Black fathers: "Your father was afraid *for* you. My father was furious *with* me." To which Baldwin consents: "Perhaps you're right—I was putting myself in danger and you were stepping outside the natural social order." They agree that all children need education and discipline to develop toughness and an ability to resist authority and pressure to conform to social norms regardless of gender.

Another moment excluded from the *Essence* article involves Lorde's description of her visit to a Black college, Texas Southern, in Houston, "about 3 weeks after my mastectomy." Her realization that she might die soon had freed her to shed her public self. "I talked about race, about sex, about sexuality; I talked as a lesbian, I talked as a Black woman. . . . In Texas, you know; the girls were still going with white gloves." The students responded strongly, especially one young woman who thanked her when they were alone together, and Lorde realized that "you see that's what happens when you have to deal with what you believe being true." Baldwin interrupts her: "Then you remember too that you yourself were once that boy . . . you were once that girl," seeing her many spinning selves as similar to his own. Remembering their lives as children makes it possible for them both to understand as adults what their fathers might have once feared. Baldwin muses that had the reverend lived, they might have become friends, understanding that he "saw something that I didn't see . . . what I was attempting to do—become a writer. It placed me in terrifying danger." Lorde is skeptical, however, and her skepticism concerning men's ability to understand women and "sissy boys" like Baldwin runs through the rest of their conversation.

By the time Lorde and Baldwin met, she was a recognized Black lesbian poet and feminist intellectual, an activist and world traveler. Beginning in 1984, her annual stays in Germany would make a long-lasting impact on the African diasporic communities and academe there alike. Like Baldwin, she wrote from her personal experience of marginalization, but her brand of auto-theory was strongly informed by gender analysis: "I usually find myself a part of some group defined as other, deviant, inferior, or just plain wrong." She called her life story, *Zami: A New Spelling of My Name* (1982), a "biomythography" and opened it with a wish that Baldwin had expressed only obliquely decades earlier, in spurious, unpublished notes, and formulated only after their conversation in "Here Be Dragons." In this essay, Baldwin is clearly inspired by Lorde's open expression of desire in *Zami*, where she writes, "I have always wanted to be both man and woman, to incorporate the strongest and richest parts of my mother and father within/into me—to share valleys and mountains upon my body the way the earth does in hills and peaks." (It is unclear whether Baldwin read *Zami*; no copy survived in his home library, but it is likely that he did before his conversation with Lorde.)

Like Baldwin, Lorde thought of the "transformation of silence into language and action as an act of self-revelation" for the writer, as something "fraught with danger." Lorde's daughter asked her to always remember what she had taught her since earliest childhood: "You're never really a whole person if you remain silent, because there is always that one little piece inside you that wants to be spoken out, and if you keep ignoring it, it gets madder and madder and hotter and hotter, and if you don't speak it out one day it will just up and punch you in the mouth from the inside." In her conversation with Baldwin, Lorde does speak out, while he seems to be waiting for that punch.

In the published *Essence* conversation, Lorde takes on Baldwin's inexplicable defense of Black men in response to her demand that they be held accountable for gang violence and the abuse of Black women and children. Baldwin's replies contradict his earlier questioning of gender divisions in his novels, even his comments in the excised parts of their recorded conversation. Here he insists on essentializing masculinity like a broken record: "[A] man has a certain story to tell . . . just because he is a man," he says, repeating his statements to Mead and Giovanni. Exacerbating the situation, *Essence* slotted them both into essentialized, representative identities, the introductory copy describing them as "Every Black Man and Every Black Woman," their queerness covered with terms that erased the personal, and branded them as "revolutionaries and visionaries." While the magazine's choice to ignore Lorde's and Baldwin's queer identities tracks with Baldwin's circumspect self-presentation, Lorde blasts it with her very clear and public self-identification as a lesbian. Like Giovanni and Mead, Lorde must coax Baldwin to embrace her feminist point of view, to do the work he once asked his readers to do with his own ideas on race and sexuality.

She begins by taking apart masculinity, which she argues functions for women much as race functions for Black men. Lorde explains that the heroic freedom dreams of Malcolm X or Martin Luther King excluded her: "I was female. And I was out. . . . Nobody was dreaming about me. Nobody was even studying me except as something to wipe out. . . . Black women are the blank." The dynamic of their conversation is fascinating, as Baldwin tries repeatedly to get the upper hand, while Lorde calmly steers the discussion back to her non-essentializing Black feminism. He heaps on his tried-and-true race man rhetoric—"you're trying to deal with the man . . . and your man or your woman has to deal with . . . facts of life in this country"; "Black men and women are much less easily thrown by the question of gender or sexual preference"; "men . . . had to be responsible for the women and the children, which means the universe." She counters with brutal realities: "We need to acknowledge those power differences between us and see where they lead us. . . . I'm talking about Black women's blood flowing in the streets—and how do we get a fourteen-year-old boy to know I am not a legitimate target for his fury? . . . My blood will not wash out your horror." When Baldwin admits, erasing his own inner woman in the process, that "a man doesn't know the way a woman looks at the world. A woman *does* know much more about a man"—Lorde counters that women's knowledge is similar to that of Black Americans as opposed to whites—it is a matter of survival for an endangered group to understand its oppressor better than the oppressor understands the group.

Referencing the title of the foundational women-of-color feminist anthology, *This Bridge Called My Back: Writings by Radical Women of Color* (1981), edited by Cherríe Moraga and Gloria Anzaldúa, Lorde explains, "We're finished being bridges. Don't you see?" A landmark publication that built a coalition of writers, activists, and artists of color, *This Bridge Called My Back* was quickly followed by another important book on Black women, edited by Akasha Gloria Hull, Patricia Bell-Scott, and Barbara Smith in 1982. Its title, *All the Women Are White, All the Blacks Are Men, But Some of Us Are Brave,* explores the space of "blankness" that Lorde occupied and that she insisted Baldwin acknowledge. Baldwin's somewhat willful ignorance concerning the women's movement, and Black feminism in particular, may have been a pose he cultivated in public, but in 1984, at least to some of the *Essence* readers, his reticence would be surprisingly off-putting.

In the end, Lorde's is the more revolutionary and expansive vision—she embraces diversity and rejects ageism and ableism, insisting on telling the truth about human relationships: "It's vital that we deal constantly with racism, and with white racism among Black people . . . [and] also examine the ways we have absorbed sexism and heterosexism." Calling these forms of discrimination "the norms in this dragon we have been born into," Lorde has Baldwin's back against the wall. (Lorde's "dragon" perhaps influenced the new title of his *Playboy* "Freaks" essay.) Brilliantly throwing Black men's so-called "special role" to elevate the race back at him, Lorde insists on Baldwin's "responsibility not just to me but to my son and to our boys," which resonates with his own attention to the "children," family, and parenting. As Lorde sees it, Black men need to work to be good role models to ensure that boys stop believing that "the sign of their masculinity is impregnating a sixth grader." She also sees all genders as connected, just as Baldwin did in his early probing pieces, "The Preservation of Innocence" and "The Male Prison."

Lorde needs the "little sixth-grade girl who believes that the only thing in life she has is between her legs" to have other options. She tells Baldwin things that he has already written about:

"In the same way you know how a woman feels, I know how a man feels, because it comes down to human beings being frustrated and distorted because we can't protect the people we love." To Lorde, "distortions" are equivalent to power being misused, to discrimination. "Do you know what happens to a lesbian who sees her woman and her children beaten in the street while six other guys are holding her? Do you know what that feels like?" He does not answer. As a writer, Baldwin has described all kinds of humans—he inhabited Julia Miller's abused body in *Just above My Head*—yet here he is left speechless and, not for the first time, trapped in self-denial.

Baldwin's most radical ideas about Black queer love and the ravages of rape, incest, homophobia, racism, even "toxic masculinity" finally found expression in his last, innovative and daring novel, *Just above My Head*, which can be read as a literary expression of his philosophy of Black queer humanism. Having largely confined his nonfiction to the politics of race, after this novel Baldwin returned to these ideas in three late essays that may be read as shaped by his three failed conversations with feminists: "Here Be Dragons," "The Price of the Ticket," and "To Crush the Serpent," the last of which, like the original "Freaks" essay, also appeared in *Playboy*, adorned with an illustration of a menacing, multicolored, coiled snake. "To Crush the Serpent," subtitled "Reflections on the Hypocrisy of Today's Fundamentalist Ministers by an Evangelist Who Came Down from the Mountaintop," is Baldwin's last publication, with the exception of the *Architectural Digest* piece about his house that will appear on Side D.

Eerily relevant in our time of mega-churches, conversion therapy, and banned books, "To Crush the Serpent" recounts Baldwin's sexual coming of age with candor, juxtaposing erotic desire and love with fundamentalist Christianity and late-twentieth-century political conservatism. Recalling his teenage years, Baldwin explains his choice to "walk disorderly" and remain friends with a boy who, in the congregation's judgment "backslid," and with whom he was in love. The essay points at racist complicity between religious institutions and the state—"the [Black] minister and the sheriffs were hired by the Republic to keep the Republic white." We can almost hear Lorde's words when Baldwin argues that the politics of racial purity on both sides of the color line are rooted in normative notions of gender and sexuality. For the policing and regulation of non-normative and female bodies—as Mead, Giovanni, and Lorde taught him—supports the power of religious as much as state institutions. In the white republic, Blackness is synonymous with outlawed sex acts, miscegenation, and sin. Thus, white people may celebrate coming out as gay, as many have done since the 1990s, but queerness is a betrayal of their whiteness—a flip side, indeed, of what Cleaver reviled as Baldwin's racial death wish. Queer and nonconforming people of all colors remain hunted by the state-and-church systems inside their communities, which criminalize all aspects of their lives. Readers feel Baldwin's anger as he writes that by attacking sexual and gender freedom, both the church and the state are making "the possibility of the private life as fugitive as that of a fleeing n[—]r" for all Americans.

In "Here Be Dragons," his humanistic imagination admits all kinds of androgynous play. As in earlier work, his ideas arise in opposition to what he defines as the American late-capitalist "rage for order." He unequivocally links that rage to the "ideal of American manhood" that spoke through this essay's original title: "Such figures as Boy George do not disturb me nearly so much . . . as do those relentlessly hetero (sexual?) keepers of the keys and seals, those who know what the world needs in the way of order and who are ready and willing to supply that order." He sees these keepers as capitalizing on chaos, which also means capitalizing on fear of the other, for "in this country, chaos connects with color," and racism has been a for-profit enterprise. In the same essay, he also points out "the burning, buried American guilt; and sex and sexual roles and sexual panic; money, success and despair"—things he had narrated candidly in his much earlier short stories "The Outing" (1951) and "Going to Meet the Man" (1965). A short story from that period, "Come Out the Wilderness," is the only fiction in which the narrative point of view is that of a Black woman, with the exception of *If Beale Street Could Talk*, whose narrator is the pregnant teenager Tish.

A notable break from his public reticence on gender and feminism came in a talk that the visibly ailing Baldwin, who died less than a year later, gave about the role of Black women writers for the National Press Club on December 10, 1986. Worried that he might "exclude someone," he claimed loud and clear that "the arrival of Toni, Maya and Paule Marshall, Alice Walker, Louise Meriwether was in many ways inevitable, because of the role that black women have played in this country . . . and in the lives of black men." The lateness of this statement seems surprising, given that he owned a copy of Morrison's first novel, *The Bluest Eye* (1970), as well as her *Beloved* (1987), although he may not have read the latter because of his illness. He also owned books by Maya Angelou and Alice Walker, whose novel *The Color Purple* (1985) instigated a national debate on its "hostility" toward Black men because of its frank depictions of sexual violence within Black families. He praised Meriwether's *Daddy Was a Numbers Runner* (1970), writing a warm foreword to it after several letters (one included Meriwether's exasperated poem-as-request) reminding him that he had forgotten to do so.

Baldwin was close friends with many other Black women writers and academics, such as Eleanor Traylor, Vertamae Smart-Grosvenor, Florence Ladd, and Ida Lewis, and he stressed in his speech to the National Press Club that theirs "has always been a troubled and dangerous role." He followed this statement with a somewhat restrictive charge that these writers needed to "respect their fathers and protect their sons and lovers without emasculating them," thus emphasizing Black women's heroic—and widely stereotyped—role in holding Black families together. Most important, women needed to tell their stories and have their voices heard. He explained that Black men—those fathers, sons, and lovers—may have had something to do with Black women's writing having to enact "a ventilation . . . of a family quarrel." For men, he said, were never questioned about writing about women, while the opposite was clearly the case. He concluded that "what they have to say is somewhat terrifying but true," and they are here "to clarify the role of black people. . . . So Toni and Maya are excavating us all from a very dangerous myth."

What that myth was Baldwin left unexplained in his speech. We can guess, though, based on many unrealized projects among his papers that focused on women's lives. He probably meant that letting Black men speak for the race was officially over. (He did not mention that Black women's voices had always been raised, but nobody wanted to listen.) Walker's collection of womanist writing titled *In Search of Our Mother's Gardens* (1983), which claimed an interracial and matrilineal legacy of women's creativity, storytelling, and love for each other, was among Baldwin's books in Saint-Paul-de-Vence. He may have read Casey Hayden and Mary King's much earlier "Sex and Caste" manifesto (1965), in which they protest the "strait-jacketing of both sexes" in the New Left and Civil Rights Movements; they report, too, that the response of most men to their feminist critique of Black nationalism when it was first expressed was laughter. Today, reading *In Search of Our Mothers' Gardens* as an achronological context for Baldwin's mother characters in novels like *Go Tell It on the Mountain, If Beale Street Could Talk*, or *Just above My Head*, or even for a single professional like Ruth in "Come Out the Wilderness," whose character was inspired by his sister Gloria and fed into Ida Scott in *Another Country*, we can see that he could be called a womanist, but only in his fiction. Hiding his love for women from public view, hiding himself *as* one, that unrealized "stranger" remained hidden deepest among his conflicting private selves.

Having dubbed himself the "aging, lonely, sexually dubious, politically outrageous, unspeakably erratic freak" in *No Name in the Street,* Baldwin developed these ideas, and grappled with their gender-sex conflicts in dramatic form in his last, unpublished play, "The Welcome Table." It was inspired by an actual late-August dinner at his home, Chez Baldwin, and a set of characters who were part of his household. It plays on the last side of his Life Album.

Side D

TRACK 1

Coda Chez Baldwin

ROM 1971 until his death in 1987, Baldwin lived in France, in an old stone house on route de la Colle, just outside the ramparts of Saint-Paul-de-Vence. He originally rented rooms there from the owner, Jeanne Faure, and later bought it, piece by piece, as money came in. Faure was a "pied noir," a white French colonist from Algeria, and a right-leaning medieval historian. After Baldwin moved in, the racist old lady barricaded herself in her room, but he soon charmed her, and she treated him like family until her death the year before his. Faure, whose photograph Baldwin kept in his study, inspired the cranky Mlle Lafarge, a character in his last play, "The Welcome Table," which was set in his own house.

Nicknamed "Chez Baldwin," the old house boasted the French cubist painter Georges Braque among its previous inhabitants. It contained a dozen rooms, with the writer's ground-floor studio and living quarters facing the back. Calling it his "torture chamber" or "dungeon," Baldwin worked long hours in a large, sunny office with a fireplace; the living space also included another small room, a bathroom, and a kitchen. A record player was always going; art, photos, books, and knickknacks complemented eclectic furnishings. The dwelling perhaps reminded him of the life he had once shared with Lucien Happersberger in Loèche-les-Bains; its comforts recalled his rented house, Pasha's Library, in Istanbul. The Black dancer and choreographer Bernard Hassel managed the house, occupying a separate gatehouse. A local woman, Valerie Sordelo, cooked for a constant bevy of guests and visiting family, while Baldwin's brother David steered his business affairs and David Leeming worked on his papers. These people formed his family—the House of Baldwin—until his death.

In his last piece, published in the coffee-table glossy magazine *Architectural Digest* in August 1987, Baldwin describes his house with love and gratitude: "It found me just in time." The former city dweller reminisced about having peasant roots, relishing the pastoral joys of a large garden, house parties, and visitors. An acquaintance, Jules Farber, recalled in *James Baldwin: Escape from America, Exile in Provence* (2016) that it was a protected, "tranquil setting. . . . Partners came, stayed, left or were chased out. . . . Doctors on a sick call . . . nonplussed when the bed was filled with another male body. . . . Nothing was said." The journalist and biographer James Campbell came to visit Baldwin around 1980, noting at a party, "Theatricality was central to his nature. No less characteristic of him than his integrity was his self-dramatization, a certain campness in his poise, an unflagging willingness to perform, and a weakness for flashbulbs and recognition in public places. . . . I remember him half-sitting on the round table in the middle of the floor, one foot up on a chair, at the center of a ring of people." Baldwin died in an elaborately frescoed room, a former dining parlor at the heart of his house—the "bastide"—where he was moved by David in the fall of 1987. He had found a home at long last and wished to be buried in the local cemetery.

Like that wish, his desire that the house become a writers' colony went unfulfilled. David Baldwin inherited Chez Baldwin, living there until he became ill with terminal cancer. His family brought him back to the United States in 1996. David died in New York on March 10, 1997. While at Chez Baldwin, the Harlem family—the estate owners—who came to settle his affairs burned some of Baldwin's belongings on a pyre in his garden, abandoning the rest. We will never know what was destroyed, but a collection of gay erotic art the writer cherished may have been among the victims. David's lover Jill Hutchinson, an English real estate agent, was not allowed to accompany him to the United States. She took care of the house and its contents, and it was she who saved Baldwin's remaining books and artwork from the dustbin. The house was forfeited to developers in the early 2000s. Neither the French nor the Americans bothered to preserve it. Broken up in 2014, with Baldwin's study and most of the building razed, the remaining bastide disappeared into luxury condos that Sotheby's sold for around 1.5 million euros per unit. This house was the heart, and in some ways the culmination, of the main themes of Baldwin's life—his Black queer humanism, his desire for a loving family and community, and his growing experiments with gender fluidity and embrace of his inner woman. On this last, single-track LP side, we remix all these themes as a coda to his Life Album.

Filled with much work, travel, and teaching, Baldwin's last sixteen years benefited from the reassuring embrace of his Black queer household in France. He wrote much, read outdoors under a palm tree, and dreamed up new projects. Leeming, who visited frequently, recalls the tender environment that Baldwin achieved under his roof. Men greeted each other with a look in the eye and kisses on both cheeks. Passionate embraces from lovers and the laying on of hands to comfort those in need were equally welcome. Baldwin wanted men to emulate feminine subtlety and care. In the epilogue to *No Name in the Street*, he wrote of Americans needing to become "midwives" and mothers to a better world. At that moment in time, he also described that world in a recapitulation of his "Stranger in the Village" conclusion from 1953, opening the second part of No Name, "To Be Baptized," with this charge: "All of the western nations have been caught in a lie . . . of their pretended humanism; . . . their history has no moral justification, and the West has no moral authority." But now women were to be that world's salvation. The epilogue features Black and white Madonnas, a symbolic couple nurturing the new world-child together. In Saint-Paul-de-Vence, inside the structure bought from the former Algerian colonist, the House of Baldwin nurtured an alternative model of domesticity in which such a vision of humanity could thrive.

Buying and maintaining the house, however, required a constant influx of cash. Accordingly, Baldwin worked hard. Beginning in the late 1970s and into the mid-1980s, he gave talks at conferences, received honorary degrees, published, and returned to the United States to teach creative writing and literature courses at universities in Bowling Green, Berkeley, and Amherst. At the University of Massachusetts he received an honorary doctorate in 1978 and celebrated his sixtieth birthday on campus in 1984, with the glamorous Black feminist poet Irma McClaurin and several faculty members, who later defended him against Julius Lester's posthumous charges of anti-Semitism. Baldwin's mother, Berdis, was the guest of honor at his celebration. A photo of them—she bespectacled, in a blue evening dress and pillbox hat, he laughing heartily in a dark navy suit, a sprig of flowers in the lapel—offers a rare glimpse of mother and son in public. That same year the university's New World Theater staged his play Blues for Mister Charlie, directed by the young Roberta Uno, whose innovative approach Baldwin loved.

Working with talented young people like Uno and the up-and-coming Black writers Suzan-Lori Parks and Shay Youngblood brought much joy. In a videorecorded interview at Hampshire College in 1984, Baldwin spoke about his learning curve as a teacher, mentioning the death of the Civil Rights Movement amid a general backlash against progress. He thought all Americans should confront issues of class; he also thought they all should vote. He pointed out that the presence of "queer white people" and Brown and Black people needed to "be felt," finally voicing his support for sexual minorities publicly, albeit to a small academic audience. He talked about these things in the classroom, regaling students with unscripted, expert instruction on writing and literature, along with colorful anecdotes, and conversations that frequently continued after class over drinks. Teaching, it seemed, provided a welcome respite from the hostility that continued to pain him, though he often found being on time too demanding. He was a warm and considerate instructor, often spending long extra hours beyond his required office duties to talk to every student who wanted his advice.

The year 1986 was filled with international trips, including one to London, where his play *The Amen Corner* was feted. In June, he went to Paris to receive the Légion d'Honneur from the French president, François Mitterrand, an event captured in many photographs in the Schomburg Center. He brought both Jeanne Faure and his cook Valerie Sordelo to Paris to attend the lavish ceremony on June 19, 1986, along with his brother David and Lucien Happersberger. A photograph of the ceremony echoes a Delaney canvas: A chic, gaunt, smiling Baldwin in a black suit and white shirt, hair dyed black, hands clasped behind him, stands close to the composer and conductor Leonard Bernstein, another recipient of the medal, who is in snowy white, with a red bowtie and pocket square accenting his starkly contrasting figure. Both petit men are framed by the rich carpet and clustered guests, with David Baldwin supporting a behatted Jeanne Faure, Valerie Sordelo nearby, and Lucien Happersberger invisible.

In October of that year he visited the Soviet Union, months before the commencement of the geopolitical shifts that led to its disintegration. At the invitation of the event's organizer, the Kirghiz writer Chinghiz Aitmatov, James and David Baldwin attended the Issyk-Kul Forum in the Central Asian Soviet Republic of Kirghizia. Baldwin's invitation to address the assembly was a well-earned honor for a working-class son of Harlem, proof of lifetime achievement for someone who was only sixty-two. Like the French Légion d'Honneur, it was the kind of recognition due to extraordinary individuals—the sort of validation his home country never granted him during his lifetime.

Though increasingly unwell, Baldwin presented a lecture on global racism and its consequences. The title of his address is missing; his handwritten notes are chaotic and belabored. They cover the "absence of Africa in the historical record" and "the necessity of envisioning a world without nations," the multi-ethnic, divided United States and its "subjugated cultures Black, Hispanic, Native American, Oriental: connecting with the doom of the poor White."

On October 20, the Forum delegates met the general secretary of the Communist Party, Mikhail Gorbachev, in Moscow. Baldwin liked the new Soviet leader, finding him refreshingly imaginative and open-minded. His sparse handwritten notes from the meeting appear in a luxurious red notebook, adorned in golden Cyrillic, "Moskva, TsK KPCC" (Moscow, Central Committee of the Communist Party of the Soviet Union). An underlined sentence in his shaky handwriting, "The greatest deficit is the deficit in new thinking," highlights the importance of including literary and artistic perspectives in Gorbachev's ambitious program of perestroika, which embraced diversity, nuclear disarmament, ecology, and concern for the disempowered peoples of the developing world. The delegates had collaborated on a general address before arriving in Moscow, and it was presented in front of Gorbachev. A copy, still among Baldwin's papers, rings with his conviction that "the future should depend not only on political decisions and confrontations of power, but also the imagination of men and women of genius." Along with other delegates, Baldwin urged the world to embrace the "initiatives and discoveries of scientists, the dreams of the poets, and the hopes of all people. . . . Only those able to see the invisible will be able to do the impossible. . . . We need the freedom to create, disseminate and teach the new ways of thinking, characterized by diversity and, above all, openness."

Baldwin's unfinished projects reflect a new burst of creativity in his late years; they include treatments for two novels ("No Papers for Mahomet" and "Remember This House") and sketches and titles for women-centered projects: "What Little I Had," "The Bloody Life and Stormy Death of a Certain Miss Shelley St. John," and "Vanessa Kingdom Hightower." As in the unpublished screenplay "The Inheritance," whose main character was a German–African American woman, which he began in the early 1970s, his focus in "The Welcome Table" was transnational, pulling away from America into the complex world around it. Perhaps inspired by Audre Lorde's charge that he try to imagine what it would be like to be a woman (and a lesbian?), his ideas were shifting toward female bodies and their ways of being in a late-twentieth-century world run by men.

The protagonist of "The Welcome Table," Edith Hemings, a Creole singer from New Orleans, is an intriguing transgender figuration of Baldwin, a veritable hybrid of the charismatic artists he knew and admired in Turkey, the United States, and France: Gülriz Sururi, Eartha Kitt, Bertice Reading, Josephine Baker, Maya Angelou, Nina Simone. The play's action takes place over a single day, from early morning until "around midnight" in a large Provençal house modeled on Chez Baldwin, as evidenced in archived set sketches that Baldwin may have drawn. The play's Turkish and transnational roots—he had been working on it since 1969—can be seen in its cast of characters, almost all of them worldly wise women and, as Leeming notes, deliberate self-portraits of the author. This complex text is a cornucopia of all the themes that ran throughout his writing. Mixing and remixing, revolving around one evening in the lives of these characters, filled with moments of dialogue that now read like a farewell from the ailing writer, the play reverberates with his philosophy of Black queer humanism.

"The Welcome Table" blends life writing with dramatic genres inspired by Chekhov's plays as well as African American musical and literary arts. Improvisational and impressionistic, it represents a departure from Baldwin's first two dramas and stands as his last literary testament. Walter Dallas, the director of the Freedom Theatre in Philadelphia, who collaborated with Baldwin on "The Welcome Table," agreed in our 2007 interview that this play was the culmination of Baldwin's previous works. Its progressive racial, gender, and sexual politics, offered a novel, impassioned appraisal of the effects of late-twentieth-century U.S. politics on the domestic lives and private desires of Black artists. Though intimate in focus, it echoed global issues—a prelude to the beginning of the end of the Cold War no one knew would come just two years later.

"The Welcome Table" could be also read as Baldwin's belated response to the younger Black queer activist Joseph Beam, whose invitation in 1985 to contribute to an edited volume on Blackness and gayness Baldwin, typically, never answered. And it could be read as Baldwin's take on what Beam defined as "nationalistic heterosexism"—an approach that would force Black queer people like Beam to prioritize race over sexuality. Baldwin would have rejected these terms, like his protagonist in the play, Edith Hemings, a confident, centered artist who always speaks her mind. Edith never doubts her abilities and charisma, telling her young protégé, Daniel, "I am a pro, bambino." She is the diva and the queen, or, as she is introduced in the Dramatis Personae, an "actress-singer/ star" who has transcended her origins. The play dramatizes Baldwin's proclamation in 1986 about the perils faced by U.S. artists and "the American . . . effort to . . . segregate art. Every artist has an effect on every other artist, you know. So on a certain level one can say that it's not so important to be a black artist. It's important to be an artist. But if you're an artist and happen to be an American black, then your experience comes from a depth and from places that the American republic does not wish to understand, does not wish to confront." And what if that artist is a woman who also happens to be Black?

Shaped by such conflicts, Edith Hemings presides over a veritable court of household dwellers, assistants, visitors, hangers-on, and admirers. In her twilight years, still at the height of her powers, she commands the scene as Baldwin did. Her employees include a cook, a maid, and a Muslim gardener, "Mohammed," whose character, though marginal, is based on an Algerian man who inspired Baldwin's unfinished novel "No Papers for Mahomet" (the spelling of the gardener's name differs between the manuscripts). Edith's strong femininity is a counterweight to the male characters who dominated Baldwin's earlier works and who in this play are placed off center.

As he aged, Baldwin embraced both a feminine persona and a transatlantic perspective—crystallized in the character of Edith Hemings—that often perplexed his more provincial U.S. readers and critics. In this last play, he invents his main character's Louisiana Creole childhood, and remixes themes familiar from his whole career: anxieties about authorship, the importance of music and other artistic forms to writing, the politics of race and racism,

U.S. Cold War imperialism, sexuality, androgyny. His gaze also turns inward, toward alternative home and family arrangements— love for children, close human connections, men shedding their machismo in favor of womanist values, liberated erotic desire. In "The Welcome Table" Baldwin's jackpot—his poor, Black, queer origins—is once more to the fore, as he spins new tunes within his beloved home. He is finally surrounded by his family of choice. Most important, this play and its mood return us full circle to where we began on Side A, with how women, their values, and their ways of being supported him. A metaphor for conviviality, safety, and care, the table in the play's title hints at how eager the writer was to welcome a new, changing world whose horizons and means of communication were expanding rapidly.

"The Welcome Table" marked Baldwin's farewell to his country, which appears as a cold, militaristic power driving conflicts and wars, the backdrop for his characters' international lives. In his last interview with Quincy Troupe, recorded days before his death, Baldwin despaired, "I don't see anything in American life— for myself—to aspire to. . . . Nothing at all. It's all so very false. So shallow, so plastic, so morally and ethically corrupt." He also bemoaned being forgotten in the United States, though Black celebrities like Toni Morrison, Bill Cosby, Maya Angelou, Bobby Short, Miles Davis, Nina Simone, and Stevie Wonder all traveled to see him in Saint-Paul-de-Vence throughout the 1980s, while the French actors Yves Montand and Simone Signoret came to visit often. Baldwin told Troupe about feeling homeless in America and France, and about Black men whose homophobia still hurt him. Though filled with plans for new projects, he knew he was dying, and his words conveyed a parting message. A color snapshot Leeming took during Baldwin's last week of life captures the frail-looking writer sitting wrapped in a burgundy bathrobe, propped up on pillows, watching his brother David across the living room table.

Like their author, all Baldwin's protagonists are misunderstood outcasts. "The morality of this age and I will never come to terms," Baldwin wrote in an untitled manuscript preserved among his archived papers. Probably dating to the late 1970s or 1980s, these handwritten pages seem to be an attempt to pen a conclusion to his life. Filled with memories of lovers, first kisses that "soak me up from the depths of my terrified solitude," and youthful enchantments with men and women, as well as detailed descriptions of early sexual encounters, these notes give us a glimpse of Baldwin's unstoppable imagination as he tried to work faster, his fierce spirit holding on while his body, ravaged by cancer, began to fail.

On the night of November 30–December 1, 1987, Baldwin died, the liminality of his passing marking the transatlantic time difference between his homes of New York and Saint-Paul-de-Vence, and reflecting his split, exilic life. His writer friend Caz (Caryl) Phillips came from London to join David at the wake. Phillips was somewhat disturbed to note that while Baldwin's body was lying in state, his brother allowed the remains to be photographed. The photos were probably taken by Nal, an Alabama-based queer artist, who was a close friend and who painted Baldwin's postmortem portrait that survived him.

An open-access digital collection, which accompanies an online exhibit at the Smithsonian Institution's National Museum of African American History and Culture, preserves images of Baldwin's house and its contents. The objects themselves, still protected by David's partner Jill Hutchinson, have yet to find a permanent home. Like his life, the matter and material embodied in these artifacts resist easy classification. Baldwin's last typewriter, marked with his inked fingerprints, some clothing, knickknacks, and furniture remain with Hélène and Pitou Roux in Saint-Paul-de-Vence. Their mother, Yvonne, whose family owned the inn La

Colombe d'Or, where Baldwin loved drinking and meeting friends over meals, was his bosom friend and the first reader of many of his works. Hélène and Pitou grew up around him and still consider him a beloved uncle.

The poet Nikky Finney once wrote, "Baldwin saw us long before we saw ourselves." A prophet in every sense of the word, Baldwin saw us the way Delaney had seen him on his doorstep in 1940. Perhaps, from the vantage point of 1986, James Baldwin could imagine the dismantling of the Berlin Wall soon after his death. He could envisage the dissolution of the Soviet Bloc and the Soviet Union itself in 1991, when Kirghizia became the independent state of Kyrgyzstan. The challenges to education, humanitarian governance, and ecology that he and others in Issyk-Kul feared might come to pass in the third millennium of the Common Era have by now become our reality. Our "information age" drowns us in internet-generated content that has replaced rigorous news reporting, books, and newspapers. Attention spans, subtlety, and imagination are in short supply, as is critical thinking, while ruthless political power-mongering assaults civil and voting rights, education, and women's bodily autonomy. In the words Toni Morrison addressed to Baldwin in her eulogy: "Those who saw the paucity of their own imagination in the two-way mirror you held up to them attacked the mirror, tried to reduce it to fragments which they could then rank and grade, tried to dismiss the shards where your image and theirs remained—locked but ready to soar."

In today's dire circumstances of war and climate disaster, Baldwin's Black queer humanism provides us with hope and courage. Drawn from the experience of marginalization and pain by a man who was born poor and queer, this philosophy is Baldwin's legacy—his ancestral gift to us. Baldwin never offers easy fixes, and his work is unlikely to spark a popular protest movement, the love-

and-read revolution he so yearned for. But his philosophy is nonetheless a guide for a new way of being, humanist in nature, arising from an anarchic joy in the pleasures of the mind and body alike, mixing intellectual pursuits with the sensual comforts of music, art, flesh, and nature, a way of seeing and feeling that connects us all. Baldwin's rich, bright, fluid philosophy, like one of Delaney's gorgeous abstractions, can be caught out of the corner of the eye, swirling with colors, textures, and rhythms: an invitation to be better than the world. Inside Chez Baldwin, music is still playing, a vinyl record spinning blues in a Black woman's voice, strong and tender. This one is called "The House of Baldwin," and it concludes his Life Album a century after his birth. Come in: there's room for all. Let's embrace good trouble.

CHRONOLOGY

——

1924   Born on August 2 to Emma Berdis Jones, father unknown, Harlem Hospital, New York City

1927   Berdis marries David Baldwin, a preacher from Louisiana, who becomes James's stepfather and gives him his last name

1929   Begins school at P.S. 24 in Harlem

1936–38   Attends Frederick Douglass Junior High School, where he edits the literary magazine *The Pilot*

1938   Begins to preach at the Fireside Pentecostal Assembly church in Harlem

1938–42   Attends DeWitt Clinton High School, where he meets Emile Capouya, Sol Stein, and Richard Avedon and edits the school's literary magazine, *The Magpie*

Begins first drafts of what will become his first novel, *Go Tell It on the Mountain*

1940   Meets the painter Beauford Delaney in Greenwich Village

1942   Graduates from DeWitt Clinton and renounces the pulpit; works at various menial jobs; moves to Greenwich Village

1943   David Baldwin, his stepfather, dies on July 29

1944   Meets Richard Wright

1945   Receives a Eugene Saxton Fellowship on Wright's recommendation

1947   His first book review, "Maxim Gorky as Artist," appears in the *Nation*

1948   Receives the Rosenwald Fellowship

1948   "The Harlem Ghetto: Winter 1948" and short story "Previous Condition" appear in *Commentary;* works with editor Robert Warshow

Leaves for France on November 11; meets close friends Gidske Anderson and Mary Painter in Paris

1949   Essay "Everybody's Protest Novel" published in Parisian magazine *Zero*

Conflict with Richard Wright

Lives in France, with intermittent trips back to the United States until 1957

1949   Meets the Swiss painter Lucien Happersberger, the love of his life, in Paris

1950–53   Visits Switzerland three times with Happersberger; finishes *Go Tell It on the Mountain* and writes the essay "Stranger in the Village," which is published in *Harper's*

1953   *Go Tell It on the Mountain* published by Knopf and nominated for the National Book Award

1954   Act 1 of first play, *The Amen Corner*, published in the Parisian magazine *Zero;* "Gide as Husband and Homosexual" (later retitled "The Male Prison") published in the *New Leader*

Receives a Guggenheim Fellowship

1955   Publishes "Me and My House" in *Harper's* and *Notes of a Native Son*, first essay collection, with Beacon Press

Play *The Amen Corner* performed at Howard University

1956   *Giovanni's Room*, second novel, published by Dial Press

Receives Partisan Review Fellowship and a National Institute of Arts and Letters Grant

1957   Returns to the United States; first trip to the South

Publishes essays in *Harper's* and *Partisan Review*

1959   Selected for Ford Foundation Grant; returns to France

1960   Befriends William Styron, at whose house he will write some of *Another Country*

Throughout the decade he will support the Civil Rights Movement, especially SNCC and CORE, as a speaker and fundraiser

1961   *Nobody Knows My Name: More Notes of a Native Son*, second essay collection, published by Dial and chosen as one of the outstanding books of the year by the Notable Books Council of the American Library Association

1961   Arrives in Turkey, hosted by the actors Engin Cezzar and Gülriz Sururi in Istanbul; he will stay in several locations for intermittent periods until 1971

1962   *Another Country,* third novel, published by Dial and selected for the Brotherhood Award by the National Conference of Christians and Jews

Travels to Africa with his sister Gloria

1963   *The Fire Next Time,* nonfiction volume, published by Dial and selected for the George Polk Memorial Award for outstanding magazine reporting

1964   *Blues for Mister Charlie,* second play, and *Nothing Personal* (with photographs by Richard Avedon) published by Dial and Atheneum, respectively; *Blues* opens at ANTA Theatre on Broadway

Receives the Foreign Drama Critics Award and an honorary Doctorate of Letters from the University of British Columbia

Elected to the National Institute of Arts and Letters

1965   *Going to See the Man,* short story collection, published by Dial

The Amen Corner opens on Broadway at the Ethel Barrymore Theatre

Debates William F. Buckley, Jr., at the University of Cambridge

1968   *The Amen Corner,* complete text, and *Tell Me How Long the Train's Been Gone,* fourth novel published by Dial

1969   Essay "Sweet Lorraine," a tribute to Lorraine Hansberry, published in *Esquire*

Directs and collaborates on stage design and music (with Don Cherry) of the play *Düşenin Dostu* (Turkish title of *Fortune and Men's Eyes*) in Istanbul; the play is shut down, then reopens and tours Turkey

1971   "An Open Letter to My Sister, Miss Angela Davis" published in *New York Review of Books*

A Rap on Race: Mead and Baldwin (Baldwin's discussion with Margaret Mead) published by Lippincott

Arrives in Saint-Paul-de-Vence in Provence and begins renting rooms at the house of Jeanne Faure, then buys the house in increments; ownership contested after his death

1971   *Soul!* TV program featuring Baldwin and Nikki Giovanni in dialogue
        first shown on WNET-TV

1972   Publishes nonfiction volume *No Name in the Street* and *One Day, When
        I Was Lost: A Scenario Based on "The Autobiography of Malcolm X"* with
        Dial

1973   *James Baldwin/Nikki Giovanni: A Dialogue* published by Lippincott

1974   *If Beale Street Could Talk,* fifth novel, published by Dial and chosen
        for the Best Young Adult Book List by the American Library Asso-
        ciation

1976   *The Devil Finds Work,* nonfiction volume, and *Little Man, Little Man:
        A Story of Childhood* (illustrated by Yoran Cazac) published by Dial

        Receives an honorary doctorate from Morehouse College

1979   *Just above My Head,* sixth novel, published by Dial

1982   Awarded honorary degree by City University of New York

1983   *Jimmy's Blues: Selected Poems* published by Michael Joseph in
        London

1985   *The Evidence of Things Not Seen,* nonfiction volume, published by
        Holt, Rinehart and Winston

        The Price of the Ticket: Collected Non-Fiction, 1948–1985, and *Jimmy's
        Blues: Selected Poems,* published by St. Martin's Press

        Go Tell It on the Mountain television film broadcast by PBS in January

1986   Receives the Légion d'Honneur from the French president François
        Mitterand in June

        Visits the Soviet Union for the Issyk-Kul Forum in Kirghizia and
        travels to Moscow, where he meets the secretary general of the Com-
        munist Party of the USSR, Mikhail Gorbachev, in October

1987   *Perspectives: Angles on African Art* with an interview by Baldwin pub-
        lished by the Center for African Art in New York

        "*Architectural Digest* Visits: James Baldwin" published in *Architectural
        Digest* in August

        Dies at age sixty-three at home in Saint-Paul-de-Vence, November
        30–December 1; funeral service on December 8 at the Cathedral of
        Saint John the Divine in New York City; laid to rest at Ferncliff
        cemetery

1989   *Conversations with James Baldwin,* edited by Fred L. Standley and
        Louis H. Pratt, published by the University Press of Mississippi

1989   *Gypsy and Other Poems,* limited edition, illustrated by Leonard Baskin, published by Gehenna Press
1997   Brother David Baldwin dies
1999   Mother Berdis Baldwin dies

NOTES

Note on Sources

Unless indicated otherwise, all manuscripts and unpublished works quoted in the text are in the James Baldwin Papers at the Schomburg Center for Research in Black Culture of the New York Public Library in Harlem.

Baldwin's correspondence with David Leeming, Mary Painter, Orilla "Bill" Miller Winfield, and Arthur Moore is located in the James Baldwin Manuscript Holdings archive at the Beinecke Library at Yale University.

Quotations from Baldwin's published nonfiction works are cited in the Notes, indexed by first words, as are scholarly, journalistic, and online references.

The essays from Baldwin's nonfiction volumes *Notes of a Native Son, Nobody Knows My Name, The Fire Next Time, No Name in the Street,* and *The Devil Finds Work* have been collected in the anthology *The Price of the Ticket* (1985), which is cited throughout.

Introduction

"When you were starting out..." : Excerpted in *The Price of the Ticket: James Baldwin,* dir. Karen Thorsen. California Newsreel, 1989. Hereafter cited as Thorsen.

"finding words hard to pin down...": Caryl Phillips, "Dinner at Jimmy's," in *The European Tribe* (New York: Vintage, 1987), 40.

"the most tweeted literary authority..." : William Maxwell, *James Baldwin: The FBI File* (New York: Arcade, 2017), 6.

"still on brand...": #Dr.JasmineAbrams.

"6 James Baldwin quotes about race": American Masters: James Baldwin, https://www.pbs.org/wnet/americanmasters/james-baldwin-about-the-author/59/ (accessed August 7, 2024).

"community hub": Neda Ulaby, "A Bookstore Named for James Baldwin Is Counting Down to His 100th Birthday," July 28, 2024, NPR, https://www.npr.org/2024/07/28/nx-s1-5020708/james-baldwin-bookstore-new-orleans?fbclid=IwZXhobgNhZWoCMTEAAR2D1u8NwJDTf4PXWgUYLR-3LOG-OwGTZEXkhPeXf7s1Pf6RzWrsx4qatpw_aem_z_30rNf3avEM2r14ZhpVmQ.

"global humanism": David Brooks, "On Staying Humane in Inhumane Times," The Opinions podcast, *New York Times*, November 23, 2023, https://www.nytimes.com/2023/11/23/opinion/brutalizing-humanity-modernity.html?searchResultPosition=1.

"ancestor": Holly Williams, "*The Prophets* by Robert Jones Jr—Outstanding Debut," *The Guardian*, January 4, 2021, available at https://www.theguardian.com/books/2021/jan/04/the-prophets-by-robert-jones-jr-review-outstanding-debut.

"drama of masculinity": Colm Tóibín. *On James Baldwin* (Waltham, Mass.: Brandeis University Press, 2024), 139.

"the book James Baldwin never finished": *I Am Not Your Negro* page, IMDb, tagline, at https://www.imdb.com/title/tt5804038/?ref_=fn_al_tt_1.

"the book that Baldwin never wrote": Raoul Peck, ed., *I Am Not Your Negro: A Major Motion Picture*, directed by Raoul Peck, from texts by James Baldwin (New York: Vintage International, 2017).

"Black ecstatic . . . ": Barry Jenkins, "Baldwin's Black Ecstatic," in *God Made My Face: A Collective Portrait of James Baldwin*, ed. Hilton Als (Brooklyn, N.Y.: Dancing Foxes Press/Brooklyn Museum, 2024), 95–97.

"Black American Socrates . . .": Cornel West, *Democracy Matters: Winning the Fight against Imperialism* (New York: Penguin, 2004), 80.

"spur today's progressives . . . spiritual activism . . .": Jamie McGhee and Adam Hollowell, *You Mean It or You Don't: James Baldwin's Radical Challenge* (Minneapolis: Broadleaf Books, 2022), front flap, 58.

"memorial mosaic": *God Made My Face.*

"man, spirit, voice": JIMMY! *God's Black Revolutionary Mouth*, New York Public Library, https://www.nypl.org/events/exhibitions/jimmy-gods-black-revolutionary-mouth.

"sociopolitical analogies . . . ": Teresa Retzer, "The Seventh Continent: 16th Istanbul Biennal," in *Art Papers*, https://www.artpapers.org/the-seventh-continent/ (accessed April 14, 2024).

"Jimmy the public figure begins . . . ": Philip Lopate, "Baldwin the Prophet vs. Baldwin the Writer: Can a Film Really Capture the Essence of Both?" *American Scholar* (April 28, 2017), available at https://theamericanscholar.org/baldwin-the-prophet-vs-baldwin-the-writer/ (accessed April 14, 2024).

"most important single literary influence": *Conversations with Caryl Phillips*, ed. Renee T. Schatteman (Jackson: University Press of Mississippi, 2009), 25.

"unknown: less read, cited, . . .": Michele Elam, "Review of New York City's 'The Year of Baldwin,'" *James Baldwin Review* 1 (2015): 203, available at https://www.manchesterhive.com/view/journals/jbr/1/1/article-p202.xml (accessed April 14, 2024).

"a strange magic . . . domesticated and reincarnated . . . a massive invasion of his integrity": Maria Diedrich, "James A. Baldwin: Obituaries for a Black Ishmael," in *James Baldwin: His Place in American Literary History and His Reception in Europe*, ed. Maria Diedrich (Frankfurt: Peter Lang, 1991), 131.

"the conscience of his generation . . . How shall we explain the exile . . . ": "Black Writers in Praise of Toni Morrison," *New York Times*, January 24, 1988, available at https://archive.nytimes.com/www.nytimes.com/books/98/01/11/home/15084.html?_r=2.

"A domicile in southern France . . .": Diedrich, "James A. Baldwin."

"true, gritty real stories of black life . . . may shoot me . . .": Percival Everett, *Erasure* (Minneapolis: Graywolf, 2001), 44.

"all countries . . . make of their trials . . . key to [their] . . . imagination . . . We all exist . . .": James Baldwin, "Here Be Dragons," in Baldwin, *The Price of the Ticket: Collected Nonfiction, 1948–1985* (New York: St. Martin's, 1985), 677–90. Further quotations from this essay will be from this edition, which is hereafter cited as *PT*.

"sanctuary for writers": Meet Our Board, La Maison Baldwin, https://www.lamaisonbaldwin.org/about. For the Centennial, see *Baldwin and Black Legacy: Truth, Liberation, Activism*, https://www.lamaisonbaldwin.org/centennial (both accessed August 7, 2024).

"gracefully lilting sentences . . . ": Caryl Phillips, "The Price of the Ticket," *Guardian*, July 14, 2007, available at https://www.theguardian.com/books/2007/jul/14/fiction.jamesbaldwin (accessed April 14, 2024).

"novel-writing and novel-reading . . .": Jacqueline Goldsby, "Closer to Something Unnameable: Baldwin's Novel Form," in *The Cambridge Companion to James Baldwin*, ed. Michele Elam (Cambridge: Cambridge University Press, 2015), 37.

"confessional school of poetry . . .": D. Quentin Miller, "Baldwin and the Rhetoric of Confession," in *James Baldwin in Context*, ed. Miller, 221–32 (Cambridge: Cambridge University Press, 2019), 221.

"thought-provoking, tantalizing . . . ": Langston Hughes, "From Harlem to Paris," review of James Baldwin's *Notes of a Native Son*, *New York Times*, February 26, 1956, available at https://www.nytimes.com/1956/02/26/archives/from-harlem-to-paris.html?searchResultPosition=4.

"Negro in extremis": F. W. Dupee, "James Baldwin and 'The Man,'" in *Modern Critical Views: James Baldwin*, ed. Harold Bloom (New York: Chelsea House, 1986), 11–15.

"nervous, slight, almost fragile figure . . .": "The Nation: Races," *Time*, May 17, 1963, 26–27.

"I have been criticized . . . ": *Cep Dergisi*, "James Baldwin Breaks His Silence," in Fred R. Standley and Louis H. Pratt, eds., *Conversations with James Baldwin* (Jackson: University Press of Mississippi, 1989), 63. This collection is hereafter cited as *Conversations*.

"homosexual funkiness . . .": Robert Reid-Pharr, *Once You Go Black: Choice, Desire, and the Black American Intellectual* (New York: New York University Press, 2007), 108.

"threw into confusion . . . ": Robert Reid-Pharr, "Tearing the Goat's Flesh: Homosexuality, Abjection, and the Production of a Late Twentieth-Century Black Masculinity," *Studies in the Novel* 28, no. 3 (1996): 378–79.

"He described not only the social . . .": Lynn Orilla Scott, *James Baldwin's Later Fiction* (East Lansing: Michigan State University Press, 2002), 170.

"schizoid wrenching": Thorsen.

"penalized for trying to remain . . . ": Eve Auchincloss and Nancy Lynch, "Disturber of the Peace: James Baldwin—An Interview," in *Conversations*, 64–82.

"parable in the form of confession . . . ": David Leeming, *James Baldwin: A Biography* (New York: Henry Holt, 1994), 350–51. Hereafter cited as Leeming.

"literary testament . . . brotherhood . . .": translation mine.

"had wanted to be a musician . . .": Jordan Elgrably and George Plimpton, "The Art of Fiction LXXVIII: James Baldwin," in *Conversations*, 232–54.

"sexless and manufactured . . . Not everything that is faced . . .": James Baldwin, "As Much Truth as One Can Bear," *New York Times*, January 14, 1962.

"impassioned pamphleteer": James Baldwin, "Everybody's Protest Novel," *PT*, 27–34. Further quotations from this essay are from this edition.

"true 20th-century literary heir": Henry Louis Gates, Jr., "Cabin Fever," *New York Times*, October 22, 2006, available at https://www.nytimes.com/2006/10/22 /books/review/Gates.t.html.

"fearful pressures . . . what the citizens . . .": James Baldwin, "A Word from Writer Directly to Reader," in Baldwin, *The Cross of Redemption: Uncollected Writings*, ed. Randall Kenan (New York: Vintage, 2011), 7–8. Further quotations from this essay will be from this volume, hereafter cited as *Cross*.

"a kind of return to my own beginnings . . .": Wolfgang Binder, "James Baldwin:

An Interview," in *Conversations*, 190–209. Further quotations from this conversation will be from this volume.

"I tried to deal with what I was most afraid of . . .": "The Last Interview: Interview by Quincy Troupe, St. Paul de Vence, France, November 1987." In *James Baldwin: The Last Interview and Other Conversations* (Brooklyn, N. Y.: Melville House, 2014): 75–117. This contains the complete interview, portions of which are excerpted in *Conversations* as "Last Testament: An Interview with James Baldwin" and "James Baldwin, 1924–1987: A Tribute—The Last Interview," which I cite below.

"Music is our witness . . . ": James Baldwin, "Of the Sorrow Songs: The Cross of Redemption," in *Cross*, 128–24. Further quotations from this essay will be from this edition.

"all those strangers": Auchincloss and Lynch, "Disturber of the Peace."

"was like a movie . . . ": Douglas Field, "Interview with David Linx," *African American Review* 46, no. 6 (2013): 731–40.

"love, rhythm, then dealing with yourself . . .": Field, "Interview with David Linx": 739.

"various contradictions . . . ": Hilton Als, "Family Secrets," *PEN America*, January 8, 2007.

"a balm of sorts": Valentina Di Liscia, "Listening to the Joy in James Baldwin's Record Collection." *Hyperallergic*, December 18, 2020, https://hyperallergic .com/606491/listening-to-the-joy-in-james-baldwins-record-collection/.

"I've changed precisely because America has not": Elgrably and Plimpton, "The Art of Fiction LXXVIII."

"victimized by my own legend . . . I was right . . .": Quincy Troupe, "James Baldwin, 1924–1987: A Tribute—The Last Interview," in *Conversations*, 287–92. (The words badly placed in time" are from his unpublished autobiographical notes.)

"Martin Luther Queen": W. J. Weatherby, *James Baldwin: Artist on Fire; A Portrait* (New York: Donald I. Fine, 1989), 169; Lee Edelman, *Homographesis: Essays in Gay Literary and Cultural Theory* (New York: Routledge, 1994), 42; Douglas Field, *All Those Strangers: The Art and Lives of James Baldwin* (New York: Oxford University Press, 2015), 67.

"an acclaimed homo sissy artist and activist": Marlon Ross, *Sissy Insurgencies: A Racial Anatomy of Unfit Manliness* (Durham, N.C.: Duke University Press, 2022), 172.

"life-long dedication to . . . ": Leeming, 338.

"two confusions . . . what is called civilization": James Baldwin, *No Name in the Street*, in *PT*, 449–552. Further quotations will be from this edition.

"I begin to hear what I see": Teju Cole, *Blind Spot* (New York: Random House, 2017), 252.

Side A

TRACK 1. OVERTURE

"minor disagreements . . . constructive dialogue": Leeming, 10–11.

"I would not describe my mother as a saint . . .": Wolfgang Binder, "James Baldwin, an Interview," in *Conversations*, 190–209.

"That *is* a good idea . . . ": James Baldwin, *No Name in the Street*, in *PT*, 449–552. Further quotations will be from this edition.

"I knew he *had* to write": Thorsen.

"I want a man . . .": W. J. Weatherby, *James Baldwin: Artist on Fire; A Portrait* (New York: Donald I. Fine, 1989), 96.

TRACK 2. IN MY MOTHER'S KITCHEN

"We can guess how old . . . ": James Baldwin, *No Name in the Street*, in *PT*, 449–552. Unless otherwise noted, further quotations will be from this edition.

"began plotting novels . . . My mother was delighted": James Baldwin, "Autobiographical Notes," in James Baldwin, *Collected Essays* (New York: Library of America, 1998), 5–9.

"I read, without the remotest discrimination . . . ": James Baldwin, *The Devil Finds Work*, in *PT*, 557–636. Further quotations will be from this edition.

"You get the full essence . . . ": "Profiles: Duke Ellington," *New Yorker* (July 1, 1944), 34.

"the greatest crisis in my whole life . . . ": *Margaret Mead/James Baldwin: Rap on Race* (Philadelphia: Lippincott, 1971), 211.

"Caught in the American crossfire . . . Georgia has the Negro": James Baldwin, "The Harlem Ghetto: Winter 1948," in *PT*, 1–12. Further quotations will be from this edition.

"the rats, the murders . . . ": Baldwin, *No Name in the Street*.

"wine-stained . . . every knife and pistol fight . . . a slow, agonizing death . . .": James Baldwin, *The Fire Next Time*, in *PT*, 333–80. Further quotations will be from this edition.

"alabaster Mary . . . despised black mother": James Baldwin, "Epilogue: Who Has Believed Our Report?" *No Name in the Street*, in Baldwin, *Collected Essays*, 475. The epilogue is not included in the *PT* collection.

"draw in [women's] potential . . .": Trudier Harris, *Black Women in the Fiction of James Baldwin* (Knoxville: University of Tennessee Press, 1987), 11.

TRACK 3. SISSY BOYS DON'T BELONG

"silence, rigidity . . . ": Jewell Handy Gresham, "James Baldwin Comes Home," in *Conversations*, 159–67.
"Once, my father gave me a dime . . . ": James Baldwin, "Here Be Dragons," in *PT*, 677–90. Further quotations will be from this edition.
"righteous in the pulpit and a monster . . . ": Eve Auchincloss and Nancy Lynch, "Disturber of the Peace: James Baldwin—An Interview," in *Conversations*, 64–82.
"frightened . . . so badly": Thorsen.
"mostly boys": "Atlanta Child Murders," FBI Records: The Vault, FBI, https://vault.fbi.gov/Atlanta%20Child%20Murders (accessed April 14, 2024).
"Whose little boy are you?": Leeming, 24.
"The young male preacher is a sexual prize . . .": James Baldwin, "To Crush the Serpent," in *Cross*, 158–65. Further quotations will be from this edition.
"For every Sammy Davis . . . ": David Frost, "Are We on the Edge of Civil War?" in *Conversations*, 93–97.
"whores and pimps and racketeers on the Avenue . . .": James Baldwin, *The Fire Next Time*, in *PT*, 333–80. Further quotations will be from this edition.
"presence of her flesh": Leeming, 28.
"slugging it out with Daddy": Thorsen.
"When I entered the church, I ceased . . . ": James Baldwin, *The Devil Finds Work*, in *PT*, 557–636. Further quotations will be from this edition.
"writing for *The New Yorker* . . . ": Teju Cole, *Blind Spot* (New York: Random House, 2017), 252.

TRACK 4. AT THE BLACKBOARD

"You think your pain . . . ": Interview with Jane Howard, *Life* (May 24, 1963), 89.
"has its roots . . . ": James Baldwin, "*Mother* by Maxim Gorky," in *Cross*, 244.
"directed my first play and endured . . . ": James Baldwin, *The Devil Finds Work*, in *PT*, 557–636. Further quotations will be from this edition.
"to which no one else . . .": Baldwin, *The Devil Finds Work*.
"utterly surprised . . .": Lynne Orilla Scott, interview, personal archive.
"with books by white devils": Leeming, 23.

Side B

TRACK 1. THROUGH THE DOOR OF MY LIPS

"A short, round brown man . . .": James Baldwin, "The Price of the Ticket" in *PT*, ix–xx. Further quotations will be from this edition.

"all the stars, all the constellations . . . ": Henry Miller, "The Amazing and Invariable Beauford DeLaney," *Outcast*, 2 (Yonkers, N.Y.: Alicat Bookshop, 1945), 24, available at https://babel.hathitrust.org/cgi/pt?id=uc1.31822041129727 &seq=7.

"principal witness": David Adams Leeming, *Amazing Grace: A Life of Beauford Delaney* (New York Oxford University Press, 1998), 68. Hereafter cited as *Amazing*.

"a Dickensian job . . . ": Baldwin, "The Price of the Ticket."

TRACK 2. THE PRINCE AND HIS SPIRITUAL FATHER

"I have, unhappily, the sort of intelligence . . . ": The interview is unpublished, but I found excerpts (although not this statement) in *James Baldwin's Testimony: Eclectic Interview by Arthur Crossman*, ed. Henry Anderson and Christy Harris (Atlanta: Yeshua Kingdom Church and Temples, 2006).

"emblematic importance to later . . . ": Henry Louis Gates, Jr., "The Black Man's Burden," in *Fear of a Queer Planet: Queer Politics and Social Theory*, ed. Michael Warner (Minneapolis: University of Minnesota Press, 1993), 230–38.

"Dante and their bohemian friends . . . ": *Amazing*, 62.

"On the surface Beauford . . . was all tranquility . . . ": *Amazing*, 51.

"'uppity' ways, his sardonic wit . . . ": Leeming, 38.

"all the time . . . the first walking, living proof . . . ": James Baldwin, "The Price of the Ticket," in *PT*, ix–xx. Further quotations will be from this edition.

"I remember standing on a street corner . . . ": Jordan Elgrably and George Plimpton, "The Art of Fiction LXXVIII: James Baldwin," in *Conversations*, 232–54.

"an example of courage . . .": Baldwin, "The Price of the Ticket."

"painterly writer": D. Quentin Miller, "Shadow and Light: Chiaroscuro in Delaney and Baldwin's 'Sonny's Blues,'" *In a Speculative Light: James Baldwin and Beauford Delaney*, University of Tennessee Humanities Center, February 20–21, 2020.

"On the twenty-ninth of July, in 1943, my father died . . . ": James Baldwin, "Notes of a Native Son," in *PT*, 127–46. Further quotations will be from this edition.

"like a spoiled son . . . ": *Amazing*, 198.

TRACK 3. LETTERS TO JEWISH EDITORS

"I . . . had simply been laughed out . . . ": James Baldwin, "The Price of the Ticket," in *PT*, ix–xx. Further quotations will be from this edition.

"Negro leaders . . . [were] created by the American . . . ": James Baldwin, "The Harlem Ghetto: Winter 1948," in *PT*, 1–12. Further quotations from this source are from this edition.

"You look exceedingly alone . . . ": James Baldwin, "An Open Letter to My Sister Angela Y. Davis," in *Cross*, 206–11.

"my first real editor . . . marvelous ": David C. Estes, "An Interview with James Baldwin," in *Conversations*, 270–80. Further quotations from this interview are from this edition.

"There is no doubt that he wanted more . . . ": Robert Warshow, "An Old Man Gone," in *The Immediate Experience: Movies, Comics, Theatre and Other Aspects of Popular Culture*, ed. Sherry Abel (Cambridge: Harvard University Press, 2002), 90.

"tender, ironic and observant . . . ": James Baldwin, "Maxim Gorki as Artist," *The Nation*, April 12, 1947, reprinted as *"Best Short* Stories by Maxim Gorky" in *Cross*, 239–41.

"I was a black kid . . . ": Estes, "An Interview with James Baldwin," in *Conversations*, 275.

"If you harm this brother . . .": "Peace with American Jews Eludes Jackson," *Washington Post*, February 13, 1984.

"He comes to collect the rent . . . ": "James Baldwin on Blacks and Jews," transcript of a lecture delivered on February 28, 1984, W. E. B. Du Bois Department of Afro-American Studies, University of Massachusetts, Amherst, printed privately, March 1988.

"I am no longer deceived . . .": Julius Lester, *Lovesong: Becoming a Jew* (New York: Arcade, 1988), dedication page.

"anti-Semitism among Negroes . . .": James Baldwin, "Negroes Are Anti-Semitic Because They're Anti-White," in *PT*, 425–34. Further quotations will be from this edition.

"Christofascism": Noah Berlatsky, "What James Baldwin Got Wrong about Black Antisemitism," *Sojourners*, August 14, 2023, https://sojo.net/articles/what -james-baldwin-got-wrong-about-black-antisemitism.

"civilizational apparatus of inequality": Jacques Berlinerblau and Terrence L. Johnson, "Blacks and Jews: Fifty-Five Years after James Baldwin's 'Negroes Are Anti-Semitic Because They're Anti-White,'" *Literary Hub*, April 9, 2022, https://lithub.com/blacks-and-jews-fifty-five-years-after-james-baldwins -negroes-are-anti-semitic-because-theyre-anti-white/.

"just twenty-nine years after . . . ": James Baldwin, "Every Good-Bye Ain't Gone,"
PT, 641–48.

TRACK 4. A LOVER'S KISS IS A VERY STRANGE EVENT

"uneasy members of the same tribe": Hilton Als, "Family Secrets," *PEN America*,
January 8, 2007.

"oblique confession . . .": James Baldwin, "The Price of the Ticket," in *PT*, xi–xx.
Further quotations will be from this edition.

"They told me to burn it!": W. J. Weatherby, *James Baldwin: Artist on Fire; A Portrait* (New York: Donald I. Fine, 1989), 120.

"It did not occur to me . . .": James Baldwin, "Stranger in the Village," in *PT*,
79–90.

"After ten years . . .": Jordan Elgrably and George Plimpton, "The Art of Fiction
LXXVIII: James Baldwin," in *Conversations*, 232–54.

"one of his few close friends": Allan Morrison, "The Angriest Young Man," *Ebony*,
October 1961.

Side C

TRACK 1. BECAUSE MY HOUSE FELL DOWN
AND I CAN'T LIVE THERE NO MORE

"a brilliant young Negro American writer . . .": Studs Terkel, "An Interview with
James Baldwin," in *Conversations*, 3–23.

"re-create the life . . .": James Baldwin, "The Discovery of What It Means to Be
an American," in *PT*: 171–76.

"musical, angular poetics": Ed Pavlić, *Who Can Afford to Improvise? James Baldwin
and Black Music, the Lyric and the Listeners* (New York: Fordham University
Press, 2016), 299.

"I don't know anything about music": James Baldwin, "The Uses of the Blues,"
in *Cross*, 56–66.

"All I had . . . was me . . . ": James Baldwin, "Notes for *The Amen Corner*," in Baldwin, *The Amen Corner* (New York: Dial Press, 1968), xi–xvii. Further quotations will be from this edition.

"children": "Civil Rights—James Baldwin—Interview—Mavis on Four, YouTube,
https://www.youtube.com/watch?v=YUMrEDNiy3I (accessed July 30, 2024).

TRACK 2. I AM ALL THOSE
STRANGERS AND A WOMAN, TOO

"tall and blonde, Baldwin dark and diminutive" James Campbell, *Talking at the Gates: A Life of James Baldwin* (New York: Viking, 1991), 55. Hereafter cited as Campbell.

"sexless and manufactured": James Baldwin, "As Much Truth as One Can Bear," *New York Times*, January 14, 1962.

"with a Dutch-boy haircut . . ." ; "Norwegian girl who saved my life" "exploring each other's souls": Leeming, 58, 69, 58.

"I was fascinated . . .": Siri Lindstad, "Fortellingen om Gidske Anderson," https://sirilindstad.com/fortellingen-om-gidske-anderson/ (originally in Norwegian).

"Put a bone through his nose . . .": Campbell, 58.

"Men and women have all but disappeared . . . ": James Baldwin, "Preservation of Innocence," in James Baldwin, *Collected Essays* (New York: Library of America, 1998) 594–600. Further quotations will be from this edition.

"apprehension of what a woman [is] . . .": James Baldwin, "The Male Prison," in *PT*, 101–5. Further quotations will be from this edition.

"an important innovator . . .": Obituary for Mary Painter, *Chicago Tribune*, October 25, 1991.

"sorriness . . . the weapons": James Baldwin, *The Evidence of Things Not Seen* (New York: Holt, Rinehart and Winston, 1985), 19–21. The Moynihan Report (full name: *The Negro Family: The Case for National Action*) was a report published in 1965 by Daniel Patrick Moynihan that explored the root causes of Black poverty. Its conclusions were and remain controversial.

TRACK 3. TRAVELING THROUGH
THE COUNTRY OF THE SELF

"I have nothing in common with them . . .": "Full Text of 'James Baldwin,'" as reported to the FBI and concerning *The New Crusader*, August 19, 1964, https://archive.org/stream/JamesBaldwinFBIFile/James%20Baldwin%20011_djvu.txt.

"this earth had acquired its color . . . ": Baldwin, "A Fly in Buttermilk," in James Baldwin, *Nobody Knows My Name*, in *PT*, 161–70.

"my unbelieving shock. . . . This man, with a phone call . . . ": James Baldwin, *No Name in the Street*, in *PT*, 449–552. Further quotations will be from this edition.

"territory absolutely hostile . . . ": Baldwin, *No Name in the Street*.

"rebaptized by the flood . . . ": Leeming, 119–20.

"What Europe still gives an American . . .": James Baldwin, "The New Lost Generation," *PT*, 305–14.

"from a distance, from another country . . .": Sedat Pakay, *From Another Place: James Baldwin*, Hudson Film Works, 1973. Further quotations will be from this film.

"rare indeed is an American artist . . . ": Baldwin, "The New Lost Generation."

"distracted look Europeans cultivate . . .": Richard Goldstein, "Go the Way Your Blood Beats: An Interview with James Baldwin," in *James Baldwin: The Last Interview and Other Conversations* (Brooklyn, N.Y.: Melville House, 2014), 55–74. Further quotations are from this edition.

"Because the responsibility of a writer . . . ": *James Baldwin/Nikki Giovanni: A Dialogue* (Philadelphia: Lippincott, 1973), 82. Hereafter cited as *A Dialogue*.

"Manhattan's notoriously expensive restaurants . . . any American writer . . . jazz musicians, dancers . . .": Fern Marja Eckman, *The Furious Passage of James Baldwin* (New York: M. Evans, 1966), 243, 242. Hereafter cited as Eckman.

"sweet Lorraine": James Baldwin, "Sweet Lorraine," in *PT*, 443–48.

"take yourself too *seriously* . . . ostentatiously inept . . . sponged on him shamelessly . . . I didn't want any of this shit . . .": Eckman, 242, 246.

"I was one of the very few black things . . .": *Margaret Mead/James Baldwin: A Rap on Race* (Philadelphia: Lippincott, 1971), 83. Hereafter cited as *Rap*.

"buried with Martin Luther King": Nick Ludington, "Baldwin, in Istanbul, Denies He's Given Up the Struggle," *New York Post*, December 12, 1969.

"Jimmy . . . makes you feel you've still got . . . ": Eckman, 244.

"became a great threat . . .": *Rap*, 83.

"pioneering archivist . . . " William J. Maxwell, "African American Modernism and State Surveillance," in *A Companion to African American Literature*, ed. Gene A. Jarrett. (Chichester, West Sussex, UK: Wiley-Blackwell, 2010), 255.

"an author who has been critical . . . rented an apartment . . . ": "James Baldwin," FBI Records: The Vault, 2 parts, https://vault.fbi.gov/james-baldwin (accessed August 5, 2024).

"white-black conflict . . . running away . . . I cannot imagine a country . . .": "James Baldwin," FBI Records: The Vault.

"feast-or-famine work . . . ": William J. Maxwell, *F.B. Eyes: How J. Edgar Hoover's Ghostreaders Framed African American Literature* (Princeton: Princeton University Press, 2015), 307.

"love affair . . . a kind of attraction": Charles Adelsen, "A Love Affair: James Baldwin and Istanbul." *Ebony* (March 1970), 46.

"racial death wish . . . little jive ass": Eldridge Cleaver, "Notes on a Native Son,"

Ramparts (June 1966): 51–56, available at https://www.unz.com/print/Ram
parts-1966jun-00051/.

"Homosexuality is a sickness just as baby rape . . . bending over and touching . . . ":
Eldridge Cleaver, *Soul on Ice* (New York: McGraw-Hill, 1968), 102.

"Baldwin is a very small man . . . ": "Huey Newton: A Candid Conversation with
the Embattled Leader of the Black Panther Party," *Playboy* (May 1973):
73–90.

"transatlantic commuter": Eve Auchincloss and Nancy Lynch, "Disturber of the
Peace: James Baldwin—An Interview," in *Conversations*, 64–82.

"the terror within": Richard Avedon and James Baldwin, *Nothing Personal*, in *PT*,
381–94. Further quotations will be from this edition.

"despair, dishonesty . . . ": Leeming, 227.

"breathtaking and prophetic witness . . . ": Imani Perry, Foreword to James Baldwin, *Nothing Personal* (Boston: Beacon, 2021), viii.

"Writing is a private endeavor . . . ": David Leeming, "An Interview with James
Baldwin on Henry James," *Henry James Review*, 8, no. 1 (Fall 1986): 51.

"We were truly . . . ": James Baldwin, *One Day, When I Was Lost: A Scenario Based
on "The Autobiography of Malcolm X"* (London: M. Joseph, 1972), 237.

"my way or not at all . . . The American public": Grace Nagata, "I Can't Blow This
Gig: Interview with James Baldwin," *Cinema* (Summer 1968): 2–3.

TRACK 4. THE HOUSES OF BALDWIN

"a fifty-year-old's evaluative reminiscence": Leeming, 332.

"Baldwin-bashing was almost a rite of initiation . . . national identity became
sexualized . . . ": Henry Louis Gates, Jr., "Looking for Modernism," *Black
American Cinema*, ed. Manthia Diawara (New York: Routledge, 1993), 203.

"the odd and disreputable . . . seem to stand forever at an odd . . . ": James Baldwin, *No Name in the Street*, in *PT*, 449–552. Further quotations will be from
this edition.

"sissy heroics": Marlon Ross, *Sissy Insurgencies: A Racial Anatomy of Unfit Manliness* (Durham, N.C.: Duke University Press, 2022), 172.

"cocksucker": Quincy Troupe, "James Baldwin, 1924–1987: A Tribute—The Last
Interview," in *Conversations*, 287–92.

"did not endear himself . . . ": Ernest A. Champion, *Mister Baldwin, I Presume:
James Baldwin—Chinua Achebe. A Meeting of the Minds* (New York: University
Press of America, 1995), 136.

"from New Guinea to Harlem . . . ": *Margaret Mead/James Baldwin: A Rap on Race*
(Philadelphia: Lippincott, 1971), 168. Hereafter cited as *Rap*.

"I am not being as vehemently romantic . . . Ha . . .": *Rap*, 90–91.

"You define people . . .Which is not exactly the point . . .": *Rap*, 91–92.

"an essential element . . . I don't agree . . .": *Rap*, 95.

"All the things you do . . .": *Rap*, 50.

"You've simply got to force the language . . .": *Rap*, 51.

"Since you're talking about . . .": *Rap*, 51–52.

"I don't understand . . . I don't like white people . . .": *James Baldwin / Nikki Giovanni: A Dialogue* (Philadelphia: Lippincott, 1973), 43–45. Hereafter cited as *A Dialogue*.

"the words 'white' and 'black' . . . Even today . . . black men say . . .": *A Dialogue*, 45–47.

"People invent categories . . . ," "He's not mad at you. . .": *A Dialogue*, 89–91.

"He's mad the same way . . . ": *A Dialogue*, 91.

"One cannot, and I'm not knocking . . . They were your brothers . . .": *A Dialogue*, 57.

"penalized by history . . . exactly like a Russian Orthodox . . ." *Rap*, 223–25.

"the band of mediocrities which appear to rule this country," *Rap*, 96

"real suffering is when the iron is on your flesh . . .": *Rap*, 236.

"all those strangers called Jimmy Baldwin . . .": Eve Auchincloss and Nancy Lynch, "Disturber of the Peace: James Baldwin—An Interview," in *Conversations*, 64–82.

"the power and the glory . . . ": James Baldwin, Introduction, in Michael Thelwell, *Duties, Pleasures, and Conflicts: Essays in Struggle* (Amherst: University of Massachusetts Press, 1986), xxii.

"few people . . . without antecedents . . .": Sedat Pakay, *James Baldwin: From Another Place*, Hudson Film Works, 1973. Further quotations will be from this film.

"All of the American categories . . . ": James Baldwin, "Here Be Dragons," in *PT*, 677–90. Further quotations will be from this edition.

"weak . . . too pat . . . refusal to accept the conventional definition of masculinity": Dennis Altman, *Homosexual: Oppression and Liberation* (London: Allan Lane, 1974), 206–7.

"Identity would seem to be the garment . . . ": James Baldwin, *The Devil Finds Work*, in *PT*, 557–636. Further quotations will be from this edition.

"love of silk . . . James Baldwin would be transformed . . .": Leeming, 377.

"He was . . . like a grand-mother . . . ": Jules B. Farber, *James Baldwin: Escape from America, Exile in Provence* (Gretna, La.: Pelican, 2016), 37.

"The discovery of one's sexual . . . ": Richard Goldstein, "Go the Way Your Blood Beats: An Interview with James Baldwin," in *James Baldwin: The Last Interview and Other Conversations* (Brooklyn, N.Y.: Melville House, 2014), 55–74.

"creative energy . . .": Audre Lorde, "Uses of the Erotic: The Erotic as Power," in *Sister Outsider* (New York: Penguin, 2020): 41–48.

"warrior poet": Audre Lorde, "The Transformation of Silence into Language and Action," in *Sister Outsider,* 30.

"forty-nine-year-old Black lesbian feminist . . .": Audre Lorde, "Age, Race, Class, and Sex: Women Redefining Difference," in *Gender through the Prism of Difference,* 6th ed., ed. Maxine Baca Zinn et al. (Oxford: Oxford University Press, 2020), 198.

"I usually find myself . . .": Audre Lorde, "Age, Race, Class, and Sex," 198.

"I have always wanted . . .": Audre Lorde, *Zami: A New Spelling of My Name; A Biomythography* (Toronto: Crossing Press, 1982), 7.

"transformation of silence into language . . .": Lorde, *Zami,* 31.

"You're never really a whole person . . . ": Audre Lorde, "The Transformation of Silence into Language and Action." In *Sister Outsider,* 30.

"[A] man has a certain story to tell . . .": "James Baldwin and Audre Lorde: Revolutionary Hope; A Conversation," *Essence* (December 1984). Further quotations will be from either this article or the original unpublished transcript.

"walk disorderly . . . the possibility of the private life . . . ": James Baldwin, "To Crush the Serpent," in *Cross,* 158–65. Further quotations will be from this edition.

"exclude someone . . . the arrival of Toni . . .": James Baldwin, speech to the National Press Club, December 10, 1986, YouTube, https://www.youtube.com /watch?v=VRTOe8UOxN8.

"strait-jacketing of both sexes": Casey Hayden and Mary King, "Sex and Caste: A Kind of Memo," *Liberation* 10 (1965): 133–36, available at https://www.freedom archives.org/Documents/Finder/Black%20Liberation%20Disk/Black%20 Power!/SugahData/Essays/Hayden.S.pdf.

Side D

TRACK 1. CODA CHEZ BALDWIN

"It found me just in time . . .": "*Architectural Digest* Visits: James Baldwin," photographs by Daniel H. Minassian and text by James Baldwin, *Architectural Digest* (August 1987): 122–25.

"tranquil setting . . .": Jules Farber, *James Baldwin: Escape from America, Exile in Provence* (Gretna, La.: Pelican, 2016), 185.

"Theatricality was central to his nature . . .": James Campbell, *Talking at the Gates: A Life of James Baldwin* (New York: Viking, 1991), 262.

"midwives": James Baldwin, "Epilogue: Who Has Believed Our Report?" *No Name in the Street,* in James Baldwin, *Collected Essays* (New York: Library of America, 1998), 475. The epilogue is not included in the *PT* collection.

"All of the western nations have been caught in a lie . . .": James Baldwin, *No Name in the Street,* in *PT,* 449–552.

"queer white people . . . be felt": "1984 James Baldwin Interview: Hampshire College Archives and Special Collections," May 1984, Hampshire College TV, YouTube, https://www.youtube.com/watch?v=fT1eh43acUo (accessed on August 16, 2024).

"nationalistic heterosexism": Joseph Beam, "Brother to Brother: Words from the Heart," in *In the Life: A Black Gay Anthology,* ed. Joseph Beam (Boston: Alyson, 1989), 230–42.

"the American . . . effort to . . .": James Baldwin and Clayton Riley, "James Baldwin on Langston Hughes," *Langston Hughes Review* 15, no. 2 (Winter 1997): 125–37.

"I don't see anything in American life . . . ": Quincy Troupe, "James Baldwin, 1924–1987: A Tribute—The Last Interview," in *Conversations,* 287–92.

"Baldwin saw us long before we saw ourselves . . . " Nikky Finney, Introduction, in James Baldwin, *Jimmy's Blues* (Boston: Beacon, 2014), xxi.

"Those who saw the paucity of their own imagination . . .": Toni Morrison, "James Baldwin: His Voice Remembered; Life in His Language," *New York Times,* December 20, 1987.

SELECT ONLINE RESOURCES

―――――

Documentaries and Podcasts

I Am Not Your Negro. Directed by Raoul Peck. Velvet Film, coproduced by Artémis Productions and Close Up Films, 2016. Trailer available at https://www.imdb .com/title/tt5804038/?ref_=fn_al_tt_1.

James Baldwin: From Another Place. Directed by Sedat Pakay. Hudson Film Works, 1973. https://www.sedatpakay.com/james-baldwin-from-another-place.

James Baldwin: The Price of the Ticket. Directed by Karen Thorsen. California Newsreel, 1989. Aired on *PBS American Masters*, August 23, 2013. https://www .pbs.org/wnet/americanmasters/james-baldwin-film-james-baldwin-the -price-of-the-ticket/2632/.

Lost Archives of James Baldwin, The. BBC SOUNDS Radio 4. Aired on July 30, 2024. https://www.bbc.co.uk/sounds/play/m0021vyz.

Martin, Aldo B., and Dr. Frank Leon Roberts. *Finding James Baldwin: The Magpie Years*. Podcast. https://open.spotify.com/show/23KTWwrrZ5Qm73SA07L0NZ.

Sunday Feature: Nobody Knows My Name: Notes on James Baldwin. BBC Radio 3 Documentary. Aired September 24, 2017. https://www.bbc.co.uk/programmes /p05h0xd1.

Take This Hammer. Documentary. Premiered on February 8, 1964. Film and transcript at https://www.pbs.org/wnet/exploring-hate/2022/04/18/full-film -more-take-this-hammer-1964/.

"Magdalena Zaborowska on James Baldwin's Turkish Decade." In conversation with William Armstrong. Podcast. July 7, 2020, Turkey Book Talk, https:// turkeybooktalk.podbean.com/?s=Zaborowska.

Interviews with Author

2023   Interview with Morteza Hajizahed about *James Baldwin's Turkish Decade*, March 18, 2023. New Books Network, https://newbooksnetwork .com/james-baldwins-turkish-decade.

2021   "James Baldwin and Being Better Than the World." Cultural Medallion Dedication for James Baldwin. Historical Preservation Society of New York, May 25, 2021. YouTube, https://www.youtube.com/watch?v=_kfa SlebH-M.

2020   Interview with Efe Oc, BBC News/Turkey. YouTube. https://www.you tube.com/watch?v=E6zFOo4wI2Q.

2018   "Tracy Sharpley-Whiting's 'Bricktop's Paris' and Magdalena J. Zaborowska's 'Me and My House,'" Black Agenda Report, BAR Book Forum, November 7, 2018. https://www.blackagendareport.com/bar-book-forum -tracy-sharpley-whitings-bricktops-paris-and-magdalena-j-zaborowskas -me-and-my-house.

"The Forum: The American Author James Baldwin." BBC World Service. September 4, 2018, https://www.bbc.co.uk/programmes/w3cswpsg.

Other

Askaripour, Mateo. "The Stylish Literary Legacy of Mr. James Baldwin." Mr Porter, February 19, 2022, https://www.mrporter.com/en-ca/journal/fashion /james-baldwin-style-legacy-american-authors-black-history-10457564.

Beauford Delaney and James Baldwin: Through the Unusual Door. Exhibition, Knoxville Museum of Art, February 7–October 25, 2020. Information available at https://knoxart.org/event/beauford-delaney-and-james-baldwin-through -the-unusual-door/ (accessed April 13, 2024).

Chez Baldwin: An Exploration of James Baldwin's Life and Works through the Powerful Lens of His House "Chez Baldwin" in St. Paul de Vence, France. Exhibition, National Museum of African American History and Culture/Smithsonian. Information available at https://nmaahc.si.edu/explore/exhibitions/chez -baldwin (accessed April 13, 2024).

Comprehensive Catalog of Works by James Baldwin, A. https://www.baldwinbib liography.com/ (accessed April 13, 2024).

James Baldwin Project. https://jamesbaldwinproject.org/.

James Baldwin Review. Available in print and online at https://www.manchester hive.com/view/journals/jbr/jbr-overview.xml.

Jones, Josh. "Listen to James Baldwin's Record Collection in a 478-track, 32-Hour Spotify Playlist." Open Culture, December 29, 2020, https://www.openculture

.com/2020/12/listen-to-james-baldwins-record-collection-in-a-478-track-32
-hour-spotify-playlist.html (accessed April 13, 2024).

Kaufman, Liz. "6 James Baldwin Quotes about Race." PBS American Masters, August 4, 2020. https://www.pbs.org/wnet/americanmasters/6-james-baldwin -quotes-race/15142/.

Ndegeocello, Meshell. *No More Water: The Gospel of James Baldwin.* CD. Blue Note. Reviewed in Stéphane Ollivier, "Album of the Week: Meshell Ndegeocello," Qobuz, August 5, 2024, https://www.qobuz.com/us-en/magazine/story/2024 /08/05/album-of-the-week-meshell-ndegeocello/.

Smith, Roberta. "Beauford Delaney: Portraits Glowing with Inner Light." Review of *Be Your Wonderful Self* exhibition at Michael Rosenfeld Gallery. *New York Times,* October 14, 2021. Available at https://www.nytimes.com/2021/10/14 /arts/design/beauford-delaney-rosenfeld-gallery.html.

Zaborowska, Magdalena J. "The Best Books on James Baldwin as a Black Queer Exile." Shepherd, https://shepherd.com/best-books/james-baldwin-as-a -black-queer-exile (accessed August 13, 2024).

Zaborowska, Magdalena J. "'Chez Baldwin' Writer's House Digital Collection." University of Michigan Library, https://quod.lib.umich.edu/b/baldwin1ic?g =photo-ic;page=index (accessed August 13, 2024).

Zaborowska, Magdalena J. "James Baldwin." In *The Literary Encyclopedia.* October 25, 2002, https://www.litencyc.com/php/speople.php?rec=true&UID=229.

Zaborowska, Magdalena J. "James Baldwin." Oxford Bibliographies. Updated June 28, 2016, https://www.oxfordbibliographies.com/display/document /obo-9780190280024/obo-9780190280024-0031.xml?rskey=qURHwf& result=1&q=James+Arthur+Baldwin#firstMatch.

Zaborowska, Magdalena J. "The Last Days of James Baldwin's House in the South of France: Where Miles Davis, Nina Simone, Stevie Wonder and More Once Met." Literary Hub, April 27, 2018, https://lithub.com/the-last-days-of-james -baldwins-house-in-the-south-of-france/.

Zaborowska, Magdalena J. "What Was James Baldwin's Life in France Like?" Slide show of the author's original photographs. The Advocate, April 27, 2018, https://www.advocate.com/books/2018/4/27/what-was-james-baldwins-life -france#rebelltitem1.

ACKNOWLEDGMENTS

I AM GRATEFUL to the Black Lives series editors at Yale University Press, Professors Jacqueline Goldsby, David Blight, and Henry Louis Gates, Jr., for entrusting me with this book. I especially thank Jackie for generously discussing, in a Zoom conversation during the worst of the COVID lockdown, my ideas about Black queer humanism. I cherish her steadfast support and her faith in my work.

Seth Ditchik at Yale University Press got me started. Since Jessie Kindig took over as the series editor, she has been a model reader, guide, and invaluable interlocutor as my shape-shifting manuscript metamorphosed into its final form. I'm also grateful to the anonymous external readers for their rigorous fact checking and thoughtful revision suggestions. Thanks to the production staff at Yale University Press, and especially Susan Laity for her superb copyediting.

I thank my intrepid family members, friends, and colleagues who have commented on the first difficult drafts, especially my partner Yeidy M. Rivero, Cazmir Thomas-Jordan Zaborowski, Kasia Kietlinska, and David Leeming. This is my first foray writing for a general audience, and I also thank Anitra Gonzales and Danielle

LaVaque-Manty for helping me wrestle early drafts into a form that let my ideas evolve and spin alongside Baldwin's.

At the Schomburg Center for Research in Black Culture I received assistance from archivists and staff, especially Bridgett Pride and Cheryl Beredo. My son Cazmir spent a week there transcribing many pages of precious material. As always, he's my heart and my most important reader. I also thank my colleagues at the University of Michigan's Institute for the Humanities, Danny Herwitz, Sid Smith, Peggy McCracken. My wonderful colleagues— Kristin Hass, Greg Dowd, Mary Kelly, June Howard, Anthony Mora—and others in the departments of American Culture and Afroamerican and African Studies have my gratitude. Frieda Ekotto and Sandra Gunning have been my feminist immigrant literary interlocutors and role models for over two decades.

Funding that enabled numerous trips to the Schomburg Center and assisted with costs of editing and production came from the University of Michigan–Ann Arbor's College of Literature, Science, and the Arts, Institute for the Humanities, and my two departments. UM's generous ADVANCE and SUCCEED programs, and colleagues, students, and staff across campus, too numerous to mention here, all have my warmest thanks.

I am indebted to the Baldwin tribe of scholars, artists, intellectuals, writers, and mentors who have nourished my thinking and helped me grow. Many are friends with whom I dearly wish I had more time to keep up: Lynn Orilla Scott, David Leeming, Ed Pavlic, E. Patrick Johnson, Nicholas F. Radel, Quentin Miller, Brian Norman, Nick Boggs, Robert Reid-Pharr, Marlon Ross, Doug Field, Sharon Holland, Meta DuEwa Jones, Patricia Parker, Hilton Als, Amy Elias, Mary Campbell, Ewa Luczak, Ania Pochmara, Agata Mlynarska, Stephen Wicks, Michelle Elam, Kathy Pakay, Helen Baldwin, Trevor Baldwin, Jill Hutchinson, Lorraine Fox, Paul Cato, Hélène and Pitou Roux, Eric Freeze. I wish the late Sedat Pakay could read this book. My students have my deepest gratitude for moments of textual revelation and delight in the classrooms that we have shared in the United States and beyond.

As always, my life has been sustained by my family in Poland, Belgium, and the United States. I hold them close and thank them for being there for me through it all.

INDEX

Abernathy, Ralph, 180
Actors Studio, and staging of *Blues for Mister Charlie*, 190–91
Adelsen, Charles, 192
Aitmatov, Chinghiz, 246
Albee, Edward, *The Death of Bessie Smith*, 150
All the Women Are White, All the Blacks Are Men, But Some of Us Are Brave (Hull, Bell-Scott, and Smith), 232
Als, Hilton, 6, 9, 11, 136, 137; on Black queer identities, 136, 137; "Family Secrets," 25
Altman, Dennis, *Homosexual: Oppression and Liberation*, 221, 222–23
Altman, Robert Mark, 87
American Civil Liberties Union, 4
American Fiction (cinematic adaptation of *Erasure*), 12
American Masters (PBS), 4
Amos 'n' Andy Show, 86–87
Anderson, Alston, *Lover Man*, 125–26
Anderson, Gidske: as influence on Baldwin's writing, 156–59, 212,

216; *Mennesker i Paris* (People in Paris), 157
Angelou, Maya, 15, 31, 52, 220, 221, 235, 250
Anzaldúa, Gloria, 29; *This Bridge Called My Back*, 231–32
Auchincloss, Eve, 219
auto-theory, and Baldwin's approach to storytelling, 15–16
Avedon, Richard, 87, 88, 191; Baldwin's collaboration with, 196, 197
Ayer, Gertrude E., 38, 77, 80

Baker, Houston A., Jr., 9, 10
Baker, Josephine, 54
Balamir, Oktay, 192
Baldwin, Barbara (grandmother), 43
Baldwin, Berdis Jones (mother), 7, 244; Baldwin's relationship with, 35–37; and marriage to David Baldwin, 42; and Bill Miller, 78–79; as presence in Baldwin's writing, 41, 50–52
Baldwin, David (brother), 6, 107, 144, 166, 171, 245; and Baldwin's business affairs, 242

Baldwin, David (stepfather), 7, 36, 78; abusive behavior of, 53–54; anti-Semitism of, 115; Baldwin's difficult relationship with, 43, 53, 57–58, 60, 99, 144–45, 161, 169; death of, 94–95, 104, 112–13; as presence in Baldwin's writing, 42, 57–60

Baldwin, James: activism of, 100–101; alcoholism of, 107; on the American literary canon, 20–21; archives of, 3, 13–14; and artistic collaborations with artists and photographers, 196–97; author's approach to biography of, 14–18, 23, 25–26, 31–32; on being a Black queer person in America, 18–20, 108–9; on Black-Jewish relations, 48, 84, 116–21, 130–33; Black queer humanism of, 25–26, 27–28, 31, 56, 106, 134, 153, 175, 219, 224, 233, 243, 248, 252–53; on Black women writers, 235–36; as book reviewer, 116, 127–28, 210; celebrations of the life of, 6, 11–12, 13–14; celebrity status of, 3–7, 183–84; childhood of, 38–39, 42, 43–44, 53–54; childhood infatuations of, 62–65; childhood trauma experienced by, 58–60, 228; conflicted sexuality as problematic for, 205–6; and confusion relating to his sexuality, 44, 54–56, 63–64, 134, 138–39, 160–61; in conversation with Giovanni, 204, 207, 211–16, 223; in conversation with Lorde, 204, 207, 226–33; in conversation with Mead, 206–11; death and

funeral of, 9, 144, 251; and decision to leave the church, 73–74; Delaney as mentor to, 91–96, 99–100, 103, 105–7, 114, 151, 159; Delaney's portraits of, 93–94, 97–98, 99–100, 109–10; depression experienced by, 2–3, 99, 107, 111, 122, 144, 167, 169, 183; documentaries about, 5, 7, 18–19, 36, 54, 58–59; as early reader, 44–45, 76–77; education of, 38, 74–75, 77–78, 80–86; emotional struggles experienced by, 99–101; family background of, 7; FBI file on, 186–88; on fiction as truth, 22; film adaptations of works by, 5; financial difficulties of, 126–27; gender anxiety as manifested by, 218–19; on gender fluidity, 159–60, 162–63; Harlem as described by, 46–49; hashtags relating to, 4; his family's expectations of, 181; honors and recognition awarded to, 8, 28–29, 167, 245; as iconic Brand, 3–4; as influence and inspiration, 4–5, 9, 30–32; inner life of, 2–3; jobs held by, 103–5; juvenilia of, 66, 94; on labels as fictions, 27–29; last days of, 241–53; legacy of, 7, 10–12; life abroad as experienced by, 8, 152–53, 154–56; on literature and love, 26–27; and love of family, 49–50; male mentors to, 91–96; music as inspiration for, 24, 150–51; origins and identity of, 1–2, 27–28; Pakay's film and photos of, 187–88, 221; poverty as experienced by, 43–44; on

prominent white authors, 20–21; and prison as metaphor, 192–93; in prison in Paris, 181–82; as prophet, 252; public role of, 8, 151–52; quotations from works by, 11; racial discrimination experienced by, 105, 133; record collection of, 26; renewed interest in, 10–11; reviews of works by, 17; on the role of writing in society, 20–21; romantic infatuations of, 62–64; and screenplays based on autobiography of Malcolm X, 199–202; as secular humanist, 127; self-awareness of, 166; sexuality of, as expressed in his writings, 8, 66–68, 69, 74, 135–36, 138–39, 140–42, 156–57, 160–61, 235; sexuality of, as part of his identity, 1–2, 15–16, 18, 25, 26–30, 39, 55, 57, 67–68, 158–59, 162–63, 181, 204–6, 226, 234; Bessie Smith as influence on, 150–51; social media presence relating to, 3–4; suicide attempts by, 111, 144, 167, 181–82; symposia and exhibitions honoring, 6; as teacher of writing, 153; teachers of, 77–83; as teenage preacher, 64–65, 66, 68–69, 79; on "the terror within," 197–99; translations of works by, 8; on *Uncle Tom's Cabin*, 46; unfinished projects of, 247; as victim of sexual abuse, 60–61; vulnerability of, 98; women's influence on, 15–16, 151, 156, 179; and writing as journey to self-knowledge, 108
—Fiction by: *Another Country*, 3, 8,

22, 25, 49, 50, 68, 112, 116, 125, 136, 139–40, 150, 155, 156, 165, 169–70, 172–73, 174, 182, 184, 188, 191, 222; "Any Boot-Legger," 107; "Be the Best," 86; "Come Out the Wilderness," 19, 235; "Crying Holy," 60; "The Deathbed Conversion," 51–52; "The Death of the Prophet," 70–71, 95, 122–24; *Giovanni's Room*, 3, 8, 22, 68, 110, 132, 140, 143, 155, 156, 157, 161, 164, 167, 169, 193, 222–23; *Going to Meet the Man*, 8, 174, 178, 235; *Go Tell It on the Mountain*, 3, 8, 23, 38, 41–42, 49, 51, 52–53, 57, 59, 65, 74, 132, 133, 142, 156; *Harlem Quartet: La Cosmopolite*, 19; "Holy City," 228; "I, John," 36–38, 40–41, 59–60; *If Beale Street Could Talk*, 5, 8, 49, 50, 51, 112, 116, 136, 172, 173–74, 190, 193, 196, 235; "An Incident in London," 88; *Just above My Head*, 8, 19, 23, 24, 31, 49, 50–51, 58, 61–62, 68, 136, 174, 185, 193, 196, 222, 233; *Little Man, Little Man: A Story of Childhood*, 47, 49, 50, 138; "Mississippi Legend," 88; "No Papers for Mahomet," 249; "One Sunday Afternoon," 86; "The Outing," 235; "Peace on Earth," 87–88; "Previous Condition," 52, 95; "The Prisoner," 52; "Spring 1949," 167–68; *Tell Me How Long the Train's Been Gone*, 8, 15, 20, 68, 136, 150, 156, 165, 184, 191, 193, 194, 196, 222; "That Evening Train May Be Too Late," 137–39, 140; "What Little I Had," 107

Baldwin, James (*continued*)
—Nonfiction by: "As Much Truth as One Can Bear," 20–21, 22; "The Black Boy Looks at the White Boy," 117; "Dark Days," 178; *The Devil Finds Work*, 8, 45, 71–72, 73, 74, 78, 79, 83, 150, 178, 202, 203, 225; "Dialog in Black and White," 117; "The Discovery of What It Means to Be an American," 149, 150, 155; "Down at the Cross," 69, 177; "Encounter on the Seine: Black Meets Brown," 155; "Equal in Paris," 182; "Everybody's Protest Novel," 20, 21, 45, 127, 134; "Every Good-Bye Ain't Gone," 134; *The Evidence of Things Not Seen*, 5, 8, 62, 175, 178, 193; *The Fire Next Time*, 5, 48, 65, 69, 71, 73, 111, 118, 177, 184, 193; "A Fly in Buttermilk," 179; "The Harlem Ghetto: Winter 1948," 47–48, 84, 94, 95, 105, 116, 117–18, 119, 132, 133; "Here Be Dragons," 12–13, 31, 58, 68, 83, 141, 160, 221–22, 224, 226, 233; "The Male Prison," 163, 172, 210; "Maxim Gorki as Artist," 127–28; "Me and My House," 79–80, 110; "Negroes Are Anti-Semitic Because They Are Anti-White," 132, 178; "The New Lost Generation," 182; *Nobody Knows My Name: More Notes of a Native Son*, 8, 149, 150, 163, 179, 181; *No Name in the Street*, 8, 29, 36, 40–41, 42–43, 48, 49–50, 108, 111, 144, 150, 175–76, 178, 180, 181, 184, 193, 195, 209, 220, 243–44; "Notes for *The Amen Corner*," 151; "Notes of a Native Son" (essay), 73, 94, 110, 112–13, 134; *Notes of a Native Son* (essay collection), 8, 17; "Notes on the House of Bondage," 178, 193; "Of the Sorrow Songs: The Cross of Redemption," 24, 150; "An Open Letter to Mr. Carter," 178; "The Preservation of Innocence," 162–63, 172, 210; "The Price of the Ticket," 91, 92, 94, 105, 106, 108–9, 116, 137, 141, 163, 224, 233; "A Question of Identity," 155; "Stranger in the Village," 142–43; "Theater: The Negro In and Out," 150; "To Crush the Serpent," 66, 162, 226, 233–34; "The Uses of the Blues," 150; "White Man's Guilt," 178; "White Racism or World Community," 178; "A Word from Writer Directly to Reader," 22, 23
—Plays and poetry by: *The Amen Corner*, 8, 19, 142, 245; *Blues for Mister Charlie*, 3, 8, 111, 184, 190–92, 244; *Jimmy's Blues*, 25, 178; *These Two*, 66–67; "The Welcome Table," 20, 31, 237, 247–49, 250
Baldwin and Black Legacy: Truth, Liberation, Activism (festival), 13
Baldwin & Co. bookstore and coffee shop, 4
Balfour, Lawrie, 11
Baraka, Amiri, 6, 9, 205; "Brief Reflections on 2 Hot Shots," 205
Basie, Count, 24
Beam, Joseph, 248
Bearden, Romare, 87
Beauvoir, Simone de, 154

Beinecke Library (Yale University), 3, 80
Belafonte, Harry, 19, 92, 145
Bellow, Saul, 121, 155
Bell-Scott, Patricia, 232
Bernstein, Leonard, 245–46
Binder, Wolfgang, 23, 35–36
Birstein, Ann, 158
Black American Writer, 219
Black Arts Movement, 205
Black feminists, 15–16; and new understandings of race, gender, and sexuality, 29
Black literature, devaluation of, 9–10
Black Lives Matter, 4
Black Panthers, 29; Baldwin's defense of, 223
Black people: evolving terminology applied to, 29; Jews as perceived by, 117–19, 120–21
Black Power Movement, 31, 177. *See also* Cleaver, Eldridge
Black Queer Studies, 30
Blacks, Jews, and race relations, as theme in Baldwin's work, 116–19, 128–33
Blint, Rich, 11
Blues for Mister Charlie (Baldwin), staging of, 190–91
Bogart, Humphrey, 72
Boggs, Nicholas, 11
Boughton, Priscilla, 155
Boyd, Herb, 11
Brandhagen, Bishop Gladys, 64
Brando, Marlon, 104, 191
Brim, Matt, 11
Brooks, David, 4
Brown, Geoff, *I Want What I Want*, 221
Brown v. Board of Education, 84

Cain, James M., 163
Calypso (restaurant): Baldwin's connection with, 103–4
Campbell, James, 11, 157–58, 242
Campbell, Mary, 111–12
Camus, Albert, 154
Caplan, Cora, 11
Capouya, Emile, 72–73, 87, 88, 104, 136
Carmichael, Stokely (Kwame Ture), 153
Cavanaugh, Inez, 155
Cazac, Yoran, 49
Cep Dergisi (Turkish literary journal), 17, 185
Cezzar, Engin, 83, 136, 164, 170, 185, 193, 194
Champion, Ernest A., 205
Cherry, Don, 192
Chez Baldwin (Baldwin's home in France), 241–43
Childress, Alvin, 86–87
Christian, Barbara, 15
Civil Rights Movement: Baldwin as fundraiser for, 178; Baldwin's involvement with, 8, 177, 178, 179; Baldwin's writings relating to, 178–79; Delaney as speaker in support of, 110; images of Black men as projected by, 16; impact on Baldwin of the murders of leaders of, 180–81
Clark, Kenneth, 77, 84
Clark, Mamie, 84
Clarke, Romeo, 62–63
Cleaver, Eldridge, 218; Baldwin's response to, 195–96, 223; on Baldwin's sexuality, 195; *Soul on Ice*, 96, 194–95

Coates, Ta-Nehisi, 9; *Between the World and Me,* 4–5

Cocteau, Jean, 154

Cohen, Elliot E., 48

Cohen, Rachel, 11

Cold War, Baldwin as critic of America's role in, 185–86

Cole, Teju, 9; *Blind Spot,* 31–32, 73

Coleman, Milton, 130

Commentary, Baldwin's publications in, 48, 70, 116, 122–24

Congress of Racial Equality (CORE), 8, 80, 178

Cosby, Bill, 250

Crawford, Cheryl, 190–91

Crisis magazine, 4

Crossman, Arthur, 44, 99, 115

Cullen, Countee, 54, 67, 86, 105

Dallas, Walter, 248

Dark Room Reading Series, 10

Davis, Angela, 116–17, 223

Davis, Bette, 52

Davis, Miles, 19, 250

Davis, Sammy, Jr., 191

Dead End (film), 72

Delaney, Beauford, 19, 88, 166, 193; background of, 100; *Dark Rapture,* 97–99, 109, 136; death of, 114; and the Harlem Renaissance, 101–2; *Jazz Quartet,* 106; mental illness experienced by, 103, 114; as mentor to Baldwin, 91–96, 99–100, 103, 105–7, 114, 145, 197; *Portrait of James Baldwin, 1944,* 109; *Portrait of James Baldwin, 1957,* 110–11, 113; *Portrait of James Baldwin, 1965,* 109–10; *Portrait of James Baldwin, 1966,* 109–10; *Portrait of James Baldwin, 1971,* 99, 109–10; portraits of Baldwin by, 93–94, 97–98, 99, 109–10, 113; as represented in Baldwin's writing, 107; self-portraits by, 102

DeWitt Clinton High School: Baldwin as student at, 17, 82, 87; literary magazine at, 87

Dial Press, 140

Dickens, Charles: *Bleak House,* 78; *Oliver Twist,* 78

Diedrich, Maria, on Baldwin's legacy, 9–10

disidentification: in Baldwin's life and his fiction, 52–54; and misogyny and homophobia, 53–54

Dos Passos, John, 20

Du Bois, W. E. B., and concept of double-consciousness, 13

DuBois, William, *Haiti,* 87

Dupee, F. W., 17

Düşenin Dostu (Fortune and Men's Eyes), Baldwin as director of, 191–92

Dworkin, Andrea, 175; *Heartbreak,* 221; *Intercourse,* 221

Eckman, Fern Marja, 11; *The Furious Passage of James Baldwin,* 183–84

Edelman, Lee, 28

Elam, Michele, 9, 11

Elgrably, Jordan, 19, 26, 106

Elias, Amy, 11

Ellington, Duke, 24; "Harlem Air Shaft," 40–41, 47

Ellis, Thomas Sayers, 10

Ellmann, Richard, 206

Estes, David C., 120, 128–29
Evans, Walker, 188, 189
Everett, Percival, *Erasure*, 12
Evers, Medgar, 177, 190; murder of, 180

Farber, Jules, *James Baldwin: Escape from America, Exile in Provence*, 242
Farrakhan, Louis, 130
Faulkner, William, 20
Faure, Jeanne, 241, 245, 246
Fauset, Jessie Redmon, 54
FBI Story, 188
Federal Bureau of Investigation (FBI) file on Baldwin, 186–88
Federal Theatre Project, 86–87
Ferguson, Roderick, 30
Fiedler, Leslie, 121
Field, Douglas 11, 24, 28
Finney, Nikky, 9, 252
Fitzgerald, Ella, 54
Fitzgerald, F. Scott, 20
Flaubert, Gustave, *Madame Bovary*, 156
Fortune and Men's Eyes, Baldwin as director of, 191–92
Franco, Francisco, 82
Franklin, Aretha, 200
Frederick Douglass Junior High: and Baldwin as editor of the school magazine, 86; Baldwin as student at, 67, 77, 85–86
Friedrich, Otto, 155
Frost, David, 67

Garin, Georges, 165
Garrett, Greg, 11
Gates, Henry Louis, Jr., 101–2; "Cabin Fever," 22; on nationalism and homophobia, 203–4
Geist, Eileen, 155
Geist, Stanley, 155
Ghansah, Rachel Kaadzi, 9
Gibson, Ernest, 11
Gide, André, 218; Baldwin's critique of, 163
Giovanni, Nikki, 15, 31, 183; Baldwin's conversations with, 204, 207, 211–16, 223; reticence about her queerness, 219–20
Glaude, Eddie, 6, 11
Glazer, Nathan, 121
God Made My Face: A Collective Portrait of James Baldwin (symposium and exhibit), 6
Gold, Herbert, 155
Goldsby, Jacqueline, 11, 15
Goldstein, Richard, "Go the Way Your Blood Beats," 226
Gorbachev, Mikhail, 246–47
Gorky, Maxim: Baldwin's review of translation of, 127–28; *Mother*, 77
Greene, Mary, 128
Griffith, D. W., *The Birth of a Nation*, 12

Haizlip, Ellis, 212
Hamer, Fannie Lou, 177
Hansberry, Lorraine, 184, 185; death of, 220
Happersberger, Lucien, 136, 140, 142, 143–44, 154–55, 165, 168, 242, 245
Happersberger, Luc James, 143
Happersberger, Suzy, 143
Harlem, as literary inspiration for Baldwin, 46–49

Harlem Renaissance, 55, 93; and
    Beauford Delaney, 101–2
Harris, Kamala, 4
Harris, Trudier, 50
Hassel, Bernard, 144
Hawthorne, Nathaniel, 17, 45
Heath, Gordon, 155
Hemingway, Ernest, 20; *The Sun Also
    Rises*, 157
Henderson, Mae G., 11, 30
Herbert, John, *Fortune and Men's
    Eyes*, 191–92
Himes, Chester, 155
Hitler, Adolf, 82
Hobson, Laura Z., 163
Hoetis, Themistocles, 155
Hoffenberg, Mason, 155
Holiday, Billie, 24, 82
Holland, Sharon P., 30
Hollowell, Adam, *You Mean It or You
    Don't* (coauthor), 5–6
hooks, bell, 15, 29
Hoover, J. Edgar, 188
Horn, Bishop Rosa Artemis, 64
Horne, Lena, 191
Howe, Irving, 121
Hughes, Langston, 18, 54, 86; on
    Notes of a Native Son, 17
Hull, Akasha Gloria, 232
Hurston, Zora Neale, 54
Hutchinson, Jill, 6, 243, 251
Hutton, Bobby, 117

Israel, Baldwin's views on, 131
Israel, Marvin, 197
Issyk-Kul Forum (Kirghizia), 246, 252

Jackson, Jesse L., anti-Semitic
    comments by, 129–30

James, C. L. R., 104
James, Henry, 20; as inspiration to
    Baldwin, 155; *Lady Barbarina*, 155
James Baldwin: From Another Place
    (film), 144, 221
*James Baldwin / Nikki Giovanni: A
    Dialogue*, 183. *See also* Giovanni,
    Nikki
*James Baldwin among the Philoso-
    phers*, 5
James Baldwin Project, 5
James Baldwin Review, 5
Jarrell, Randall, 9, 128
Jedrowski, Tomasz, 9; *Swimming in
    the Dark*, 4
Jewish editors, Baldwin's mentorship
    by, 115–16. *See also* Blacks, Jews,
    and race relations
Jews, as perceived by Black people,
    117–19, 120–21. *See also* Blacks,
    Jews, and race relations
*JIMMY! God's Black Revolutionary
    Mouth* (exhibition), 6
Johnson, E. Patrick, 11, 30
Jones, Emma Berdis. *See* Baldwin,
    Berdis Jones
Jones, LeRoi. *See* Baraka, Amiri
Jones, Robert, Jr., 6; *The Prophets*, 4
Jones, Saeed, 4
Jordan, June, 9, 10
Joseph, Michael, 140
*Jubilee for Jimmy: A Celebration of
    James Baldwin*, 6

Kaplan, Harold, 155
Kazan, Elia, 190, 193
Keen, Mary, 155
Kenan, Randall, 9, 11
Kennedy, John, 28

Kennedy, Robert, 8, 28
King, Martin Luther, Jr., 117, 177; murder of, 180, 200
Kitt, Eartha, 104

Ladd, Florence, 31, 235
La Maison Baldwin, 13
Lee, Spike, *Malcolm X* (biopic), 201–2
Lee, Stan, 87
Leeming, David, 11, 19, 35, 41, 55, 66, 83, 85, 111, 165, 166, 182, 191, 199, 203, 205; *Amazing Grace,* 100; as Baldwin's assistant, 108, 242, 243; on Baldwin's sexual ambiguity, 222, 225; on Beauford Delaney, 100, 102–3
Leonard, Zoe, 6
Lester, Julius, 244; "James Baldwin—Reflections of a Maverick," 117; *Lovesong: Becoming a Jew,* 129, 132
Levister, Alonzo (Lonnie), and assault on Painter, 170–73
Levister, Lucille, 171
Levitas, Sol, as editor of the *New Leader,* 95, 116, 128
Lewis, Ida, 235
Ligon, Glenn, 6
Lincoln, Abraham, 45
Linx, David, 24–25
Locke, Alain, 104, 122
Looking for Langston (film), 102
Lopate, Philip, on *I Am Not Your Negro,* 6–7
Lorde, Audre, 15, 29, 31; Baldwin's conversations with, 204, 207, 226–33; and Baldwin's defense of Black men, 230; on masculinity, 231; *Sister Outsider,* 227; "Strange Gods," 228; *Zami,* 229–30

Lost Archives of James Baldwin (radio program), 6
Lover's Question (record album), spoken word performance by Baldwin, 24–25
Lowe, Janice, 10
Lowell, Robert, 15
Lynch, Nancy, 219

Mabanckou, Alain, 9, 19
Macbeth (Shakespeare), Welles's all-Black cast of, 78
Magpie (literary magazine at Baldwin's high school), 87–88
Mailer, Norman, 117, 155, 218
Maison Baldwin, La, 13
Malcolm X, 104, 177; Avedon's photograph of, 197; Baldwin's screenplays on, 196, 199–202; murder of, 180
Malcolm X: His Own Story How It Really Happened (documentary), 200
Malloch, Douglas, 86
Margaret Mead / James Baldwin: A Rap on Race, 206, 217
Marlowe, Christopher, *The Jew of Malta,* 125
Martin, Florence, 104
Martin, Tom, 104
Martin Luther King Memorial Medal, 28–29
Maxwell, William, 4, 11, 186
McBride, Dwight, 11, 30
McCarthy, Joseph, 82
McClaurin, Irma, 244
McGhee, Jamie, *You Mean It or You Don't* (coauthor), 5–6
McGruder, Aaron, *The Boondocks,* 46

McKay, Claude, 104
McPhatter, Clyde, 25
Mead, Margaret, 48, 185, 186;
    Baldwin's conversation with,
    204, 206–11, 216–19, 220; on
    gender discrimination, 208;
    on race and gender, 210–11
Meeropol, Abel, 38; as Baldwin's
    teacher, 82–84; "Bitter Fruit,"
    82; "Strange Fruit," 82
Meeropol, Michael, 82, 84
Meeropol, Robert, 82
Meredith, James, 177
Meriwether, Louise, *Daddy Was a
    Numbers Runner*, 235
Miller, D. Quentin, 11, 15, 111–12
Miller, Henrietta, 79
Miller, Henry, 93
Miller, Orilla "Bill," as Baldwin's
    teacher and friend, 38, 74–75,
    77–81, 83, 96, 158, 225
misogyny: in Baldwin's fiction, 107,
    156–57; and homophobia, 222; as
    perceived by Baldwin, 53–54, 69,
    174–75
Mitterand, François, 245
Mock, Janet, *Reinventing Realness*, 4
Montand, Yves, 154, 250
Moore, Arthur, Baldwin's infatuation
    with, 64–65, 135
Moraga, Cherríe, 29; *This Bridge
    Called My Back*, 231–32
Moreau, Jeanne, 154
Morrison, Allan, 143, 165
Morrison, Toni, 4, 9, 10, 16, 250, 252;
    Beloved, 235; *The Bluest Eye*, 235
Morton, Jelly Roll, 24
Movement for Black Lives, 4
Muhammad, Elijah, 177, 201

Mullen, Bill, 11; *James Baldwin: Living
    in Fire*, 178
Muñoz, José, *Disidentifications*, 52
Murray, Albert, 205
Mussolini, Benito, 82

National Association for the Ad-
    vancement of Colored People
    (NAACP), 29
National Museum of African
    American History and Culture
    (NMAAHC) / Smithsonian, 14
Nation of Islam, 177–78
Native Son (film), 73
Native Son (Wright), 20, 95
Newton, Huey, 153, 195, 196, 203,
    208–9
Norman, Brian, 11
Nothing Personal (Baldwin / Avedon),
    196, 197–99
Nyren, Magnus, 192

O'Grady, Gerald, 26
Ohm, Kirsten, 158
O'Keeffe, Georgia, on Beauford
    Delaney, 102
Oliver, Smith, 104
*One Day, When I Was Lost: A Scenario
    Based on" The Autobiography of
    Malcolm X"* (screenplay by
    Baldwin), 196–97, 200–202
Onyewuenyi, Ikechúkwú, 26
Oprah Daily, 4
Oral, Zeynep, 83, 193

Painter, Mary, 111, 142; background
    of, 164–65; as Baldwin's friend
    and supporter, 156, 164–67, 170,
    190, 212; Baldwin's letters to,

166, 168, 169, 179–80, 181; sexual
assault experienced by, 170–73,
218
Pakay, Sedat, 83, 144, 183, 185; on
American male behavior, 189;
*James Baldwin: From Another
Place,* 187–88
Paris, France, Baldwin's experiences
in 154–56
Parker, Charlie, 23
Parker, Dorothy, 197
Parks, Suzan-Lori, 9, 16, 245
Pavlić, Ed, 41, 150
Peck, Raoul, *I Am Not Your Negro*
(documentary), 5, 7
Perl, Arnold, 200
Philips, Tony, 6
Phillips, Caryl, 15, 251; *The European
Tribe,* 2
Pierson, Ann, 191
Pinckney, Darryl, 9
Plimpton, George, 26, 106
Poitier, Sidney, 19, 191
Porter, Billy, 5; *Unprotected,* 31
Porter, Herman W., 85
Porter, Horace, 38
Poyrazoğlu, Ali, 192
Price of the Ticket (documentary), 5
Psalms, book of, 91
PUSH/Rainbow Coalition, 130

"queer," concepts signified by, 30
quotefancy.com, 6

Rahv, Philip, 121
Rainey, Ma, 24
Reed, Ishmael, 205
Reid-Pharr, Robert, 11, 17, 30
Reine Blanche (gay bar), 154–55

"Revolutionary Hope: A Conversa-
tion Between James Baldwin
and Audre Lorde," 227–33
Robeson, Paul, 104
Robinson, Ruth, 104
Rocchi, Jean-Paul, 9
Rodriguez, Richard, 9
Rosenberg, Ethel, 82, 120
Rosenberg, Julius, 82, 120
Rosenwald Fellowship, 133
Ross, Marlon B., 11, 28, 30, 205
Roth, Philip, 155
Roux, Hélène, 205–6, 251–52
Roux, Pitou, 205–6, 251–52
Roux, Yvonne, 205–6, 251–52
RuPaul, *The House of Hidden
Meanings,* 31
Rustin, Bayard, 16

Saint-Paul-de-Vence, Baldwin's
home in, 13–14, 241–53
Sanchez, Sonia, 16
Sartre, Jean-Paul, 154
Saxton Foundation Fellowship, 133
Schomburg Center for Research in
Black Culture (New York Public
Library), 3
Schulberg, Budd, 117
Schwarz, Bill, 11
Scott, Lynn Orilla, 11, 30, 80; *James
Baldwin's Later Fiction,* 18
Scott-Heron, Gil, 87
sexuality/sexual orientation, evolving
terminology applied to, 30
Shabazz, Betty, 200, 201
Shagaloff, June, 191
Short, Bobby, 250
Signoret, Simone, 154, 250
Simone, Nina, 82, 250

Smart-Grosvenor, Vertamae, 31, 235
Smith, Barbara, 232
Smith, Bessie, 200; "Backwater
  Blues," 149, 150; "Empty Bed
  Blues," 150; as influence on
  Baldwin's writing, 149–51, 212;
  "Long Old Road," 150; "Ship-
  wreck Blues," 150; "Sing Sing
  Prison Blues," 150
Smith, Jerome, 177
Sordelo, Valerie, 242, 245, 246
South: Baldwin's experiences in,
  179–81
Soviet Union, Baldwin's visit to,
  246–47
Stein, Sol, 87, 88, 121
Stone, Wilmer, 82
Stowe, Harriet Beecher: *A Key to
  Uncle Tom's Cabin,* 45–46; *Uncle
  Tom's Cabin,* 20, 21–22, 45–46
Strange, Sharan, 10
"Strange Fruit" (poem/song), 82
Strasberg, Lee, 190–91
Strawbridge, Mary, 191
Student Nonviolent Coordinating
  Committee (SNCC), 8
Styron, William, 18–19
Sururi, Gülriz, 83, 193, 194

20,000 Years in Sing Sing (film), 78
Tacer, Cengiz, 189, 221
Tale of Two Cities (film), 78
Terkel, Studs, 149–50
Thelwell, Michael, *Duties, Pleasures,
  and Conflicts,* 219
Thorsen, Karen, *James Baldwin: The
  Price of the Ticket* (documentary),
  18–19, 36, 54, 58–59, 142
Till, Emmett, 190

Tóibín, Colm, 11; *On James Baldwin,* 5
Toomer, Jean, 54
Traylor, Eleanor, 31, 235
Trilling, Lionel, 121
Troupe, Quincy, 23–24, 26, 205, 250
Ture, Kwame (Stokely Carmichael),
  153
Turkey: Baldwin as dark-skinned
  curiosity in, 184–85; Baldwin
  as theater director in, 191–92;
  Baldwin's experiences in, 3, 6,
  108, 144, 184–94; Pakay's film of
  Baldwin in, 187–88

Uno, Roberta, 244

Van Dormael, Pierre, 24
Vogel, Joseph, 11

Walker, Alice, 15, 29; *The Color Purple,*
  31, 235; *In Search of Our Mothers'
  Gardens,* 31, 236
Ward, Jacky, 25
Warshow, Robert, 87, 95; as mentor
  to Baldwin, 120–26, 197; "An Old
  Man Gone," 125; publications of,
  119–20
Waters, Ethel, 54
Weatherby, W. J., 11, 28, 38
Weir, Stan, 104, 121
Weissman, Marty, 155
Welles, Orson, 73, 78
West, Cornel, 5
Whitman, Walt, 24, 221
Williams, Connie, 103–4
Williams, John A., *Night Song,* 23
Winfield, "Bill" Miller. *See* Miller,
  Orilla "Bill"
Winfield, Evan, 79, 80–81

Winfield, Ken, 81
womanism, 29
women: Baldwin as advocate for the
    role of, 163–64; brutality against,
    144, 174–76; sexuality of, 69–70;
    as strong characters in Baldwin's
    fiction, 50–51, 236–37
Wonder, Stevie, 250
Works Progress Administration
    (WPA), 78
Worth, Eugene, 136–37, 139, 173
Worth, Marvin, 200
Wright, Richard: as advocate for
    Baldwin, 133; Baldwin on, 20,
21–22, 155; "The FB Eye Blues,"
186; *Native Son*, 20, 73, 95; *Uncle
Tom's Children*, 46

Yerby, Frank, 155
Youngblood, Shay, 9, 245
Young People's Socialist League
    (YPSL), 127

Zaborowska, Magdalena J.: on
    Black queer humanism, 18–20,
    27–28; *Me and My House: James
    Baldwin's Last Decade in France*,
    27